A Guide to Accountir

A small price to pay for a complete accounting package.

£7

Here are a few of the many excellent general features offered in this fully integrated accounting package:-

- Nominal Ledger
- Accounts Receivable
- Accounts Payable
- Inventory Control
- Billing
- Purchase Order
- Forecasting

And some specifics:-
- Hundred's of different reports
- Password Protected
- Extensive manual with accounting primer
- List of accounts
- Cash flow analysis
- Physical inventory routine with count sheets
- Full back order control
- Hundreds of different reports
- Financial statements
- Unlimited accounts
- Open invoice or balance forward
- Flexible ageing
- Mailing labels
- 99 items per purchase order
- Full purchase journals
- Unique forecasting module

Awards

- 1st – 1986 – PC World Magazine "World Class Award" – 300,000 Readers voted for DAC Easy Accounting with a margin of 5:1 over any other accounting package.
- 1st – 1985 – PC World Magazine "World Class Award".
- 1st – 1985 – Infoworld "Product of the Year" and "Best Software Value".
- 1st – PC Magazine "Editor's Choice".

Press

"Dac-Easy is a genuinely amazing deal" – PC Magazine
"Remarkable, amazing, revolutionary, and sensational" – Computer Buyers Guide
"Dac-Easy is an incredible value" – PC Week
"I enthusiastically award four stars and recommend the purchase" – Business Software
"Dac Software has taken the industry by storm" – Dun & Bradstreet Reports
"Dac-Easy is a program we highly recommend" – InfoWorld

To receive your copy of the world's favourite accounting package simply fill in the coupon or call (0753) 47021

Dac-Easy for only £7

I enclose a cheque for £9.55 (£7 for Dac-Easy, plus 15% VAT and £1.50 postage), for each copy I require.

Name _____ Company _____

Address _____

_____ Tel no: _____

Cheques should be made payable to ACM and sent to 31 High Street, Datchet, Berkshire.
Offer ends June 30th 1988. Please allow 14 days for delivery.

ACM ADVANCED COMPUTING MANAGEMENT
31 High Street, Datchet

A GUIDE TO ACCOUNTING SOFTWARE
EVALUATION TECHNIQUES FOR ACCOUNTANTS AND MANAGERS

JL Muggridge PA Malton and SJ Thomson

KOGAN PAGE

The Institute of Chartered Accountants of Scotland
INCORPORATED BY ROYAL CHARTER IN 1854

© Institute of Chartered Accountants of Scotland 1988
All rights reserved. No reproduction, copy or transmission of this publication may be made without written permission.

No paragraph of this publication may be reproduced, copied or transmitted save with written permission or in accordance with the provisions of the Copyright Act 1956 (as amended), or under the terms of any licence permitting limited copying issued by the Copyright Licensing Agency, 7 Ridgmount Street, London WC1E 7AE.

Any person who does any unauthorised act in relation to this publication may be liable to criminal prosecution and civil claims for damages.

First published in 1988 by
Kogan Page Ltd, 120 Pentonville Road, London N1 9JN
in association with the Institute of Chartered Accountants of Scotland
Reprinted 1989

Printed in Great Britain by
Dotesios Printers Ltd, Trowbridge, Wiltshire

British Library Cataloguing in Publication Data
Muggridge, J.L.
  A guide to accounting software.
  1. Accountancy. Applications of computer
  systems. Software packages
  I. Title   II. Malton, P.A.   III. Thomson, S. J.
  IV. Institute of Chartered Accountants of Scotland
  657'.028'553

ISBN 1-85091-526-1

Contents

About This Book	9
Part 1 General Principles	**11**
Introduction	13
Using accounting software	20
Selecting a system	27
Accounting software	34
Part 2 Detailed Evaluation	**41**
Introduction	43
Principle 1: Suitability	45
Principle 2: Functionality	49
Principle 3: Integrity	71
Principle 4: Support	89
Principle 5: Ease of use	93
Principle 6: Efficiency	98
Principle 7: Flexibility	102
Part 3 Reviews and Checklists	**105**
Introduction	107
Low-price packages	110
MAP Integrated Ledger Package	112
Sagesoft Accountant Plus	115
SNIP	118
TAS	121

Medium-price packages	174
Finax Gold Plus	176
Multifacts	179
Multisoft	184
Pegasus Senior	187
High-price packages	238
Omicron Power Systems	240
SMB Datasolve	242
Tetraplan	246
Sun Account	249
Other packages	302
BOS	304
FACT	304–5
PAXTON Business Desk	304
Shortlands	305
Part 4 Appendices	**355**
1. IT statement	357
2. Checklists	389
3. Test data	398
Glossary	*413*

Shelling out for accounting software?

With Sage you've cracked it.

	Single User	Multi User	Upgrade
ACCOUNTANT	£149	£299	£150
ACCOUNTANT PLUS	£199	£399	£200
FINANCIAL CONTROLLER	£299	£599	£300
SAGENET	£149 per PC		

Prices shown do not include VAT

Sagesoft plc, NEI House, Regent Centre, Newcastle-upon-Tyne NE3 3DS
Tel: 091-284 7077 Telex: 53623 SAGESL G

SAGE
PC BUSINESS SYSTEMS

About this book

Based on the much respected guidelines and evaluation checklists developed by the Institute of Chartered Accountants of Scotland, which outline the features to be expected in good accounting software, this practical new book comprises:

* The only authoritative and totally independent guide to the most commonly-used UK packages
* An analysis of the advantages of computerising the accounting function
* Clear, detailed and comprehensive advice on selecting and evaluating the right system and software
* Reviews carried out by experienced accountants using a standard set of data to provide comparability between the packages
* Checklists for nominal, purchase and sales ledgers which will enable you to make your own software evaluations

Written by experts with typical business people in mind, this book provides an invaluable source of reference for those who are either about to set up a computer-based system or who wish to upgrade from a basic to a more advanced system.

The Authors

J L Muggridge is the Institute's Director of Information Technology. He has over 20 years' experience of computers in business and is involved in a number of companies as a consultant for software development.

P A Malton and **S J Thomson**, both chartered accountants, are advisers in the Institute's Computing Centre. They have experience in public practice and advise on computing systems to members of the Institute.

Part I
General Principles

Chapter 1
Introduction

The boom in business micros has brought about an explosion in the number of accounting packages coming on to the market. These range from simple, basic and usually cheap packages to complex and flexible multi-user packages which supply a basic shell for the user to tailor to his own requirements.

The purpose of this book is to steer potential users of accounting software and their financial advisers through the maze of accounting packages which have been written for micro-computers. The book uses methods developed by The Institute of Chartered Accountants of Scotland (ICAS) for evaluating accounting software. Each user's needs are unique and require a unique solution. Ideally, this would be a tailor made system. However, as most systems have the same basic accounting requirements they can be suited to a greater or lesser degree by an appropriate accounting package. Thus the most cost effective solution for the majority of businesses is to choose the most suitable off-the-shelf package at the price they can afford.

The majority of accounting packages will do the job for which they were designed and will cater for the basic accounting functions. However, all the packages differ in detail and in the facilities they offer. They will have different ways of producing reports, different code structures, screen layouts and methods of producing the final results. Some packages offer only the basic sales, purchase and nominal ledgers, either in separate modules or all in one. Others offer an extensive range of modules which include purchase and sales order processing, stock control, payroll, asset registers and many others, all integrated with their associated ledgers. Most packages offer at least the integration of the sales and purchase ledgers with the nominal so that transactions only need to be posted once in detail, though the update to the nominal may be run as a separate process.

In the following chapters we will outline the principles behind software evaluation and give examples of the essential features of good accounting software.

Most people start with one or more of the three basic ledgers – purchase, sales and nominal or general ledger – and add extra modules at a later date.

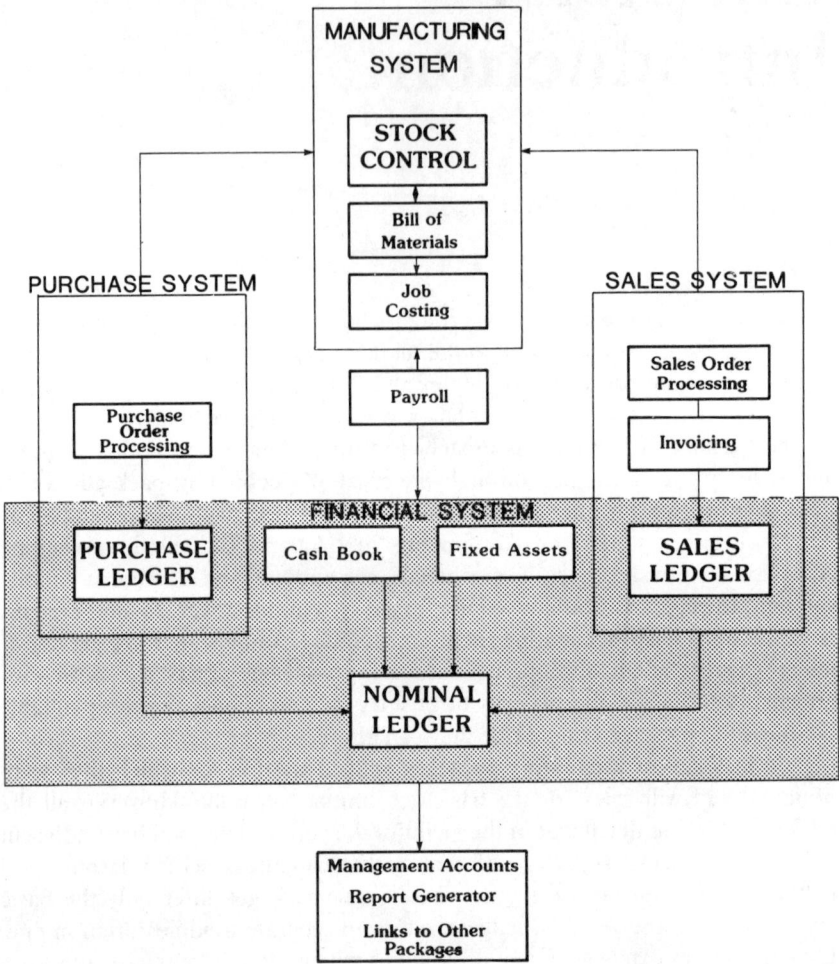

They are, therefore, almost certainly committed to a particular system at the initial stage. We have accordingly confined our evaluation to systems comprising the three ledger modules.

With a few exceptions, package accounting software mimics double entry bookkeeping and books of prime entry such as daybooks, journals and cashbooks, familiar to users of good manual accounting systems. 'Integration' of the sales and purchase ledgers with the nominal ledger allows update of both

ACCOUNTING SOFTWARE?
Spot the Paxton user

The 'no worry' accounting system

Over 3000 companies use Paxton Business Desk to give them what they need – a solid, dependable accounting system – and peace of mind.

Peace of mind that comes from Business Desk's proven routines and solid architecture. Peace of mind that comes from Paxton's quality of support – the plus factor which has proved a vital ingredient in Business Desk's continuing success story.

Making sense of the real world

Modern business is a complex of transactions; orders, invoices, payments and receipts, stock movements, VAT and journals. Business Desk helps you make sense of your current situation at a glance by organising your book-keeping into a series of easy to understand entry routines and management reports.

Seven integrated modules

Business Desk is a modular package. There are seven modules:–
- Sales ledger
- Nominal ledger
- Stock control
- Purchase orders
- Purchase ledger
- Invoicing
- Sales orders

Each module is fully featured and yet easy to follow and easy to operate – your staff will be amazed how quickly they will become proficient Business Desk users.

Single or multi-user operation

Business Desk runs on most popular business computer systems from desktop PC's through to true multi-user systems running under C-DOS or UNIX.

Safeguarding your future

Circumstances do change – businesses expand, requirements change, technology advances. Business Desk aims to protect your investment in your accounting system.

Many Business Desk users have come back again and again as their business has grown. For specific requirements, Paxton offer a full software tailoring service for those special facilities that you might need. As technology has advanced, Paxton have kept Business Desk at the forefront.

At Paxton we expect a long term relationship with our customers

For further information on Business Desk call us on 0480-217777

Paxton Computers Ltd., 28 New Street, St. Neots, Cambs PE19 1AJ
Telephone: 0480 217777   Fax: 0480 405475

the individual sales or purchase ledger account and the appropriate nominal accounts, including a control account from a single entry. Good accounting software contains checks to ensure that the control accounts are always in balance with the total of the amounts outstanding in the sales and purchase ledgers. Also that all transactions are carried through to the nominal ledger and that the control accounts cannot be altered directly within the nominal ledger but only by a transaction or journal through the sales or purchase ledger.

Most systems allow for some form of tailoring to the user's needs. This is usually done by means of sets of parameters in the form of tables or lists of questions. This allows the user to specify the system set up – including the password structure, backup and spooling procedures – and to set up multiple companies and departments. Within the ledgers the parameters allow control accounts and analysis formats to be set up, period lengths and timings to be set, and some tailoring of the standard printed reports provided within the module. More detailed or more specific reports can often be set up by using a report generator which is provided either within the module or as separate module.

Nominal ledger

The nominal ledger module will provide the functions to maintain and control a nominal ledger and produce a trial balance, management and annual accounts. Exploiting the full potential of the nominal ledger depends on the effectiveness of the account structure. This has to be defined at the outset and cannot usually be altered easily once the system is running. For this reason it is essential that a package with an account structure suitable to the user's needs is chosen. A great deal of thought must also be given to the detailed coding before the nominal account structure and layout are set up on the computer. A full understanding of the coding can often add an extra dimension to the level of analysis and useful management information that can be extracted from the system. As a general rule, dealers should not be relied upon to understand the full potential of a package's nominal coding structure. Manuals often show examples that are far too simple to demonstrate what may be very powerful features. Time spent with a pencil and a sheet of paper is well rewarded.

Account structures for the nominal ledgers vary, but are usually based on a six- to eight-digit alpha-numeric or numeric code. Some systems have a special code which denotes a change of category from, say, fixed asset codes to current asset codes and the use of this code will total the previous range and set up a heading for the next range. Other systems have complicated hierarchical codes which allow the nominal ledger to be broken down into departments and cost centres. Nearly all systems require that the nominal ledger accounts are coded in the order in which they should appear in the balance sheet or profit and loss account. Very basic systems rely on this to get a meaningful printout of the final accounts. Gaps should always be left in the coding so that new account codes can be added at a later date.

Postings to the nominal ledger are effected either by an update from one of the sales or purchase ledgers or by means of direct input using a nominal ledger posting routine. Update from the sales and purchase ledgers may be by individual transaction at the time of input or by some type of batch update routine. This may be user controlled through an option on the nominal ledger menu or a part of the automatic end-of-day procedure of the system. In either case a system of controls to ensure that the update is complete and accurate must be set up. Such controls are likely to be a combination of machine controls set up by the author of the system and manual controls by the user to ensure that all the necessary procedures for update have been carried out, especially before a period or year end.

Direct posting to the nominal ledger is either by journal entry or through a cash receipts/payments routine on the menu. All good accounting systems have some sort of total check for cash transactions and only accept balanced journal entries.

Input screens should be well set out, easy to follow and should request enough information to identify a transaction easily from the subsequent printout. On the better systems such a printout is mandatory. Systems vary, so make sure that the space provided for reference and narrative is sufficient for your particular needs. Ensure also that what gets through onto the printout will identify your transactions – not everything which appears on the input screen is always transferred to a printout.

Provision is usually made for period-end adjustments using special or reversing journals which reverse after the period-end routine has been run. These journals can be used for accruals, prepayments and stock. Recurring journals may be provided for standing orders and direct debits and can be set up for the whole year or part year.

Most systems have a budget facility built into the nominal ledger but these vary so much that it is difficult to give a general description. Budgets for cheaper systems are usually fairly simple, with in some cases just an annual total for each account split evenly over the year. More complex budgets may take into account seasonal fluctuations or previous years. They may be allocated to departments or flexed during the year based on year-to-date figures. Some systems have all of these features.

For the average business user the standard nominal ledger reports set up in the package will be sufficient. However, not all packages incorporate standard management reports. The only printouts available from such packages are the nominal ledger transaction reports (audit trail) and a trial balance. It is then up to the user to construct his own reports using a built-in report generator. While this does mean that the reports will be laid out in the way the user wants, not all report generators are particularly easy to use. Most packages have a report generator built into the individual modules (or as a separate module) so that users can write management reports in a format useful to their particular organisation.

Sales and purchase ledgers

Sales and purchase ledgers in computer systems are normally mirror images of each other and, with a few exceptions which reflect their different functions, incorporate exactly the same features. For this reason they can be considered together.

Sales and purchase ledgers may integrate with the nominal ledger or may be run as stand-alone modules. Starting off with a stand-alone ledger is usually no barrier to converting to an integrated system at a later date. From the other direction, invoicing, sales order processing and stock control modules are usually available to integrate with the sales ledger, and purchase order processing, job costing and stock control with the purchase ledger. Specialist or vertical market software such as time recording packages for accountants and solicitors or contract costing for building contractors often interface with standard ledger packages to make up an accounting system suited to a particular profession or industry.

Good sales and purchase ledgers hold all the information necessary to record and control transactions with customers and suppliers. A system usually allows accounts to be set up as open item or balance forward. Most people find an open item format, with its listing of all unmatched transactions, to be the most useful. Recently, many ledgers have included a facility for handling foreign currency transactions and for accounting for exchange gains and losses.

The minimum standing data that you can expect the ledger to hold for each individual account is name, address, contact details, credit limit and some form of analysis code for ledger reports. Many systems also supply comment areas, discount facilities and separate delivery addresses.

Postings to the sales and purchase ledgers use standard routines selected from a posting menu within the ledger. Standard postings include invoices and credit notes, adjustments, cash and cash allocation. The cash allocation routine allows cash receipts or payments to be allocated to the aged balance or individual invoices, depending whether the ledger is set up as balance forward or open item. Allocation can be done automatically as part of the cash posting sequence or allocated manually as a separate routine. Automatic allocation usually allocates the cash to the oldest balance or invoice unless the system provides an over-ride for invoices in dispute. Good software will have built-in checks to prevent you from allocating more cash than has been entered but will allow you to allocate cash on account and part-pay invoices.

Standard, zero-rated and exempt items for VAT purposes will be dealt with automatically through the system and reports from the ledgers suitable for completing VAT returns should be available as standard. Most systems should have been adapted to cope with new VAT legislation to give users the option of accounting for VAT on a cash basis.

Reports from the sales and purchase ledgers should be available both as screen enquiries and printed output. Many ledger modules will incorporate or be linked to report generators to give user designed analyses of sales and purchases. This analysis may be based on a special code assigned to each invoice entry or to the individual account, or based on a coding structure within the account number.

Standard reports include invoice and credit note listings which form the computer equivalent of daybooks; summaries of receipts, payments and adjustments; aged debtor and creditor prints for cash control; statements for the sales ledger and remittance advices for the purchase ledger.

There are about a thousand accounting packages in the UK market, ranging in price from under £50 to over £50,000. They run on everything from small home computers to large mainframe systems. The most popular packages are priced in a range from £100 to approximately £1,000 for each module and are designed to run on standard business microcomputers such as the IBM range of personal computers.

The majority of these packages are produced and supported by small software houses supporting a specialised vertical market or local area. A relatively small number of packages have become established to the extent that they are available nationally through a network of agents and dealers. These are the accounting systems likely to be acquired by a large number of small businesses and so an analysis of their features will form the major part of this book.

The best known example of the basic package is probably Sagesoft's 'Accountant' which was originally designed as a one disk, integrated set of ledgers for twin or even single floppy machines. Tetraplan and Omicron 'Powersystems' are examples of the sophisticated packages aimed at businesses large enough to employ an accountant and which have fairly complex requirements. There is a middle range of packages which can be tailored to some extent by the user while keeping the accounting functions standard and menu controlled. Such packages can have quite sophisticated built-in features and controls and cover the widest market for accounting software. Middle range packages such as Pegasus and Multisoft are used in both their single and multi-user version. Firms often start with the single-user version and upgrade to multi-user as they expand.

Chapter 2
Using Accounting Software

You will probably have to change your methods of working in some way to accommodate a computer system. But the methodical approach imposed by a computer is often beneficial when compared to the informal manual systems which operate in many small businesses. It is essential to overhaul the manual system and get it running smoothly *before* a computer is installed: computerising a mess results almost invariably in a computerised mess. At worst, this can mean abandoning the system and starting again from scratch. At best, it results in vast amounts of work before accurate reports are available.

It is a common mistake to expect a computer to replace staff. This rarely happens. A well-used computer will almost certainly allow existing staff to use their time more efficiently and may allow you to increase the size of the business without having to take on extra staff.

A computer is the ideal tool for doing repetitive, mundane work fast and consistently and for collating large masses of data into useful reports. It will not make up for management deficiencies or a basically bad system.

Within a typical accounting system consisting of a sales and purchase ledger integrated with the nominal ledger, a stock control module and perhaps a payroll module, the major time saving will come when processing data and retrieving information from the system. You can expect virtually no time saving when entering data into the computer since input will be barely faster than recording the information manually. In the following paragraphs we will look at the various modules in turn and consider the advantages to be gained from a computer system.

Sales and purchase ledgers

A fundamental truth about a computer system – or indeed any accounting system – is 'garbage in, garbage out'. Too many people expect to plug in a computer, switch it on and leave it to work and think for itself. Many computer accounting systems do have built-in checks which will cause the software to reject incorrectly coded items or items which fall outside a reasonable range,

PLUSMARK BUSINESS MANAGEMENT SYSTEM

SOFTWARE TO ACCOUNT ON

Invoicing
Sales Order Processing
Sales Ledger
Sales Analysis
Purchase Ledger
Nominal Ledger
Cash Book
Management Accounts
Stock Control
Costing
Payroll
Spreadsheet & Database Links

The Plusmark Business Management System is available through your local Plusmark Authorised Dealer:-

Computer Services (Scotland) Ltd.
89/90 Westlaw Place
Whitehill Industrial Estate
Glenrothes, Fife KY6 2RZ
Telephone: 0592 773710

but no computer can authorise invoices for payment or replace human judgement when setting credit limits. Far from reducing clerical procedures at the point of entry to the system the computer may in fact increase them.

Purchase invoices will still have to be authorised and checked to receipt of goods; sales invoices based on delivery notes will still have to be typed out and checked; credit notes have to be authorised and customer credit limits monitored. Many systems allow for credit limits to be included in the customer information in the sales ledger but unless a current balance is available when an order is placed by the customer, the computer can only be used for credit checking after the order has been sent out and the invoice has been prepared. In addition, invoices will have to be batched and coded with account numbers, analysis codes and nominal ledger account numbers before they are ready for posting. During input, data keyed in will have to be checked to the original documents before being accepted. Batch totals need to be checked at the end of each session.

If the bottleneck which prompted you to consider a computer in the first instance was an increase in the volume of sales invoices beyond the capability of the manual system, then the solution may be a sales ledger with an invoicing or sales order processing module.

An invoicing module will allow you to design and produce professional looking invoices on preprinted stationery. Input will normally be from delivery notes. Prices and discounts can be pre-set so that calculations including VAT will be automatic. The sales and nominal ledger will be updated from the same input either as a batch update or item by item.

Sales order processing with invoicing starts with the order enquiry from the customer. The operator can then check the stock position and customer credit status before allocating the goods to the customer or placing them on back-order for later delivery. The system can produce delivery notes and invoices and take care of all ledger updates. While this type of system eliminates a good deal of the clerical work it does require a lot of routine maintenance to keep stock prices, discounts and credit limits up to date.

Substantial savings in time and effort can be expected during processing and reporting. Provided the system has been correctly installed and set up the programs can be relied upon to process the information consistently and correctly. From a control point of view, the great advantage of package software over bespoke software and software written and maintained in house is the absence of any source code or facilities for altering programs. This means that it can be relied on to function as expected, barring system failure or data corruption. A good system has methods of minimising the effects of such eventualities.

Output in the form of printed reports or screen displays is available quickly and is as up to date as the information that has been fed into the system. Once they have been set up, reports appear in the format most useful to the business. For example, sales analyses by region, salesman or product that took days to collate from manual records are available virtually on demand. Cash control can be tightened up by printing monthly or bi-monthly aged debtor listings so that slow payers can be identified and chased up.

On the purchases side, many systems have a facility for automatic cheque runs or suggested payment listings based on a pre-input latest payment date so that you can take full advantage of early settlement discounts. Control can still be maintained by authorising the payments listing and by retaining a hand-written signature for the cheques. For systems with large volume of payments, most packages have a BACS facility which will write to a payments file for direct transmission or – more usually with a micro-based system – onto a floppy disk.

All systems should account for VAT and produce reports suitable for preparing VAT returns.

Nominal ledger

Many small businesses will have confined themselves to an analysed cashbook and a system of sales and purchases recording, and will not have used a formal nominal ledger before installing a computer. This type of business often relies on its accountants to produce management accounts. The owner may not even be sure he has made a profit until the annual accounts have been prepared.

Sales and purchase ledgers are fairly straightforward and can probably be set up with help and training from the software supplier. If the business does not employ an accountant, installing and setting up a nominal ledger will require professional assistance. This should ensure that it is set up correctly and that proper controls are installed to ensure the nominal ledger forms a valid basis for preparing the accounts. It is pointless and expensive to spend money on a nominal ledger module if at the end of the year your accountant has to redo all the work from the basic entries to prepare the accounts.

Properly set up and used a nominal ledger will produce management accounts regularly and accurately. If coded to be compatible with the system your accountant uses to prepare the annual accounts then the year-end data can be input to his system with the minimum of effort. This can save a great deal of time and effort but requires close liaison between accountant and client before the system is installed.

Input to the nominal ledger will often come directly from the sales and purchase ledgers. With proper safeguards, direct cash posting to the nominal ledger for non-sales/purchase ledger items can eliminate the need to keep a detailed cash book. The printouts from the direct posting routine and from cash posting to the sales and purchase ledgers will form the detailed cashbook pages for reconciliation and checking, while the manual cashbook can be reduced to summary form. Such a system can save time and duplication of records, but again it will require professional expertise. No manual records should be abandoned without professional advice.

As with the sales and purchase ledgers however, the main time saving in a computerised nominal ledger is during processing and especially from report production. Provided receipts and payments information is kept up to date, the bank account can be monitored daily by simply requesting a printout or screen report of the nominal account. Reports can be set up to give regular profit figures for departments, cost centres or particular products. There is, however, a trade off here: the more detailed the information output, the more detailed the information that has to be keyed in. Cost benefit analysis of any proposed reports should be done so that only the most beneficial are set up.

Payroll

A computer payroll system will not replace the knowledge needed to run a manual payroll system. However, it will reduce the scope for calculation error and greatly speed up payslip production. As a general rule, the larger and more stable the workforce, the greater the benefits to be gained from a computerised payroll system. The pay structure can be fairly complex without reducing the benefits to be gained from a computer provided that the hourly rates or basic pay remain largely unchanged from week to week.

A computer payroll will not reduce the clerical work needed to administer changes in individual tax codings or addresses and dealing with joiners. When dealing with leavers, some systems will print P45 information. Many will allow you to put through a percentage pay rise for all employees. Changes to tax rates, NIC rates and tax band widths are easily dealt with and are usually supplied on disk as a part of the maintenance agreement. The permanent information held for each employee includes the rate(s) of pay; standard hours worked if there is a standard working week; several overtime rates; regular deductions, both before and after tax; tax coding and pension information. PAYE and NIC is deducted automatically during the payroll calculation and all systems should be able to deal with holiday pay, SSP and maternity pay. Once each employee has been set up, the only regular weekly inputs will be actual hours worked, if different from the standard hours, overtime information and possibly expenses and subs.

Outputs include individual payslips and payroll summaries noting the total amounts due to the Inland Revenue and any pension contributions to be paid over. For cash paid employees, most systems give a coin analysis both in total and for each individual payslip. Other payment methods provided for are bank giros, cheques and autopay printouts, all with their relevant summaries.

Preprinted stationery for all methods of payment is usually available from the software supplier. Modern payroll systems are also able to prepare output for payment via the BACS system. Year-end printouts include P14 and P35 information in a form acceptable to the Inland Revenue. Payroll modules are often more easily run as stand-alone systems but payrolls can be integrated with the nominal ledger and many can also be linked to a job costing module. Many suppliers have developed payrolls suitable for building contractors and others with special requirements.

Stock control

A well-run computer stock control system should allow the business to function at the optimum stock level, thus saving on unnecessary storage costs but avoiding late delivery and part delivery of sales orders. The stock system can function either as part of a full purchase and sales order processing system or as a stand-alone module. Stock systems do require a lot of maintenance to make sure that costs and stock movements are kept up to date and this can be at least as time consuming as a manual system. The main advantage in time saving comes from having information on stock levels and suggested order quantities almost instantly.

Chapter 3
Selecting a System

It is rarely a good idea to implement a complete computer-based accounting system in one operation. Although you may plan to expand the computer facilities to cover the whole accounting system eventually, it is best to concentrate on getting each module running successfully before going on to the next. This does not mean that you should not look at the system as a whole when planning. In fact it is essential to do so.

Once you have identified the area or areas where the business might benefit from a computer, use the results of your investigation as a basis for writing an outline of the system as you would like it to be. Although you may have to modify your requirements at a later date, start off by specifying your ideal system.

This system outline has a twofold purpose, it allows you to get a clear picture of your requirements and their relative importance and it gives suppliers a document to work from when preparing proposals.

To make a start on narrowing down the choice to a manageable number of packages, the first thing to think about is special requirements related to the nature of the business which might need to be met by 'vertical market' software. Vertical market software is designed to cope with the specialised requirements of certain sections of industry and the professions. Advertising agencies with their job-bag system and advertising sales ledger; solicitors who need to account separately for client and practice monies; time recording systems used by accountants – all are users of vertical market software.

Computer magazines aimed at the business market are good sources of information, as are software guides and lists maintained by trade associations. If you need such a specialised suite of software it is often better to use the 'Turnkey' approach suitable for larger, mini-based systems. Suppliers quote for the whole system installed and ready to use, and maintain it afterwards. They should be experienced in the type of system that you have in mind and be able to give you the names of other users within your industry or profession.

The next major step is to decide how much of your system you are likely to transfer to the computer. Will there be a need for job-costing, stock or production control modules either now or in the near future? Will these extra modules integrate with the main accounting system? Can they run more efficiently as completely separate systems either within a network/multi-user environment or on stand-alone micro-computers?

The payroll, for instance, is often more easily run as a separate system on a separate machine – possibly a cheap IBM clone which can also be a word processor or run a financial modelling package. The payroll needs priority at some point each week and may hold up other applications such as invoicing and customer inquiries on a single user system for half a day. Though the actual processing time involved may be short, the payroll sequence requires frequent stops for paper changes and pauses for checking. It usually cannot be interrupted once the cycle is started, even when the machine is standing idle. Assuming that it is compatible with the main system, an additional machine can provide an emergency backup in case of breakdown and be used for other non-accounting functions. The payroll update to the nominal ledger is usually a matter of a simple weekly journal, so using a separate machine is not going to cause much in the way of extra work.

You will have to change your methods of working in some way to accommodate the computer, but it is easier to cope with these changes if they are not too radical. The next point to consider, then, is which packages will fit in best with your particular method of working. However, even if you find a package which appears to fit well and meets most of your selection criteria, it is still essential to overhaul the manual system and get it running smoothly before the computer is installed.

Lastly, you should decide from the start whether you want a single or multi-user system. If you opt for single-user, ask yourself if this is likely to change in the next few years. If the answer is yes, look for a system that will provide an easy upgrade path to either a network or a multi-user system with a central processor and dumb terminals. At the same time, think about operating systems and IBM-compatibility. For single user systems staying with the IBM standard gives access to a wide range of both accounting and non-accounting packages. There are however, several good accounting packages which are non PC or MS-DOS packages. If one of these meets all your requirements and is supplied by a reputable firm then the low cost of IBM-compatible hardware still keeps other non accounting software options open.

Widely used multi-user operating systems include Unix, Xenix, Pick and BOS. Networking micro-computers is a more difficult area to give general advice on. No real industry standard has yet emerged though names to look out for are probably Novell whose 'Netware' runs on many different network configurations and IBM with its 'Token Ring'. If you are considering a network then take expert advice and insist on seeing the network operating with your chosen accounting software installed, preferably at a user site.

Once you have given some thought to these initial considerations you are ready to make contact with possible suppliers. It is at this point that your *system outline* becomes invaluable.

For smaller systems, where the requirement is for a suite of standard accounting modules, set out the system outline in the form of a checklist for each module. Compare this checklist with the supplier's literature and use it as a basis for asking questions during demonstration and when talking to existing users. Suitable packages should emerge when you evaluate your checklists.

For larger systems and where there are special requirements not met by standard accounting packages, set out the system outline as a formal document so that suppliers can prepare a proposal or quotation. If at all possible, have the system outline included as part of the contract between yourself and the supplier. This ensures that the contract is based on your requirements rather than the contents of the package being supplied. If this is not possible (and the cheaper the package the more likely it is to be supplied under a standard and non-negotiable contract) make it clear *in writing* that the supplier is being asked to provide a system based on your specification and that any deviation from this must be agreed *in writing*. The supplier should also be requested to state in his proposal where any of your requirements cannot be met by a standard package.

The system outline should include the following sections:

Company background

You should give a brief description of your business and some indication of its size, perhaps in terms of turnover or number of employees.

A summary of the areas to be computerised and the reasons for doing so together with the proposed implementation schedule should be included.

This information will help suppliers assess the likely nature of their proposals and allocate appropriate staff to deal with your requirements.

Supplier background

You should next ask a number of questions about the supplier's background in order to assess their reliability and record for supporting their customers.

You should ask for details of other customers using the proposed system in order that you can discuss the software with them.

You should also determine the level of support and training you will receive and whether you will have to pay for it.

If you are in any doubt about the supplier's ability to give you continuing good quality support or suspect that their business may not be financially secure, you should supplement this information with a company search.

Applications

This section should define the individual applications – e.g. nominal, sales or purchase ledger – in enough detail for suppliers to be clear about your exact requirements and so that you can use it to check against proposals for the best package for your requirements. Include a separate sub-section for each application.

Go into as much detail as you need, erring on the side of excess rather than insufficiency. If your regular suppliers expect you to re-order using stock numbers then the length and format of stock numbers will be important and should be included as part of the specification. If you use more than one bank account, more than one purchase ledger or need multi-currency accounting these facts should be included. Though the Institute checklists were devised to help in assessing the facilities provided by packages they are also useful as a checklist when setting out your requirements.

It is often useful to divide your detailed specification into input, processing and output sections. In the input section include the type of input required (e.g. batch input, on-line enquiry linked input for sales order processing) plus any essential details such as length and format of account codes and the detail that should be included in the screen layout if you have any non-standard requirements.

The output section would include the type and format of reports and screen enquiries. If statements etc. need to be tailored to fit your standard stationery then this information should be included.

The processing section would include other ledgers/packages that are to be updated from the application and the method of update preferred, e.g. a daily run centrally controlled or updating all applications from a single entry at the time of input. Include in this section any other information about the way that you would like your system to function.

Volumes

Finally, the specification should give an estimate of the volumes expected. Give both the average and maximum volumes, especially if there are marked seasonal fluctuations or if an increase in volume is expected in the near future. For the sales and purchase ledgers give an estimate of the number of accounts, the number of invoices each month and the average number of lines in each invoice. For the nominal ledger give the number of accounts and the average number of monthly transactions. A stock system would require an estimate of the number of stock lines and the number of expected stock movements in a month. Set the volumes out in the form of a table for clarity and ease of reference.

Once you have completed your system outline select five or six suppliers from a list of specialist suppliers in your area or contact the suppliers of general accounting software in this book. They will put you in touch with their local dealers. Before making up your list read as many reviews and talk to as many people as possible. Weed out those which are obviously unsuitable until you have a manageable number. You should use a recommended local dealer as he will have the backing of the manufacturer and will be supplied on the most favourable terms. He will also be backed by the manufacturer's training and support system. They have an interest in his giving you a good service.

However, in rural areas you may have to choose between a recommended dealer some distance away and a local dealer with a sound reputation but who may not be able to support the preferred package so well. If you are in this situation and have fairly standard accounting needs it might be better to choose from packages which your local dealer is familiar with.

Using the proposals sent back from suppliers, look closely at any that seem out of step with the general trend of replies. Given the same criteria, most suppliers should come up with broadly similar solutions so eliminate any proposal which indicates that the supplier has grossly over- or underestimated your needs. If you are doubtful then get in touch with the supplier and find out why he made the proposal. If he cannot justify it to your satisfaction then it is safer to discard it.

Eliminate any proposal where the supplier has sent a standard reply showing no thought about your requirements.

Unless the proposal has other overwhelming elements in its favour discard any quotation where some part of the system is being supplied from a separate source and under a separate contract. Severe problems can arise where there is no overall contract – and therefore responsibility – for the entire system.

Any proposal which includes a great deal of tailored or bespoke software should be looked at carefully. This is especially true if other suppliers can offer tried and tested package software which will already meet your requirements.

Consider the response overall. Have you been treated professionally? Does the proposal meet your system outline in a way that shows it has been well thought out? A repeat of the glossy handout that your initial enquiry produced may mean that no thought has been given to your individual needs. A badly presented proposal obviously thrown together at the last moment may indicate a shortage of staff and point to difficulties in providing support once the system is installed.

Make an initial shortlist of all the packages which still look worth further investigation. Using your outline and the ICAS checklists, set out your requirements in the form of a checklist with a column for each supplier and mark off yes/no against each point from the supplier proposals. Clear up with the supplier any points marked with queries.

Include a column for hardware and software costs, upgrade costs, support and training costs. Note the number of training days proposed, response times for support and whether 'hotline' support is offered. Look at the implementation timetable proposed and the cost timescale for any amendments.

Make a shortlist of two or three packages and arrange for detailed demonstrations. Contact user sites with a view to making a final selection. Probably no one of these packages will fit your requirements perfectly but it should be possible to pick the 'best fit' compromising on the least important areas.

Chapter 4
Accounting Software

While a user's individual requirements must be carefully considered before deciding what software is suitable in a particular case, it is possible to consider in general terms what constitutes good accounting software.

Performance of requisite accounting functions

The first obvious requirement must be that the software performs all accounting functions properly. Different packages will have different capabilities (hence the need for part three to this book!) but any good package should be able to perform all normal ledger entries. It will be essential, for example, that a payment not exactly equal to an invoice amount can be posted to a purchase ledger account. However, it is not essential, though it is desirable, that this payment can be allocated as part-paying an invoice.

The features available in a package should be clearly detailed in the documentation and it is essential that the software does in fact do all that is claimed. All standard requirements, as well as being possible, should be capable of being carried out in a straightforward manner that is clear from the manual. It is all very well to know it is possible to enter 12 different monthly budget figures but unless you are told how to do so, the feature may as well not be there.

In certain cases some accounting functions will be required by statute. It is therefore essential that these functions are carried out by the software in the manner required. This applies particularly to payroll packages which must satisfy certain statutory requirements.

The way in which a package carries out its accounting functions must be consistent with good accounting practice. It must, for example, be possible to post adjustments to sales ledger accounts so that a bad debt can be written off in the normal way. It is not sufficient to be told that bad debts can be written off, if the only method of doing so is by putting through a credit note or a dummy payment. Neither of these methods should be acceptable in a manual system and should therefore not be acceptable in a computerised system either. In a

ACCOUNTING SOFTWARE 33

For the world leader in medical lasers the accounting package had to be spot on

Pilkington Medical Systems expected from its accounting software what surgeons and clinicians expect from its own medical lasers – technical excellence, quality performance and reliable support.

It comes as no surprise then that PMS chose FACT 2000. A fully integrated financial management system supported by the resources of CMG, Europe's leading independent software company.

When Pilkington and BOC recently joined forces to form Living Technology as the successor to PMS there was no problem. In a short four hour operation, the CMG systems installer set up the new company's accounts structure on the existing FACT 2000 system.

For an accounting system that's powerful, dependable and adaptable to your changing needs, find out the facts on FACT 2000 today from CMG.

CMG

We make sure systems really work

CMG – Computer Management Group
CMG Business Services Scotland Ltd

Magnet House
52 Waterloo Street
Glasgow G2 7BP
Tel: 041-221 8193

20 Stafford Street
Edinburgh EH3 7BD
Tel: 031-225 6828

IS THERE NO ACCOUNTING FOR GROWTH?

ACCPAC PLUS — DEMONSTRATION PACK VOUCHER

Yes - ACCPAC™PLUS, the world's leading micro accounting software system, is now available as a complete integrated suite or as separate modules.

ACCPAC™PLUS meets your current needs and those into which your business will grow. You select the facilities that match your size and style, without the crippling pains of shoe horning your business needs into software that won't always fit.

For a FREE demonstration pack send the voucher and your business card to the Micro Products Division of Computer Associates.

FROM THE MAKERS OF SuperCalc

COMPUTER ASSOCIATES
Software superior by design.

- World's largest independent software company.
- Broad range of integrated business and data processing software for mainframes, minis and micros.
- Worldwide service and support network of more than 70 offices.

HEAD OFFICE - SYSTEMS & MICRO SOFTWARE - 0753 77733 • Edinburgh House • 43-51 Windsor Road • Slough • Berkshire • SL1 2EQ
DATABASE/GRAPHICS & APPLICATIONS SOFTWARE - 0895 74090 • Harman House • 1 George Street • Uxbridge • Middlesex • UB8 1TW
NORTHERN OFFICE - 061 928 9334 • Lynnfield House • Church Street • Altrincham • Cheshire • WA14 4DS

Financial management solutions

for the most prestigious clientele in the World

Multi-currency, multi-company turnkey accounting solutions supplied on UNIX, XENIX, NETWORKS, PC DOS and MS DOS*

Shortlands

Shortlands Computing Services Ltd.

HEAD OFFICE:
Clyde House
Reform Road
Maidenhead
Berkshire SL6 8BU

Telephone: 0628 75227
Telefax: 0628 782234.
Telex: 849457 SHORTL G

REGIONAL OFFICE:
Seventh Floor
Station House
Stamford New Road
Altrincham WA14 1EP

Telephone: 061 941 6801
Telefax: 061 941 6820
Telex: 665190 SHORTA G

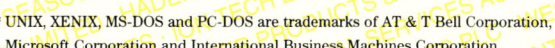

* UNIX, XENIX, MS-DOS and PC-DOS are trademarks of AT & T Bell Corporation, Microsoft Corporation and International Business Machines Corporation.

one-off situation it may be necessary to create an artificial entry in a computerised ledger but normal good practice should not be sacrificed.

The way in which accounting transactions are processed and stored should be such that full accounting records are kept. It should always be possible to trace any individual item from its entry into the system to its incorporation in the final accounts. In other words, a full audit trail should be maintained. This will be necessary, not only for audit purposes, but also so that all necessary information can subsequently be extracted from the system, e.g. for completion of VAT returns or compilation of statutory accounts. Such information can be kept either on paper in the form of various printouts or on disk. In either case information should appear in a logical fashion so that retrieval of particular sections or items should be straightforward.

Reliability, security and continuity of processing

Good accounting software will perform its functions consistently, accurately and predictably. It will ensure that once data is entered it will be processed accurately and completely, and that once stored on disk data will be reasonably secure.

There will be certain accounting controls built into the system but these must be supplemented by manual controls. A good computer system should ensure, for example, that the trial balance stays in balance by only permitting journal entries to be posted if they are square. A better system will check, for example, that the balance in the debtors' control account equals the total of the accounts in the sales ledger and that the ledgers can be advanced through the period end only if all subsidiary ledger transactions have been updated in the nominal ledger once and only once. The extent to which manual controls are necessary will depend on how good the computer system is. Even in the best system control must not be left solely to the machine. As an aid to the manual control, the computer system should produce reports of any errors, discrepancies or unusual situations.

The accounting data, once held on disk, is not invulnerable. It may, for example, be deleted (either accidentally or deliberately) or files may be corrupted due to a power failure or other mishap. A good system should deal with these situations in a way which causes the minimum of inconvenience. The user should be prompted to take back-up copies. At crucial points such as the period end this may be enforced. These copies can then be used by the system to restore the position although some re-inputting of information will probably be required. No matter how the system deals with the loss or corruption of data it should be able to demonstrate, after such a recovery, that the files are all fully restored.

User documentation and support

A good system will be of little use unless it is adequately documented and supported. Unless users can find out how to use their system it will be no good to them. The principal method of familiarisation with the software will be by reference to the user manual. This will probably be supplemented by some initial training, either from the dealer or software house. Some subsequent assistance should also be available. This often takes the form of hot-line support directly from the software house. Whatever the source, it is essential for users to be able to get answers to queries as they arise. They should never be in the position of being unable to continue processing because they do not know how to deal with a particular situation.

To be useful, the documentation produced should be comprehensive and presented in a logical and well-indexed manner. It should be easy to read and understand and it should be a simple task to locate any particular point required. All too often, time can be wasted by being unable to locate the answer to a query in the manual either through inadequate indexing or confusing structure. Unfortunately, the quality of the documentation is often inferior to the quality of the software it is designed to support.

To be of most use a manual should contain sample screens and reports, details of error messages and appropriate remedial action and guidance on how to make best use of the system as well as the standard information on installing, operating and controlling the system. It will also be of assistance if demonstration data and a tutorial are provided to help the user become familiar with the system. Many systems also come with on-line help screens. These may take the form of a simple reference to the appropriate page in the manual, or give detailed information to the user relevant to his current position in the system – e.g. what his options are at this point and what they do.

Adequate support should be available not only to guide the user until he becomes familiar with the software but also to provide any maintenance and upgrading necessary in the future. This may be necesary due to changes in the user's requirements (such as expansion of business) or to changes in some external factors (such as changes in the system of indirect taxation).

Accounting software should therefore come from a good software house and/or supplier. The organisation providing this continuing support should be sound and stable so that it is still around when the support is required. The company should be of a reasonable size with sufficient competent staff, be profitable and able to provide local support. The software itself should be written in a commonly-used programming language. Ideally, master versions of the software should be held by some third party so that all will not be lost in the event of the demise of the original support organisation.

Ease of use and flexibility

There comes a point when adding extra features to a package only makes it more complex and cumbersome to use. Inevitably the more a package can do, the more difficult it is to learn and operate. However, good documentation and interactive processing can make a complex package easier to use than a badly documented non-interactive, simpler one. An interactive system provides the user with helpful prompts and messages. He therefore knows at any time what to do next, what process is being currently performed or what error has caused a problem. In deciding which package to choose, it is usually a matter of striking the right balance between ease of use and complexity.

Whilst package software comes off the shelf as fairly standard there will be some flexibility in the system. There will often be a set of parameters for each ledger system so that it can be tailored to the requirements of a particular enterprise. This could include such things as the type of printer being used, the company name and address, and whether or not the system is to write cheques. It will usually include such things as the VAT rate. Changes to a company's needs can therefore be incorporated easily. A good system will print out these changes as they are made so that it can be checked that the system is operating as intended.

Another area where there will be greater or lesser flexibility is in the reporting facilities provided. A poor package will produce reports in one standard format. A good package will let the user have some say in how his reports are produced. Again, inevitably, the more flexible the reporting the more difficult the system is to set up and it may again be a matter of striking a balance in deciding on the most suitable system. The best type of package will be one where usual reports come as standard but the user has the option of designing any further reports he wishes. This is often done by means of a separate report generator integrated with the ledger systems.

To sum up, good accounting software should be capable of doing all that is reasonably required of it in a reliable fashion. It should be well documented and easy to use with good support being provided, both in the initial stages of setting up the system and during the life of the software. It should be capable of producing all the information that the user now requires and might reasonably require in the future.

ACCOUNTING SOFTWARE 39

You could be forgiven

for thinking there was little

choice in accounting

software.

TETRAPLAN | *Chameleon*

Fortunately, the choice includes Tetra – the leading business software specialist.

With packages of the calibre of Tetraplan and Chameleon to choose from, there's no need to look any further. **TETRA**

Tetra Business Systems Limited
Foundation House Norreys Drive
Maidenhead Berkshire SL6 4BX
Telephone (0628) 770939

**FOR A DEMONSTRATION THAT WILL REALLY SET YOU THINKING,
RING MCQUEENS – TETRA'S SPECIALIST ACCOUNTING CENTRE
IN SCOTLAND – ON 031 558 3333.**

Stockcare
Computer Systems

The One Stop Computer Centre
Keeping

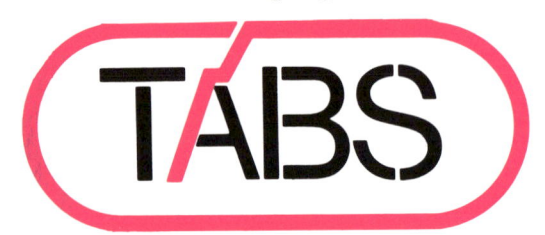

TABS

On Your Business

Whatever the size of your business Stockcare and TABS, the fully integrated accounting system, combine to offer a computer solution tailored to meet your current and future accounting requirements.

Stockcare — the Complete Solution

**Consultancy ⇒ System analysis ⇒
System Selection ⇒ Testing ⇒
Installation ⇒ Training ⇒
Free Telephone Support**

ASHTON·TATE

Opus.   apricot

**PHONE US FREE ON 0800-844855
OR 031 440 2822
Unit 9   Pentland Industrial Estate, Loanhead**

Part II
Detailed Evaluation

Introduction

This part of the book is based on checklists developed by the Institute of Chartered Accountants of Scotland for evaluating accounting software. These are based in turn on the Institute's Information Technology Statement on Good Accounting Software which gives an outline of the features which can be reasonably expected of a good software package. We have called these 'principles' and have structured this next section around them. Each principle is taken in turn and the questions in the checklists which relate to it are explained in detail. There are four checklists, one for assessing each of the three basic ledgers – sales, purchases and nominal – and one general checklist for an overall appraisal of the system. Copies of the checklists and the Information Technology Statement can be found in appendices 1 and 2.

You will find that some questions in the checklists appear more than once under different headings. Sometimes questions from one heading may be relevant to more than one attribute of good accounting software. For clarity and to save confusion we have matched each attribute to a section or sections of a checklist rather than to individual questions. For individual questions we have simply indicated when that particular question might relate to more than one aspect of accounting software. Where a whole block of questions clearly relates to more than one attribute we have included it under both headings.

The checklists were written in such a way that they could be used for any size of system, including systems running on large machines. Because of this, some of the questions relating to controls are not really relevant to smaller package systems and a few of the features mentioned may not be available. Larger systems, especially those written or maintained on site where staff have the opportunity and expertise to alter programs, require controls that are not needed by the more rigid, menu driven packages. As we review this aspect of the questionnaires we will indicate the controls it is reasonable to expect from package software and suggest supplementary manual procedures to complement those that are written into the software.

Sales purchase and nominal ledger – general questions

Each individual checklist has a section of questions which are general rather than specfic to any particular function or aspect of the software and which help the user to assess whether the package is going to be suitable, easy to run and control. For example, almost all packaged software is menu-driven. This helps to ensure that processing is done in the correct sequence. Make sure any enhancements or bespoke applications are also menu-driven.

A user log is a record of who did what, when, and can be used to monitor unauthorised access, pinpoint the source of errors, and make sure that all processing has been completed in the correct sequence. If this log is not automatic a manual computer log should be kept. Back-up and restore facilities provided by the software vary from relying on the operating system through basic diskcopying to controlling and managing files so that the minimum of work needs to be redone if there is a system failure. The facilities tend to improve with the price of the package.

Principle 1: Suitability

The suitability of accounting software for each particular user will always be dependent upon that user's individual requirements.

This is covered in the general points checklist under requisite accounting functions.

The questions listed in this section are a guide to the points to bear in mind when looking at brochures, attending demonstrations, reviewing proposals and talking to dealers and current users of the software. As the whole of this section is devoted to your personal appraisal of the proposed software, a negative answer to any question should be seriously considered as it probably means that the software is unsuitable for your needs.

General points checklist – requisite accounting functions

Functions

> 1. Does the software perform the functions which the user wants performed?

This is the crucial question in this section. It should be asked twice, once at the beginning of the appraisal – when a negative answer will save wasting any further time – and once at the end to make sure that your original reaction has held up under a more detailed scrutiny.

Size and complexity of the system

> 2. Can the software be used by more than one user at the same time?
> 3. Can the software support groups of companies/departments/branches?
>   How many such branches or companies can be supported?
>   Can they be consolidated?
> 4. Is multi-currency processing available?
>   What are the maximum number of currencies available?
>   Is conversion to sterling automatic?

These questions relate to the size and complexity of the system required rather than the quality of the software. A negative answer will only be detrimental if those particular attributes are essential to the user.

Accounting periods

> 5. Are sufficient accounting periods provided by the system?
>   Can these periods be adjusted to suit different user requirements?
> 6. Are the ends of accounting periods detemined by the user rather than being set by the system?
> 7. Can data from all accounting periods be accessed at any given moment?
> 8. Does the system prevent posting to more than one accounting period at a time?
>   Is it impossible to allocate transactions to future periods or to previous closed months?

The software should at least allow for 12 monthly periods based on calendar months. Better software will allow 12–13 periods or 52–53 weekly periods and the best packages allow flexible, user defined periods. Most software allows some tailoring of periods within the package 'parameters'.

Where disk space permits, a good package will allow transaction detail to be held for enquiry for up to a year if the user requires it. The length of time that transactions are to be retained can often be set by the user through the system or module parameters.

Some packages allow forward posting to the ledgers so that, for example, the purchase ledger can be held open for late invoices. This is a function that should be used with care. Many packages allow the user to set up monthly repeating journals for standing orders and depreciation and 'reversing' journals for accruals prepayments and stock adjustments. These are presented as separate selections on the menu options and are useful tools for producing accurate management accounts.

Budgets

> 9. Does the system permit use of budgets and provide comparisons between budgets and actuals?

A good package should always allow for the input of budgets. The facilities for comparing budget and actual figures vary from package to package. As a rough guide you can expect a simple comparison report from the cheaper packages and a more complicated type of variance analysis at the top end of the range.

Volumes

> 10. Is the maximum value of transactions that can be handled by the system sufficient?
> 11. Is the maximum number of accounts on each ledger (e.g. sales ledger, purchase ledger, nominal ledger) sufficient?
> 12. Is the size and format of account numbers adequate and sufficient for analysis purposes?
> 13. Does the associated hardware incorporate enough memory, disk storage and peripherals for the software to operate satisfactorily?
> 14. Does the system offer adequate expansion potential as regards terminals, memory, disk storage capacity and other peripherals?

If the answer to these questions is not YES then you have the wrong package. Additionally, if you deal in a small number of very large invoices or currencies with small denominations, check that the system can handle sufficient digits for a single transaction.

Controls

> 15. Are the control features provided by the software adequate to support effective user controls?
> 16. Are complementary clerical procedures to be imposed and effectively monitored by management?

An appraisal of your present system should have shown up any control weaknesss. Questions 15 and 16 should be addressed as one – the combination of package and clerical controls should be sufficient for your size and type of business. The lack of controls in a cheaper packate could be serious in a large multi-user environment but might not matter so much in a small business where the proprietor checks everything personally.

Detailed control questions are included in each individual checklist but some basic controls to look for are:

- enforced printing of all transactions including update to standing data (master file information);
- no deletion of accounts until they have been clear of transactions or balances for at least one accounting period;
- controls over period end processing so that updates between ledgers are not 'lost';
- prevention of direct postings to debtors' and creditors' control accounts in the nominal ledger;

- batch input controls such as pre-input batch totals;
- reconciliations between the ledgers and control totals and warnings if they are out of balance.

PEGASUS & SAGE
Accounting Software

AMSTRAD & APRICOT
Micro Computers & W.P.

EPSON & HEWLETT PACKARD
Matrix & Laser Printers

DISCOUNT PRICES PLUS EXPERT ADVICE

KYLE MICROS

18 Royal Terrace, Glasgow G3 7NY 041-332 2505
2 Bedford Square, London WC1B 3RA 01-580 4766

Principle 2: Functionality

Accounting software should be capable of supporting the accounting functions for which it was designed.

This is covered in the sales and purchase ledger checklists under the headings of:

- customer details
- supplier details
- transactions
- matching/allocation
- integration
- output

and in the nominal ledger checklist under the headings:

- account details
- transactions
- integration
- output

The individual checklists for each application have detailed questions on the format and content of the account information held in each ledger and the controls over standing data to be expected from good accounting software. Some of the questions, those on code formats and maximum numbers of accounts available, will relate to Principle 1. The questions relating to deletion of accounts and printouts of changes to account details cover essential controls for accounting software. Each detailed checklist then goes on to cover transactions, input controls, processing including integration with other modules, and output. Input controls, processing and integration do form part of the accounting function and they will be considered in detail later as part of Principle 3. In the following paragraphs we go into more detail about what it is reasonable to expect from an average price accounting package.

The sales and purchase ledgers will be covered together as their features are essentially the same. Minor differences reflect their differing functions.

The numbering of the questions in the sales and purchase ledger questionnaires is not always identical. Where this is the case both numbers are shown against the question, the purchase ledger questionnaire first.

Sales and purchase ledgers – customer and supplier details

Account code

> 1. What is the format of the supplier/customer account code?

The account code format should be one which has enough digits to assist with customer, supplier identification and allow for some sales analysis. An alphanumeric format is probably more useful than numeric only. Four digits is probably the workable minimum for smaller systems. If you need a specific coding structure, include this information in your systems outline.

Account detail

> 2. What other supplier/customer details are held?
>   Do these seem to be sufficient in general?

For sales and purchases expect the ledger to hold at least name, address, space for comment or contact name and whether the account is open item or balance forward. Most systems will include a credit limit, discount allowed, possibly an analysis coding and turnover details – and often a separate delivery address for the sales ledger.

Volumes

> 3. What is the maximum number of accounts that can be held?

The maximum number of accounts that can be held is not usually a problem unless you have very high numbers. However, check whether the maximum number applies to each individual ledger or varies within an overall total for all ledgers.

Maintaining customer and supplier details

> 4. Can customer/supplier details be added/deleted/amended at any time?
> 5. Is file re-sorted automatically when a new customer/supplier is added?
>   If NO, can a re-sort be initiated?
> 6. Is deletion of a customer/supplier prevented if the account has
>   an outstanding balance?
>   a zero balance but a b/f turnover?
> 7. Is a hard copy of changes in customer/supplier details automatically produced?
>   If NO, can a hard copy be taken?

For maximum efficiency the answers to questions 4 and 5 should be affirmative, so that a new customer or supplier can be set up during the invoicing routine. However, as all new accounts should be authorised and checked it is not too much of a disadvantage to use a separate routine for setting up the new accounts.

If the answers to questions 6 and 7 are negative then there is a fundamental control weakness in the software. Negative answers to question 6 (especially the first part) and the second part of 7 would almost certainly lead to rejection of the software.

Sales and purchase ledgers – transactions

The transaction questions are a check that the software will perform all the basic functions normally expected of the accounting module and that the transactions are held in the file for at least one accounting period. Most of the better packages will hold information for considerably longer. The limiting factor is usually the size of the disk.

Open item or balance forward

> 1. Can the system be open item?

Most systems are able to record transactions in an open item format. As it shows the list of invoices which make up the balance, most people prefer open item to the balance forward method. Many packages allow both open item and balance forward accounts. Some allow both within the same ledger.

Inputs

> 2. Are the following inputs possible:
>   invoices?
>   credit notes?
>   manual payments?
>   cash refunded?
>   discounts?

Listed above are the basic requirements for a sales and purchase ledger. Software that does not have all these inputs is suspect.

Analysis of sales and purchases

> 3. Can an invoice be analysed to several different sales or expense categories?
> 4. Are different VAT codes possible for different items within one invoice?

The reaction to a negative answer here depends on your requirements. If you have one type of sale only and all outputs are taxable at standard rate, there is no problem. However, most packages do have some sales or purchase analysis and you will therefore have to make sure that the scope for analysis is wide enough for your needs. The better packages also allow separate VAT rates for each line of an invoice.

Transactions details

> 5. Are all transactions retained on file for at least one period?
> 6. Can a ledger date pre-date existing transactions?
> 7. (Purchase ledger only) Can two references be input for an invoice (own and supplier's reference)?

You must be able to interrogate for all transactions (including invoices which have been matched to payments) and be able to print transactions listings until at least the period end. Many packages can be set up to hold a list of paid invoices for up to a year for answering queries. There may be times when a particular batch of invoices will be held back and entered out of date sequence by, say, a week. A good system will prevent backdating to the previous period but allow input of batches out of date sequence but within the correct period, usually after a warning that the date does not follow on from the last batch.

Sales and purchase ledgers – matching/allocation

Balance forward

> 1. Is the balance b/f aged?
> 2. Can cash be allocated automatically?
>   If YES, how is the allocation made?
>   Can this be overridden?
> 3. Can cash be allocated manually?
>   If YES, does the package check that cash allocated equals the amount paid?
>   How is any such difference treated?
> 4. Can credit notes/journal entries be allocated to previous periods?
> 5. Can cash in advance be held and later allocated to subsequent periods?
> 6. (Sales ledger only) Can cash be held unallocated?

Open item

> 6,7. Are outstanding transactions displayed for allocation?
> 7,8. Can cash be allocated automatically?
>   If Yes, how is the allocation made?
>   Can this be overridden?
> 8,9. Can cash be allocated manually?
>   If YES, does the package check that cash allocated equals cash paid?
>   How is any difference treated?
> 9,10. Can an over/underpayment of an invoice be recorded?
> 10,11. How often are settled items deleted from file?
> 11,12. Can credit notes be set against the invoices to which they refer?
> 12,13. Can journal entries be set against the invoices/credit note to which they refer?
> 13,14. Can cash in advance be held and later allocated to invoice?
> 14,15. Can cash be held unallocated?
>   How is this treated?

The sales and purchase ledger questionnaires both cover the methods used by the software to match cash posted either to balances or individual invoices. Automatic allocation usually allocates cash to the oldest invoice/aged balance first, so there should be a facility to allow invoices or balances in dispute to be flagged to prevent cash allocation. The cash allocation facility is one of the reasons for preferring an open item system: individual invoices can be paid and the current position is always clear.

For manual allocation the package should check that all cash entered is accounted for and hold 'extra' cash as an unallocated amount for future invoices/repayment. There ought to be a definite indication from the operator that an amount is to be left unallocated. An allocation of more cash than has been entered should not be accepted and the package should reject such an entry. This is not the same as a part-payment where the correct amount of cash is allocated to pay part of an invoice.

Settled items are usually deleted from the file during the period end run. Part paid invoices are usually marked as such and shown as the reduced amount. Overpayment should result in an amount of cash being held as unallocated.

It is usual for credit notes to be set against individual invoices and the items treated in the same way as cash allocation.

Sales and purchase ledger – integration

Integration

> 1. Can the purchase ledger be integrated with a job costing module and the sales ledger with an invoicing module?
> 2. Can the purchase and sales ledgers be integrated with a nominal ledger module?

If the modules are available it would be usual to have integration between the sales invoicing module and the sales ledger, and between job costing and the purchase ledger. There are no package systems worth considering where the sales and purchase ledgers cannot integrate with the nominal ledger – even if the user intends to run one or more as stand-alone modules.

Update to the nominal ledger

> 3. Can the nominal ledger be updated as often as desired?

Some packages update the nominal ledger using batch posting as a separate operation either user controlled or as a part of the processing routine. Others update both sales and nominal ledger as part of the same transaction, i.e. in batches of one. Whichever way the system works it is unusual not to be able to update the nominal ledger as frequently as desired.

> 4. Is a hard copy automatically produced at the end of each nominal ledger update?
> 5. Is there a purchase and sales ledger printout (as well as a nominal ledger printout) of the nominal ledger update?

If a printout is not automatically produced for all input you will have to set up a system for ensuring that all printouts are taken. A batch book or batch sheets, with a column for the operator to initial when the printout is complete and consecutive numbering of printouts cross-referenced to the book/sheet, could be used. If no printout is available then the software has serious shortcomings.

There is, however, usually a sales ledger printout in the form of a daybook

PRINCIPLE 2: FUNCTIONALITY 55

plus a nominal ledger printout of the update. The nominal update printout may include several sales batches. But the printouts should reconcile, and be reconciled to ensure the update is complete.

Discounts and bad debts

> 6. Are the following automatically posted to the appropriate nominal ledger accounts:
>   discount?
>   discount written back?
>   bad debts written off?
>   contras with other ledgers?

Automatic posting of discounts and bad debts does not usually present a problem. Contras between the sales and purchase ledgers usually have to be dealt with separately as ledger adjustments in both ledgers. Discount written back may have to be dealt with as a journal adjustment.

Unvalidated entries

> 7. Are any invalid/unidentified entries posted to a suspense account?
>   If NO, how are they treated?
>   If YES, how is the suspense account treated?

All entries should either be validated on input or, if not – and they are subsequently found to be invalid – they should be posted to suspense and identified on the printout as items requiring further action.

Control accounts

> 8. Is the ledger control balance agreed to the total of the balances in the individual ledger?

Control account balances in the nominal ledger should always be agreed to the sales and purchase ledger totals by the system at the end of processing. In addition, it should not be possible to post journals directly to the control accounts in the nominal ledger except by some special procedure to correct balances that are out of step. This facility should not be available through normal processing menus.

Current and future periods

> 9. Can current and future periods be maintained simultaneously?

In the larger package systems, current and future periods can often be maintained simultaneously so that ledgers can be held open for late invoices. It is a useful but not essential feature. Where forward posting is allowed the package should report on items entered for periods excessively in the future e.g. for the wrong year.

Nominal ledger update

> 10. Is there a check that transactions cannot be posted twice to the nominal ledger?
> 11. Must the nominal ledger be updated from the purchase/sales ledger before the period end is run?
> 12. Must the nominal ledger and the purchase/sales ledger be in the same period for the update to be carried out?
> 13. Is there any report/warning that transactions posted to the purchase/sales ledger have not yet been posted to the nominal ledger?

Questions 10, 11, 12 and 13 above all relate to essential controls. There should at least be a warning that the nominal ledger update has not been run before the period end is allowed to proceed. Ideally it should abort if transactions are outstanding. Transactions should be marked as updated once the update is run. Twin floppy systems should have a check – such as a generation number check – between the disks, so that the update cannot be accidentally run twice by processing from the wrong disk. Most systems update all unposted batches as soon as the update routine is invoked. It should however be possible to get a report listing batches awaiting update.

Whether update is allowed when the ledgers are in different periods depends on the complexity of the system. A system without the proper checks on its particular method of working to ensure updates are posted to the correct period is seriously weak.

Sales and purchase ledgers – output

The output requirements detailed here for both modules should be available from all accounting packages. If there are more than a couple of negative answers and those answers cover anything other than minor points, the software will have already shown major shortcomings in other areas.

Audit trail

> 1. Is it necesary to produce an audit trail before the period-end procedure is run?
> 2. Does the audit trail enable all transactions to be traced fully through the system?
> 3. Can the actual run date, or batch reference – as well as current ledger date – be shown on reports?

The audit trail is a list of all transactions that have been input (entered) to the ledgers. Using audit trail printouts it should be possible to trace all transactions through the system to the final printout or screen enquiry.

Ideally the system should ensure that the audit trail (called the daybooks by some systems) is printed out either during input or just after, as part of the exit routine. It is essential that the audit trail is printed before the period-end procedure which clears down or purges all matched transactions in open item systems, and clears down all transactions into the carried forward balance in balance forward systems. If the audit trail is not printed at or before this stage, all record of transactions can be lost. This is especially true in more basic systems where transactions are not stored for enquiry purposes beyond the current period.

Detailed list of reports

> 4. Can the following be produced:
>   list of master file information?
>   aged creditors/debtors report?
>   VAT report?
>   ledger detail report?
>   remittance advices/customer statements?
>   supplier/customer name and address labels?
>   suggested payments?
>   cheques?

All packages should have the first five reports (listed in question 4) in the sales and purchase ledgers. Most sales ledgers now also have a selection of debtors' letters or a word processing facility so that you can compose your own reminder letters.

Many purchase ledgers now have automatic payment runs and links to BACS payments. Packages which have these facilities should also have a suggested payments listing for review before the actual payments routine is run.

Statements, remittance advices

> 5. Can remittance advices show:
>   individual invoices?
>   discount?
>   supplier's reference?
> 6. Does the customer statement:
>   show discount separately?
>   show ageing?
>   allow special messages?
>   allow for suppression of erroneous postings and their corrections?

Most packages will have a fairly well designed statement layout and some allow you to design your own. Ask for a specimen statement from the supplier/dealer. The same applies to remittance advices where they are provided.

Account ledger details

> 6,7. Can the following screens be seen:
>   customer/supplier details?
>   customer/supplier transactions?
> 7,8. Can hard copies of the following be obtained for individual accounts/ selected ranges of accounts:
>   customer/supplier details?
>   customer/supplier transactions?
> 8,9. Does the ledger account detail report show:
>   the source of all postings?
>   how part-payments and allocations have been treated?
>   either the full account history or balance b/f together with current period transactions?

Screen enquiries and printouts for account details are a standard facility and can be expected from all good packages. You can expect a good system to show full details of the ledger account. Look at a specimen copy of the report to check that the details are sufficient.

Aged analysis

> 9,10 and 11. Is ageing strictly by transaction date?
>   If NO, how is ageing done?
>   Does the aged analysis show for each customer:
>   total balance outstanding?
>   credit limit?

Ageing may be by month or period, depending on how the system has been set up and whether the ageing facility is flexible or strictly by period. Check that the ageing is valid. Transactions may be input in the following calendar month if the purchase ledger has been held open for late invoices. In this case, ageing by transaction date may not be valid if the system uses the calendar date for input date.

> 10,12. Does the aged analysis show unallocated cash separately?
>   If NO, how is it aged?

For control purposes unallocated cash should be shown separately and aged as a normal transaction. In balance forward systems it may simply be deducted from the period balance which may then show up as a negative figure as a result.

Report layouts

> 11,13. Do all outputs show clearly the distinction between debits and credits?
> 12,14. Are all reports adequately titled?
> 13,15. Do reports provide totals where applicable?
> 14,16. Can report production be varied by:
>   printing a range of accounts?
>   printing by, for example, area?
> 15,17. Is the period number shown on reports?
> 16,18. Are all report pages sequentially numbered with the end of the report identified?

Look at a specimen copy of each report to satisfy yourself that it gives enough information for your needs. All reports should contain titles and totals. Reports should be available both as screen and printed output and should be sufficient for both management and control purposes.

Sales and purchase analysis

> 17,19. Is a purchase/sales analysis possible?

Some form of analysis will almost always be available. Whether or not it is sufficient for your needs is a matter of judgement.

Spooling of reports

> 18,20. Can reports be temporarily retained on file for subsequent printing?
>   If YES, are such files protected from deletion?

Spooling is available on better packages and requires a hard disk machine to be practical. Good accounting software should protect spooled reports until they have been printed. This protection almost always only applies to attempts to delete unprinted files using the accounting software routines. Users should be aware that such files can still be accidentally deleted using operating system commands or utility routines.

Report generator and transaction enquiries on previous periods

> 19,21. Is a report generator available for use with the purchase ledger/sales ledger module?
> 20,22. Can transaction files for previous periods be retained in the system to permit enquiries and reports?

Good software will have these facilities. The length of time you can store transactions on a hard disk machine will depend upon disk storage space available and the volumes of transactions.

Purchase ledger – payments/cheque writing

> 1. Can the system write cheques?
>   If YES, is the payment posted automatically to the purchase ledger?
> 2. Is there an automatic cheque writing facility?
>   If YES:
>   is a list of suggested payments printed in advance of the cheques?
>   is the total cash requirement printed in advance of the cheques?
>   can the automatic payment routine be aborted if either of the above is not satisfactory?
> 3. Can the following payment/report options be selected:
>   individual invoice selection?
>   supplier selection?
>   pay all invoices of a certain age?
>   pay according to due date?
>   pay all invoices except those marked 'not to be paid'?
>   other (specify)?
> 4. Is discount automatically calculated by the payment routine?
> 5. Can invoices be held as disputed?
>   If YES, can a report of disputed invoices be produced?

This section contains additional questions for purchase ledger packages which have facilities for printing cheques and posting such payments to the purchase ledger. Such systems save a great deal of time if there are large volumes of the payments but they do need extra controls. A suggested payments list is essential (question 2); it must be possible to hold disputed invoices back from payment. Total cash requirements information may be essential for cash control; it should be possible to run more than one suggested payments listing with totals before the final cheque print. The method of selection of invoices to be paid depends on individual needs but the options listed in question 3 can be expected from a good system. Systems which hold details of supplier terms and pay according to due date for claiming discount should calculate discount automatically.

This section can also be used for evaluating a BACS payment option in the purchase ledger.

Nominal ledger – account details

Coding structure and chart of accounts

> 1. Is the chart of accounts flexible?
> 2. What is the format of the nominal account code?
> 3. Is cost centre accounting available?
> 4. What is the maximum number of accounts that can be held?
> 5. What is the maximum balance that can be held?

The nominal coding structure and chart of accounts are crucial. Effort put into a thorough understanding of this aspect of each package is well worthwhile. The chart of accounts should be flexible enough to give you the reports you need and – as with the sales and purchase ledgers – an alpha-numeric coding is often the most useful format. If you need cost centre, divisional or departmental reporting make sure this can be done using either the account coding structure or a separate analysis coding. If you have complicated reporting needs, it is probably best to set out a trial coding structure on paper to test the software before committing yourself. As with the sales and purchase ledgers the number of accounts and maximum balance is not usually a software problem, especially on hard disk machines where the disk is normally the limiting factor.

Account maintenance

> 6. Can accounts be added/deleted/amended at any time?
> 7. Is the file automatically re-sorted when a new account is added?
>   If NO, can a re-sort be initiated?
> 8. Is deletion of an account prevented if it has:
>   a non-zero balance?
>   a zero balance but postings in the current period?
>   a zero balance but postings in the year-to-date?
> 9. Is a hard copy of changes in account details automatically produced?

For maximum efficiency the answers to questions 6 and 7 should be yes, so that a new account can be set up during posting routines. However, as all new accounts should be authorised, it is not too much of a disadvantage to have to set up a separate routine for new accounts and checking printout.

If it is possible to delete a nominal ledger account which contains a balance or transactions then there is a fundamental control weakness in the software. Negative answers to both questions 8 and 9 should almost certainly lead to rejection of the software.

Accounting periods and budgets

> 10. Are 12 or 13 (or more) accounting periods available?
> 11. Can budgets be entered for all revenue accounts?
> 12. Can separate budgets be entered for each accounting period?
> 13. Can this year's results be used to calculate next year's budgets automatically?

All packages should have at least a choice of 12 or 13 accounting periods and some form of budgeting. Budget facilities vary a great deal from package to package. The cheaper packages often provide no more than an even split of the budget over the year. You can expect the more expensive packages to provide facilities for departmental and cost centre split and to cater for seasonal fluctuations and revised budgets.

Nominal ledger – transactions

Standard journal postings

> 1. What is the maximum transaction value that can be entered?
> 2. Can each journal entry contain an unlimited number of debits and credits?
> 3. Is each input line numbered?
> 4. In a long journal entry, is it possible to move between screens to view data already input?
> 5. Can previously entered journal lines be edited before accepting the whole journal?
> 6. Does each journal entry have a reference number?

The limit on the maximum transaction value and the number of debits and credits is usually only a problem with the most basic systems. Even then the only real problem is encountered when entering the opening trial balance. In any case, journals should be authorised and totalled for control purposes before being entered and can be split into several smaller journals if necessary.

For small systems it is probably not essential for each input line to be numbered (question 3) as journals should be drafted so that each journal covers a single transaction. However, a reference number for each journal is an essential control (question 6). Questions 4 and 5 relate to ease of use. Reviewing data during input is desirable but not essential and – except for entering the opening trial balance – not a limitation often encountered during normal postings. Editing facilities are more important as most package systems should not and do not accept unbalanced entries.

Reversing and recurring journals

> 7. Are accruals and prepayments routines available which reverse automatically at the start of the next accounting period?
> 8. Can recurring journal entries be provided for automatically?

Nearly all systems have accrual and prepayment routines so that period end adjustments can be entered without having to remember to reverse the journal in the following periods. The same routine can be used to make period end stock adjustments. Recurring journals will allow you to provide for standing orders and direct debits.

Narrative

> 9. Is a narrative available for:
>   each journal entry?
>   each line of the journal entry?

Some form of narrative is available even in the most basic systems for both the journal entry and each line of the journal.

Posting to future and past periods

> 10. Can journal entries be posted to future periods?
> 11. Can journal entries be posted to previous periods?

This option is more likely to be provided within a top-of-the-range system where it is expected that the system will be installed and controlled by someone experienced in accounting procedures. If available it should be used with care and tightly controlled.

Transaction details

> 12. Are all transactions retained on file for at least one period?
> 13. Can transactions be retained at the period end?
> 14. Can a ledger date pre-date existing transactions?

You must be able to interrogate individual nominal ledger accounts for transaction details and to print transaction listings until at least the period end. Some packages can be set up to hold transaction details for up to a year for answering queries. There may be times when a particular batch of journal entries will be held back and entered out of date sequence by, say, a week. A good system will prevent backdating to the previous period but allow input of batches out of date sequence within the correct period (usually after a warning that the date does not follow on from the last batch).

Nominal ledger – output – general

Audit trail

> 1. Is it necessary to produce an audit trail before the period end procedure is run?
> 2. Does the audit trail enable all transactions to be traced fully through the system?
> 3. Can the actual run date or batch reference, as well as the current ledger date, be shown on all reports?

Ideally the system should produce the audit trail or transactions listing automatically during input or as part of the exit routine after posting. If this is not the case the period end routine should abort unless the audit trail has already been printed by the user. Where the audit trail is spooled, the period end routine should abort if all printouts have not been taken. The period end routine clears down the transaction detail into a balance for carrying forward into the next period. Therefore, systems which do not ensure that audit trails are printed before this detail is lost should be avoided. If such a system is used, strict manual controls must be enforced.

An audit trail that does not enable all transactions to be traced fully through the system is not an audit trail. Such packages shoud be avoided. The only way to really test the audit trail is by tracing one of each kind of transaction through the system using the audit trail prints. It would be unusual to find an accounting system which has been available for some time and which has a reasonable number of users with a totally inadequate audit trail. However, you should satisfy yourself that the method used to trace the transactions – and the references used on the printout to identify transactions – are sufficient for your needs.

Run dates and current period or ledger dates should be on all printouts. Batch references should be available; either system-generated, which is the ideal, or keyed in by the operator at the time of input. They should appear on all reports. Manual cross-reference to the input documents is a last resort.

Account details

> 4. Can the following be seen on screen:
>   account details?
>   account transactions?
> 5. Can a printout of the following be obtained for individual accounts/selected ranges of accounts:
>   account details?
>   account transactions?
> 6. Do all outputs show clearly the distinction between debit and credit entries?

Account details and transactions should be available both as printout and screen enquiry from all systems. The distinction between debits and credits on output is essential for the nominal ledger where the normal method of transaction input is by journal.

> 7. Are all reports adequately titled?
> 8. Do reports provide totals where applicable?
> 9. Is the period number shown on reports?
> 10. Can the following be produced:
>   trial balance?
>   ledger account detail report?
>   profit and loss account?
>   balance sheet?

The reports listed in question 10 are standard reports to be expected in a basic format from all nominal ledger packages without the need to resort to a report generator. Good systems will ensure that all reports are adequately titled and show totals and period numbers.

> 11. Does the ledger account detail report show the source of postings and narrative input?
> 12. Does the ledger account detail report show either the full account history or balance b/f together with current period/transactions?

Ledger account detail should always show the source of postings and some identifying narrative. Whether this is sufficient for individual needs is a matter for individual judgement. Control considerations only require that it is sufficient for tracing transactions. Ledger account detail should enable you to trace transactions to the account in detail for at least the current period.

Reports

> 13. Are all reports pages numbered sequentially, with the end of report identified?
> 14. Can reports be temporarily retained on file for subsequent printing?
>   If YES, are such files protected from deletion?

All report pages should be numbered sequentially for control purposes. Most systems will retain reports for subsequent printing using a spooler facility. While the better systems will prevent deletion of unprinted files from within the application, very few package systems are capable of preventing files from being deleted when using operating system commands. Some systems are weak in that unprinted reports can be lost when the period end is run.

> 15. Is a report generator available for use with the nominal ledger module?

Report generators are useful but not essential if the standard reports meet your needs. They are often fairly difficult to use. A package with a good set of standard reports which allows for some user selection to tailor the exact format may be more useful.

Retained transactions

> 16. Can transaction files for all previous periods be retained in the system to permit enquiries and reports?

The ability to store transactions beyond the period end for future enquiries and reports depends on both the software and the hardware. Provided that you have a hard disk machine and enough storage space for your volume of transactions then good software should allow you keep transactions detail for several periods. If you have a large volume of postings to the nominal ledger you may want to limit the storage of transaction details for future reference to certain accounts in order to save space. Broadly speaking, the very cheapest software packages will not allow you to keep transaction detail beyond the current period. Mid-range packages are usually capable of storing detail for a specified period of up to a year but only to all accounts. Only the most expensive and sophisicated packages will allow selective storage by individual accounts.

Trial balance; profit and loss and balance sheet
Formatting

> 1. Does the package provide for flexible formatting of profit and loss account and balance sheet?

Flexible formatting is provided by most packages using either options chosen from a list within the main module or a report generator. The first option is more limiting but often easier to cope with.

> 2. Can the following be produced for both the current period and the year-to-date?
>   trial balance?
>   profit and loss account?
>   balance sheet?
>   If YES, is it clearly shown whether a report is for the current period or year-to-date?

The three basic reports, trial balance, profit and loss and balance sheet should be available for current period and year-to-date in even the most basic systems. All reports should clearly show their purpose.

Budgets and comparatives

> 3. Can the following show budgets:
>   trial balance?
>   profit and loss account?
>   If YES, can budgets be omitted if wished?
> 4. Can the following reports show comparative figures:
>   trial balance?
>   profit and loss account?
>   balance sheet?
>   If YES, can comparatives be omitted?
>   Can two years' comparatives be shown?
> 5. Are budgets worked out from the period number as calculated by the number of period end procedures run?
> 6. Are budget variances calculated?
>   If YES, are they shown as:
>   value?
>   percentages?
>   both?
> 7. Do budget reports provide for exception reporting?

Budgets and comparative figures should be available from even the most basic systems. However, basic systems are inclined to have basic budget facilities and two year comparatives should not be expected in most micro-accounting packages. Budget variance reports can usually be constructed using a report generator but are not generally available from the more basic package systems as standard reports. Exception reports are only usually available through a report generator.

Cost centre accounting

> 8. Does the package provide for a trial balance to be produced for each cost centre?
> 9. Does the package provide for a profit and loss account and balance sheet for each cost centre?
> 10. Does the package provide for totalling of like items across cost centres?

If cost centres are available within the chart of accounts then standard reports usually cater for cost centre reporting. Cost centre accounting can be looked for in mid-range packages and is almost certainly available from top-of-the-range packages.

Trial balance

> 11. Can trial balance production be varied by:
>   printing a range of accounts?
>   subtotalling on any chosen digit of the account code?

Trial balance reports vary considerably from package to package. Subtotalling depends on the type of account code and the functions assigned to the account code within the particular package.

Percentages and breakdown

> 12. Can vertical percentages be calculated in the profit and loss account?
> 13. Can a report be produced to show the breakdown of profit and loss account and balance sheet figures?

Vertical percentages are usually possible using report generators but may be available as standard in mid- and top-range packages. There is usually a facility for a detailed trial balance report in even the most basic packages. Have a look at sample reports to make sure that they give enough detail for your needs.

Year End

> 1. Can balance sheet items be carried forward and profit and loss account items cleared automatically at the year end?
> 2. Can the destination of individual account balances be specified or are all balances cleared at the year end transferred into one account only?

Most packages will carry forward balance sheet items and clear down the profit and loss accounts into a designated account. Some will allow the year end reports to be run in draft form to be finalised when audit adjustmens are to hand. A few still exist where the year end clears all accounts to zero and the opening trial balance has to be re-input the following year.

General points questionnaire – performance of requisite accounting functions

The section in the general questionnaire, 'Performance of requisite accounting functions', has already been covered in detail when looking at users' individual requirements. It would be useful to reappraise the questions at this point after having completed the individual checklists.

PRINCIPLE 2: FUNCTIONALITY 69

Perfect Balance...

Dillon Technology's accounting systems are a perfect balance between state of the art software and reliable proven accounting packages that accountants can understand.

Dillon are able to provide a complete accounting solution covering Sales, Purchase, Nominal, Stock and Order Processing and Fixed Assets, all linked to data manipulation tools that give complete control over storage and reporting of accounting data.

For the more sophisticated user there is full multi-currency, multi-company capability conforming to the recognised International standards set out in FASB 52/8 and SSAP 20.

Dillon are able to supply software for all popular PC's, as well as multi-user versions for Networks, UNIX and XENIX systems.

Insist on fitness and flexibility for your company's accounting records by contacting Dillon Technology on (0628) 75751, or in Ireland on 01 712570, or by completing the coupon and sending it to
Dillon Technology International Ltd
McGraw-Hill House,
Shoppenhangers Road,
Maidenhead, Berks SL6 2QJ

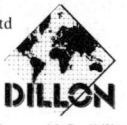

DILLON
Power with flexibility

Please send more information on Dillon Technology's accounting systems

Name _____

Position _____

Address _____

_____

Telephone _____

Principle 3: Integrity

Good accounting software should provide facilities to ensure the completeness, accuracy and continuing integrity of the accounting functions.

This principle is covered in the general points checklist under reliability, security and continuity of postings; and in the individual ledger checklists under input controls, integration and output.

In the following paragraphs we will first review the general points of reliability, security and continuity of processing which cover back-up, recovery procedures and processing problems. We will then go on to discuss the individual ledger checklists.

General points checklist – reliability, security and continuity of posting

1. Does the system facilitate back-up storage?
   How much time will complete back-up of the system require?
2. Does the system facilitate recovery procedures in the event of system failure?
3. If system failure occurs part way through a batch or transaction, will the operator have to re-input only the batch or transaction being input at the time of the failure?
4. Are there any features provided with the software to help track down processing problems?
5. Are back-up procedures provided within each specific software application or within the operating system?
   Are any of these back-up procedures automatic?

Machines and package programs can be replaced within a day or two. Your data is the lifeblood of the business and can be irreplaceable. At best, recreating data is time consuming and costly. At worst it is impossible. Back-up of data is vital. Many systems have a menu-driven back-up procedure and the better systems can also be set up to enforce back-up on a regular basis. At the very minimum the system should prompt back-up when the 'exit' option is selected from the main or system menu. Unfortunately, too many systems will force the user to rely on the operating system (usually DOS) commands for back-up. For systems where back-up is not enforced or enforceable a regular routine of back-up, either daily, weekly or at other suitable time intervals, should be set up and followed. Where back-up relies on the operating system you will need to provide a written back-up procedure for the operator to use. The tapes or disks used for back-up should be stored away from the machine, preferably in a suitable fireproof safe or another building. Not all fireproof safes maintain a low enough temperature to protect diskettes, and the majority of document safes would not be suitable for disk storage. Clearly labelled and neatly filed input documents will make it much easier to re-input the data should it be necessary.

At the end of each accounting period, a complete back-up should be taken and stored away from the premises e.g. taken home or deposited with the bank. THIS SHOULD BE DONE FOR ALL SYSTEMS REGARDLESS OF HOW GOOD THE BACK-UP CONTROLS ARE.

Recovery procedures to look for in good software include the following:

Menu-driven recovery which requests specific disks and rejects any others inserted into the drive.

A system log which shows the date of the last back-up and the disk used.

A complete automatic recovery procedure which will check the entire system and only back-up the files it requires. Such systems will often be able to take up processing at the point they left off, with only the last few transactions to be re-input. This is not a feature usually found in reasonably-priced packaged accounting software for micro-computers.

Within the individual checklists we will consider input controls and controls over processing. Processing controls are almost exclusively machine controls built into the software. One of the advantages of package software is the lack of opportunity for interfering with the original programming. Because of this, well written package software can be relied on to process accounting information accurately and consistently. Though most accounting software provides some control over input, the accuracy and completeness of input is ultimately dependent on manual controls set up by the user.

Some of the controls contained in the checklists are more common in larger systems than in micro-packages. Where it is probable that a control may not be available from most packages we have suggested possible alternative manual controls.

Sales and purchase ledgers – input controls

Passwords

> 1. Is password control used?
>   If YES, give details.

Password controls vary considerably between packages. Passwords can be personal, linked to terminals, linked to applications or hierarchical – with each member of staff given a password at the appropriate level. The password structure may include combinations of several types so that a personal password is tailored to allow a member of staff into different levels in different applications.

The level of password security needed depends on the size and structure of the business. If one part-time book-keeper does all the processing then the system only needs to be protected against unauthorised access. A larger organisation where division of duties is part of overall control will need a password system either linked to applications or tailored for individuals. Passwords alone cannot be relied upon to protect the system and should be accompanied by physical controls and supervision.

Audit trail

> 2. Is a hard copy automatically produced for all input?

If a printout is not automatically produced for all input you will have to set up a system for ensuring that all printouts are taken. A batch book or batch sheets with a column for the operator to initial when the printout is complete (and consecutive numbering of printouts cross referenced to the book/sheet) may be used for this purpose.

Batch totals

> 3. Are batch totals automatically produced for all transactions input?
>   If YES, what is the procedure if this does not agree with a pre-list total?
> 4. Is it necessary that invoices, cash and adjustments are input in separate batches?
> 5. Are batches automatically sequentially numbered?
>   If NO, can they be so numbered?

Batch totals are a fundamental control to ensure completeness of processing. Ideally, the batch total should be pre-input and checked by the system at the end of input before it accepts the batch. An over-ride will be provided in case the pre-total was wrong but the details should be reported as part of the audit trail. If this control does not exist and you wish to use the software, then create it manually by using a batch sheet and checking the totals against the total on the printout. A manual control account using the manual batch totals should have a balance which agrees with the computer control balance in both the nominal and individual ledgers. Separate batches should be used for each type of input – even if the system allows individual input of a single invoice followed by a cash item, followed by an adjustment. Some form of sequential numbering should be used to ensure all batches are processed. Write on the printout if necessary.

Reconciliation reports

> 6. Is a report produced at the end of each processing run to reconcile b/f total transactions processed and c/f total?
> If NO, is a control balance produced at the end of each posting run?

Either a reconciliation report or a control balance should be printed as a machine check on the completeness of processing. Unfortunately, omission of this basic control is common in cheaper packages. This can be overcome by reconciling a manual control from batch totals to the computer balance for the ledger. If the answers to questions 2, 3, 5 and 6 are all negative then this is a strong reason for rejecting the package. This is especially true if you intend to install it in an organisation of any size where management will have to rely to some extent on machine controls.

Validation

> 7. Are the following validated:
>   date?
>   customer account number?
>   VAT code?
>   goods value?
>   sales analysis code?

Validation of the date, customer account number, VAT code and sales analysis code, if any, is common to most systems, even at the cheaper end of the market. Validation of goods value is unlikely from a basic ledger package but is usually available if sales invoicing or sales or purchase ledger processing is integrated with the ledger.

> 8. Is VAT calculated to check figure input?
> 9. Is the gross figure agreed to goods+VAT?
> 10. Is discount calculated to check the figure input?

Similarly, a stand-alone ledger may not have a VAT calculation check, though most up to date versions check VAT using a VAT code related to a percentage table. Most package systems do no check VAT line-by-line unless linked to an invoicing module. They normally complete only an overall check on the invoice

CYCOM SBS

Multi-Currency Accounting and Management Information Systems for Single or Multi-User Computers

SYSTEMS
- General Ledger
- Sales Ledger (Debtors)
- Purchase Ledger (Creditors)
- Management Reporting
- Stock Control
- Sales Orders / Invoicing
- Purchase Orders Processing
- Job Costing
- Payroll
- Fixed Assets Register

FEATURES
- Multicompany / Multicurrency
- Comprehensive Audit / Trails
- Interface with Spread Sheets
- Interface with Word Processors
- Query Language Interface
- Available for MS-DOS, XENIX Networks, UNIX & VMS
- Report Generators
- User Friendly
- Highly Parameterised

CYCOM SBS provides the management controls required to efficiently run your business whether that is a local company trading internationally or a multinational corporation. The software has been developed according to the highest accounting standards and is already being used by hundreds of users in a number of countries.

* Distributor & Dealer Enquiries welcome.

Cycom Computer Products Ltd

Head Office
Nicosia
Marilena Building, 5th Floor
12 Princess De Tyra Str, P O Box 5732 Nicosia
Tel: 02-454448, Tlx: 2099 Centre Cy

UK Distributors
Granta Computers Ltd, Tel: 0223-207921
Micronet Computer Consultants, Tel: 061 480 3090
Structured Software Ltd, Tel: 0582 841501

total. Therefore, to avoid rejecting input for a mixed invoice where VAT may not be 15 per cent of the goods total, these systems may confine themselves to a 'reasonableness' check.

All systems should reject an input where goods+VAT does not equal the gross figure. This fundamental input control should be expected even from the cheapest, most basic systems.

Discount checks are not always available on the smaller systems especially if no invoicing module is installed. However, systems that include discount in the customer/supplier standing data should be able to cope with discounts. This is likely to be only one discount percentage per account. More complex systems may have discount tables but they are usually related to products and quantities via order processing or stock control.

Printouts

> 11. Can the actual date of posting or batch reference be shown on hard copies of transactions input?

Posting dates and batch references, either system generated or input by the operator, should appear on printouts. It is reasonable to expect this from all package software.

Input screens

> 12. Does the screen always indicate that the sales ledger as opposed to the purchase ledger is running?
> 13. Do all input screens show clearly:
>   type of entry?
>   the distinction between debits and credits?

Cheaper systems are normally used by the more inexperienced first-time users. Therefore it is important that input screens should show clearly which application is running and which type of entry is being used. Most package systems automatically deal correctly with the debit/credit aspect of postings and try to avoid worrying the user with it. The only type of posting where debit and credit entries are required from the user is adjustment to the ledger where debits and credits are usually entered in separate, labelled columns.

Multiple entry of the same item

> 14. Is there any check that the same entry is not input twice?

Most ledger packages allow entries to be input more than once without any warning unless the ledger is integrated with an order processing module which matches invoices to delivery notes. Cash matching routines should show up cash postings entered twice. If the system uses a pre-input batch total then the input total would exceed the batch total and lead to rejection of the uncorrected input. However, this would only pick up multiple input within the same batch.

Credit limits and overpayment

> 15. Is there a warning if a customer exceeds the credit limit or a supplier is overpaid?
> If YES, what action is required?

A credit limit warning is available from most packages but this is usually an operator warning designed to be easily over-ridden. In any case, with a stand-alone ledger, this is really not a meaningful check as the invoice has been issued/received along with the goods before the credit limit is checked. If a supplier is overpaid and the amount of cash available for allocation agrees with the total cash input, most package systems will hold the overpaid amount within the account as unallocated cash. Control over overpayments is only realistically available from purchase ledger modules with automatic cheque runs or which print suggested payments listings.

Masterfile amendments

> 16. Is it impossible for new accounts to be created during processing?
> 17. Is a reconciliation of numbers of accounts produced after amendment of the supplier/customer detail file?

From a control point of view it is not desirable to have accounts set up during processing. It is too easy at this stage to end up with duplicate accounts and for operators to over-ride the normal authorisation procedures. This option is often available from packages for user convenience and the software ensures that it does not disrupt processing, but controls over the actual amendments can be weak.

Most smaller users have no appreciable division of duties. Control over account set up is maintained through close supervision by management or proprietor. There is therefore no drawback to having accounts set up during processing routines. With more sophisticated package systems intended for the larger business, control over account creation can be maintained with password protection or by reviewing hard copy printout of master file amendments. Whether the added control of having accounts set up as a separate routine is essential, depends upon the user's needs. A reconciliation of numbers of accounts should not normally be expected from standard package software.

Abnormal termination

> 18. Does the system prevent the abnormal termination of programs?

Most package software is menu driven and the exit from the system is by stepping back through the menus to the final exit point. This ensures that all files are closed and all updates complete. The only abnormal exit available from most package software is by pulling the plug – a situation that good software should deal with by forcing the user to return to his last set of uncorrupted data. For sophisticated software this may be the last transaction before the power loss, but for most commonly available packages it is likely to be the last back-up taken.

Sales and purchase ledger – integration

The following points from integration sections of the sales and purchase ledger checklists relate to essential controls and have been included below.

Audit trail

> 4. Is a hard copy automatically produced at the end of each nominal ledger update?
> 5. Is there a sales purchase ledger printout (as well as a nominal ledger printout) of the nominal ledger update?

If a printout is not automatically produced for all input you will have to set up a system for ensuring that all printouts are taken. A batch book or batch sheets with a column for the operator to initial when the printout is complete (and numbering of printouts cross-referenced to the book/sheet) should be sufficient. If no printout is available then the software has serious shortcomings.

There is more usually a sales/purchase ledger printout in the form of a daybook plus a nominal ledger printout of the update. The nominal update printout may include several sales or purchase batches but the printouts should reconcile and be reconciled to ensure completeness of update.

Unvalidated entries

> 7. Are any invalid/unidentified entries posted to a suspense account?
>   If NO, how are they treated?
>   If YES, how is the suspense account treated?

All entries should either be validated on input or posted to suspense and identified on the printout as items requiring further action.

78 A GUIDE TO ACCOUNTING SOFTWARE

Control accounts

> 8. Is the sales/purchase ledger control balance agreed to the total of the balances in the sales/purchase ledger?

Control account balances in the nominal ledger should always be agreed to the sales and purchase ledger totals by the system at the end of processing. In addition, it should not be possible to post journals directly to the control accounts in the nominal ledger except by some special procedure to correct balances that are out of step. This procedure should not be available through normal processing menus.

Nominal ledger update

> 10. Is there a check that transactions cannot be posted twice to the nominal ledger?
> 11. Must the nominal ledger be updated from the sales ledger before the period-end is run?
> 12. Must the nominal ledger and the sales ledger be in the same period for the update to be carried out?
> 13. Is there any report/warning that transactions posted to the sales ledger have not yet been posted to the nominal ledger?

Questions 10, 11, 12 and 13 above all relate to essential controls. There should at least be a warning that the nominal ledger update has not been run before the period end is allowed to proceed. Ideally it should abort if transactions are outstanding. Transactions should be cleared from the file once the update is run. Twin floppy systems should have a check, such as a generation number check between the disks, so that the update cannot be accidentally run twice by processing from the wrong disk. Most systems update all unposted batches as soon as the update routine is invoked. It should however be possible to get a report listing any unposted batches.

Whether update is allowed when the ledgers are in different periods depends on the complexity of the system. A system without the proper checks on its particular method of working – to ensure updates are posted to the correct period – is seriously weak.

Sales and purchase ledgers – output

The following questions in the output section of the sales and purchases checklists relate to essential controls and have been included below.

Audit trail

> 1. Is it necessary to produce an audit trail before the period-end procedure is run?
> 2. Does the audit trail enable all transactions to be traced fully through the system?
> 3. Can the actual run date or batch reference, as well as current ledger date, be shown on reports?
> 4. Can the following be produced:
>   List of master file information?

The audit trail is a list of all transactions that have been entered to the ledgers. Using audit trail printouts it should be possible to trace all transactions through the system to the final printout or screen enquiry.

Ideally, the system should ensure that the audit trail (called the daybooks by some systems) is printed out either during input or just after, as part of the exit routine. It is essential that the audit trail is printed before the period-end procedure which clears down or purges all matched transactions in open item systems, and clears down all transactions into the carried forward balance in balance forward systems. If the audit trail is not printed at this stage, all record transactions can be lost, especially in more basic systems where transactions are not stored for enquiry purposes beyond the current period. Additionally, a list of all master file amendments should be available as a printout.

Nominal ledger – input controls

Password controls

> 1. Is password control used?
>   If YES, give details.

Password controls vary considerably between packages. Passwords can be personal, linked to terminals, linked to applications, or hierarchical – with each member of staff given a password at the appropriate level. The password structure may include combinations of several types so that a personal password is tailored to allow a member of staff into different levels in different applications.

Broadly speaking, the strength and complexity of password controls usually increase with the price of the package. Most software products have improved password facilities within the last few years in response to user demands. Most sysems – even those with weak password controls – protect the nominal ledger and especially period-end routines.

The level of password security needed depends on the size and structure of the business. If one part-time book-keeper does all the processing then the system only needs to be protected against unauthorised access. A larger organisation, where division of duties is part of overall control, will need a password system either linked to applications or tailored for individuals. Passwords alone cannot be relied upon to protect the system and should be accompanied by physical controls and supervision.

Audit trail

> 2. Is a hard copy automatically produced for all input?

Even systems which do not enforce an audit trail in other modules usually recognise the importance of doing so for nominal ledger journals. If a printout is not automatically produced for all input you will have to set up a system for ensuring that all printouts are taken. A batch book or batch sheets with a column for the operator to initial when the printouts are completed may be used for this purpose. The printouts should be numbered and cross referenced to the batch book/sheet so that they can be easily traced.

Numbering of journal entries

> 3. Are journal entries automatically sequentially numbered?
> 4. If integrated, are automatic postings from other modules included in the numbering sequence?
> 5. If accruals and prepayments automatically reverse, is the reversal included in the numbering sequence?

Automatic numbering of journal entries is common to even the most basic of systems and should include all journals.

Journal totals

> 6. Are totals of debit or credit entries produced for all journal entries?
>   If YES, is it necessary that this agrees with a pre-list total?
> 7. Is it necessary that all journal entries balance before posting?

The common format for journal entries is a screen showing debit and credit columns whose totals must agree before the entry is accepted. The exceptions to this are often cash posting routines and reversing journals where the system posts the totals of a single sided entry to a designated account. Controls in this area are often weak and it is common to supplement machine controls by using additional manual controls.

Pre-list totals for journal input are sometimes used, but pre-list totals for standard two-sided journal entries are not a common feature at the lower end of the market. Some systems will ask for a check total at the end of posting. More often, the system will put a running total on screen for the operator to check before accepting the batch.

Trial balance

> 8. Is production of an out of balance trial balance prevented?

You can expect even the most basic systems to ensure that the trial balance stays in balance.

Input screens

> 9. Do all input screens show clearly:
>   type of entry?
>   the distinction between debits and credits?

Again, even the most basic systems now have well labelled input screens showing debit and credit entries for the nominal ledger.

Transactions listings

> 10. Can the actual date of posting, or a batch reference, be shown on hard copies of transactions input?

Transactions listings can be expected to show the batch reference, date and a title showing the transaction type e.g. journal postings, cash receipts etc.

Validation

> 11. Are the following validated:
>   date?
>   nominal ledger account code?
>   cost centre code?
>   If NO, are unidentified/invalid entries posted to a suspense account?
>   How is suspense account treated?

A check for an invalid nominal code is usual at the input stage. Date validation varies: some systems automatically take the system date unless you over-ride it. Most systems will check that the date is reasonable, i.e. within the same year, and many that it is within a calendar month of the correct period. If cost centres are available, the code should be validated.

Most systems provide a suspense account for unidentified entries which has to be cleared out by journal. This is normally only used where the nominal ledger code is not validated from another module – such as the sales ledger – at the input stage.

Reconciliation reports

> 12. Is a total produced of all debit/credit transactions processed?
> If YES, is a report produced at the end of each processing run to reconcile b/f total, transaction processed and c/f total?

Many packages are weak in this area and reconciliations may have to be done manually.

> 13. Is a reconciliation of numbers of accounts produced after amendment of the accounts detail file?

Abnormal termination

> 14. Does the system prevent the abnormal termination of programs?

Most package software is menu-driven; exit from the system is by stepping back through the menus to the final exit point. This ensures that all files are closed and all updates complete. The only abnormal exit available from most package software is by pulling the plug which is a situation that good software should deal with by forcing the user to return to his last set of uncorrupted data. For sophisticated software this may be the last transaction before the power loss, but for most commonly available packages it is likely to be the last back-up taken.

Nominal ledger – integration

The following points from the integration section of the nominal ledger checklist relate to essential controls and have been included below.

Hard copy of update

> 3. Is a hard copy automatically produced at the end of each nominal ledger update?
> 4. Is there a sales/purchase ledger printout of the nominal ledger update?

A printout of all nominal ledger updates should be standard on all systems. This printout should show the update in detail including the origin of the transaction.

Control balances

> 5. Are sales ledger and purchase ledger control accounts agreed to the totals of balances in the individual ledgers?

Control account balances in the nominal ledger should always be agreed to the sales and purchase ledger totals by the system at the end of processing. A good system should also prevent direct update to the control accounts from within the nominal ledger through normal posting routines, other than during the input of the opening balances. A good system will force the user to resort to back-up if the data gets corrupted and the ledgers out of balance. As this is such a fundamental control, it should be backed up by a manually prepared control account which is agreed to the machine totals.

Completeness and accuracy of update

> 6. Is there a check that the nominal ledger cannot be updated twice with the same sales/purchase data?
> 7. Must the nominal ledger be updated from the sales and purchase ledgers before the period end is run?

A good system will ensure that all transactions for the nominal ledger are updated once and only once by other modules – and that all update has been made before the period end is run. There is usually no problem with a hard disk system as the update file is deleted once the update has been run and the system checks for existing update file during the period-end routine.

Floppy disk systems should have an inbuilt check, such as generation numbers between the disks, to ensure that the correct disks are being used and that update can neither be missed nor done twice. Check with the dealer that system controls can cope where the system has been restored from back-up in one of the ledgers because of corrupt data (a situation where data, say in the sales ledger, has to be re-input after the nominal ledger has been updated with the original data.)

Period considerations

> 8. Must the nominal ledger be in the same period as the sales and purchase ledgers for the update to be carried out?

Systems which allow multi-period running should have controls to ensure that update is done to the correct period. Simpler systems will require that the nominal ledger is the last to close down at the period end. If the sales ledger has been advanced into the next period, update to nominal ledger for the new period will have to wait until the other ledgers have caught up. Most such systems will only allow update in the same period. It is up to the user to control the period ends so that the ledgers do not get out of step with update files still to be pulled across.

The control check between the nominal ledger control accounts and individual control totals should help ensure that all transactions have been posted.

Unidentified entries

> 9. Is there any check that all data processed in the sales purchase ledgers has been posted to the nominal ledger?
> 10. Are unidentified/invalid entries held in a nominal ledger suspense account?
>   If YES, how is this treated?

All good package software will have a system for dealing with unidentified entries. This is normally a suspense account for each ledger. Transactions within this suspense account should be properly identified with their ledger of origin and the batch number so that they can be corrected by journal. Many systems validate the nominal ledger coding during input to the ledger of prime entry which reduces to a minimum the likelihood of there being entries in the suspense account.

Batch update

> 11. Can the user select whether to update the nominal ledger with individual sales/purchase ledger entries or in total?
>   If NO, is the update made in detail or in total?

Most packages update the nominal ledger using a batch update but show the entries in detail on the printout. The transaction detail shown in individual nominal ledger accounts may be either the total per batch or individual items depending on the system.

Control accounts

> 12. Is it impossible to post directly to the sales/purchase ledger control accounts?

Apart from exceptional circumstances it should never be possible to post directly to the sales or purchase ledger control account, except during the input of the opening trial balance. Facilities to correct erroneous balances should be outside the normal processing menus. A good system will resort to back-up if data becomes corrupted or if the update to the nominal ledger is incomplete because of power or system failure.

Nominal ledger – output – general

The following points from the output section of the nominal ledger checklist relate to essential controls and have been included below.

Audit trail

> 1. Is it necessary to produce an audit trail before the period end procedure is run?
> 2. Does the audit trail enable all transactions to be traced fully through the system?
> 3. Can the actual run date, or batch reference, as well as the current ledger date, be shown on all reports?

Ideally the system should produce the audit trail or transactions listing automatically during input, or as part of the exit routine after posting. If this is not the case, the period end routine should abort unless the audit trail has already been printed by the user. Where the audit trail is spooled, the period end routine should abort if all printouts have not been taken. The period end routine clears down the transaction detail into a balance for carrying forward into the next period. Therefore, systems which do not ensure that audit trails are printed before this detail is lost should be avoided.

An audit trail that does not enable all transactions to be traced fully through the system is *not* an audit trail. Such packages should be avoided. The only way to really test the audit trail is by tracing one of each kind of transaction through the system using the audit trail prints. It would be unusual to find an accounting system which has been available for some time, and which has a reasonable number of users, with a totally inadequate audit trail. However you should satisfy yourself that the method used to trace the transactions – and the reference used on the printout to identify transactions – are sufficient for your needs.

Run dates and current period or ledger dates should be on all printouts. Batch references should be available, either system generated, which is the ideal, or keyed in by the operator at the time of input. They should appear on all reports. Manual cross-reference to the input documents is a last resort.

Ledger account detail

> 11. Does the ledger account detail report show the source of postings and narrative input?
> 12. Does the ledger account detail report show either the full account history or balance b/f together with current period transactions?

Ledger account detail should always show the source of postings and some identifying narrative. Whether this is sufficient for individual needs is a matter for judgement. Control considerations only require that it is sufficient for tracing transactions. Ledger account detail should enable you to trace transactions to the account in detail for at least the current period.

Reports

> 13. Are all report pages numbered sequentially, with the end of report identified?
> 14. Can reports be temporarily retained on file for subsequent printing?
>   If YES, are such files protected from deletion?

All report pages should be numbered sequentially for control purposes. Most systems will retain reports for subsequent printing using a spooler facility. While the better systems will prevent deletion of unprinted files from within the application, very few package systems are capable of preventing files from being deleted when using operating system commands. Some systems are weak in that unprinted reports can be lost when the period end is run.

1800 users

Orchard

Our roots are in Accountancy

Orchard Business Centre (Scotland)

4th Floor · Elliott House · 8-10 Hillside Crescent · Edinburgh EH7 5EA
Telephone 031-557 1225

JIM CRUICKSHANK CA

QUALITY SOFTWARE AND SUPPORT FOR PROFESSIONAL ACCOUNTANTS AND FOR THEIR CLIENTS

Orchard Business Centres:

Horsham 0403 210625	LONDON 01-434 0480
Ireland 0001 850300	East Midlands 0788 823943
Edinburgh 031-557 1225	Kent 0622 56076
Dorset 0202 291826	East Sussex 0424 212903
Swansea 0792 476143	Middlesbrough 0642 22726
Channel Islands 0534 33561	Leeds 0532 45401

NW London 01-262 7377

Orchard Business Systems, 158 Crawley Road
Horsham, W. Sussex RH12 4EU

A GUIDE TO FIVE STAR SOFTWARE

Introducing the Omicron 'PowerPlus' Financial and Management Software System...

...Now, there is a flexible and powerful software system which can be specifically adapted to your business environment.

...A system designed to grow with you. Without compromise, without complication, without effort.

Demands placed on management information in individual organisations are – not surprisingly – unique.

PowerPlus, the unique system that can satisfy your needs today and expand to meet those of tomorrow.

– is simple to install, easy to operate, and is backed by comprehensive services, from your local Scottish Business Centres.

OMICRON
PowerPlus Systems
ACCOUNTING & FINANCIAL MANAGEMENT SOFTWARE

For further information contact your local Authorised Omicron Business Centre.

MICROAGE BUSINESS CENTRE	GATE COMPUTER SYSTEMS	REEVERA (SCOTLAND) LIMITED
TEL: 0382-561501	TEL: 041-204-2461	TEL: 041-221-5484

Principle 4: Support

Good Accounting should be effectively supported and maintained.

This is covered in the general points checklist under support and maintenance and software installation and training.

General points checklist – support and maintenance

The term 'supplier' refers to the supplier of the support and maintenance, whether or not this is the same as the supplier of the software.

Program corrections

> 1. Will the supplier provide corrections to the program?

Arrangements for corrections to programs where necessary should form part of the supplier's proposal and the subsequent contract. For package software that has been in use for some time, corrections to programs should be rare. For bespoke work or special tailoring the contract should specify the type and extent of acceptance trials and part of the payment should be withheld until the software performs satisfactorily.

General enhancements

> 2. Will the supplier provide general enhancements to the program?
>   Will these be provided automatically?
>   Will they be given free of charge?

The treatment of general enhancements by the supplier depends on the conditions within the software agreement. You should be kept up to date with developments and offered updates and enhancements. This service may only be available to those who take out software maintenance.

Hotline support

> 3. Will the software supplier provide 'hot-line' support to assist with immediate problem solving?
>   If so, at what cost?
> 4. Is the supplier capable of giving sufficient ongoing education, training and other support?
> 5. Can the supplier provide all the hardware, software and maintenance requirements of the user?

Hotline or telephone support should be available at between 10 per cent and 15 per cent of the cost of each module. There is sometimes a minimum charge. Hotline support is usually only available to users who take out a software maintenance agreement, but it depends on the terms of the agreement. Check the quality of support by contacting existing users. Details of proposed support and level of maintenance offered should be included in the proposal.

Local support and back-up

> 6. Can the supplier provide support in the user's locality?
> 7. Is a warranty offered in rspect of specification and performance of the system?
> 8. Would there be adequate back-up in the event of hardware or software failure?

Local support and back-up may not be easy for some locations. The choice may have to be made between a local supplier, who is not completely familiar with the software, and fairly remote support. If possible, choose a package/hardware combination which already has a number of users in your area.

If possible, make the system warranty part of the contract. It is not always possible with standard, packaged software and you may have to rely upon the reputation of the dealer/supplier.

Source code

> 9. Will the software supplier make the program source code available to the user, either directly or by deposit with a third party?

Source code is not usually available for packaged software but should be included in the contract for any specially written software. The higher the cost of the software, the more likely that some arrangement can be made for installing source on your machine or depositing a copy with a third party.

Licence agreements

> 10. If the software is acquired under licence, are there any unduly restrictive conditions in the licence?

Licence agreements are usually fairly standard, but ask for a specimen agreement to be sent with the proposal and review it for any unduly restrictive clauses.

General points checklist – software installation and training – involvement of software supplier

Most of the questions included in the software installation and training section of the general points checklist raise points that relate to the organisation that is installing the software, rather than to the software itself. This is an extremely important area, and the questions raised here are highly relevant for anyone installing a computer system. But they are outside the scope of this book and will not be discussed in detail. We will therefore concentrate on the supplier's proposed contribution to installation and training.

Training and support

> 5. Is the supplier capable of giving sufficient initial education, training and other support?

The supplier should have included a realistic budget for training and initial support. Details of proposed support and level of maintenance offered should be included in the proposal. Check the quality of the service with existing users.

Evaluation copies of software

> 6. Are potential users permitted to test the software for a trial period before commitment to acquire it?

A trial period for testing the software can sometimes be arranged. It is worth asking if you can have a demonstration copy for a few weeks of evaluation. The supplier may not let you have a full copy but specially restricted versions are often available.

Setting up the system

> 7. If required, does the supplier have sufficient capable personnel to assist users to convert to the new system?
> 8. If required, will the supplier provide machine time to enable users to set up files of input data before installation?

The degree of help offered beyond basic training in the use of the software depends on the individual supplier and the size of the system. Extended help with conversion and setup is a service more usually found for larger systems and would be included in the quotation. Quotations from suppliers of package software usually include an average of a day's training per module plus a day for basic training. Extra installation support, if available, will be supplied at market rates.

PACT
Associates Limited

You owe it to yourself to find out more about the ACCOUNTANT COLLECTION.

It could save you a lot of time and money.

The **Accountant Collection** from **PACT Associates** has a sound pedigree, it has been developed from the successful **Pulsar** and **Apricot Accountant** packages and the number of registered users exceeds 10,000 in the U.K. alone. **The Accountant Collection** consists of :

- Sales Ledger
- Payroll
- Data Analysis
- Purchase Ledger
- Invoicing
- Report Generator
- Nominal Ledger
- Order Processing
- Stock Control

Future developments include Job Costing, Standard Costing, Bill of Materials and Asset Register.

The Accountant Collection runs on most PC's (including all IBM compatibles), across most proprietary networks and multi-user under XENIX and PCMOS.

INTERESTED ? Then please contact PACT Associates for full details of the ACCOUNTANT COLLECTION and the other services we offer.

PACT Associates Ltd.,
Lygon Court,   Dudley Road,
Halesowen,   West Midlands,
B62 8AN
Sales : 021-503 0022   Telex : 333759 PACT G

Accounting for your business. Caring for your needs.

Principle 5: Ease of Use

It is desirable that good accounting software should be easy to learn, understand and operate.

This is covered in the general points checklist under ease of use, interactive processing and user documentation. Sales, purchase and nominal ledger are covered under documentation.

General points checklist – ease of use – interactive processing

Operating systems

> 1. Does the software run under an operating system which is a commonly accepted standard?

Going away from a commonly accepted standard may lock you into a particular supplier and restrict the scope for future expansion. Unless you are looking for industry specific, i.e. vertical market, software (or at a mini-computer installation) the practical micro-computer standard for single users is MS-DOS or its IBM equivalent, PC-DOS. For multi-user systems based on micros, either a PC/MS-DOS based network or a multi-user operating system such as Unix or Xenix are the most common standards.

Multi-user and multi-tasking software

> 2. Is the software available concurrently to more than one user?

True multi-user software will allow more than one user to access files using the same program at the same time, e.g. two operators entering invoices to the sales ledger at once. Data integrity will be maintained by the use of file locking or, more efficiently, record locking so that the same data cannot be accessed by more than one person simultaneously. The record, e.g. a customer account, is temporarily closed to the second person until the first has finished with it.

> 3. Can more than one system function be performed cocurrently?

Multi-tasking allows different users to run different programs or parts of programs at the same time. Good multi-user software will be both multi-user and multi-tasking with safeguards for data integrity. If you are buying multi-user accounting packages you should see them working in that mode during demonstrations or, if possible, at a user site. Make sure any additional software such as word processing or spreadsheet software is a true multi-user version. At least be aware of the possible problems and limitations if it is not.

Data entry

> 4. Does the software effectively lead the user through the data entry procedure?
> 5. Is the software menu-driven?
> 6. Are the user screens adequately titled?

Questions 4, 5, and 6 cover points to consider during demonstrations or discussions with existing users.

> 7. Does the system inform the operator which programs or files are being loaded?

Messages informing the operator which programs are running are more usual from command operated programs in mini-based systems. Micro-systems rely on menus and screen headings.

Back-up

> 8. Does the software facilitate file maintenance, back-up and archive copying?

Good package software should have menu driven back-up and restore facilities, menu-driven file maintenance and a reminder/enforcement procedure to ensure regular back-up.

General points checklist – ease of use – user documentation

User manuals

> 1. Is the manual clearly laid out and understandable?
> 2. Is the manual comprehensive and accurate?
> 3. Is there an index to the manual?
> 4. Is it easy to locate specific topics in the manual when required?
> 5. Is it easy to follow through all procedures in the manual?
> 6. Are completed examples included in the manual?

Try to acquire a copy of the manual as part of your selection process. Manuals vary considerably in quality and layout. Ask other users how they found the manual. Avoid systems where existing users have had problems acquiring manuals or where manuals are still being revised/printed after the software has been released.

Help screens

> 7. Are help screens available?
>   Do they provide detailed on-line instructions on how to use particular features of the software?
>   Can they be edited or prepared by the user?

Good software will have instructions on each screen to guide the operator, or help screens available at the press of a function key; better still, both. Look out for these features, or the lack of them, during demonstrations.

Documentation

> 8. Does the documentation clearly specify the actions to be taken by users at each important stage of processing?
> 9. Will the software supplier provide regular updates of documentation in the event of modifications or revisions?
> 10. Will the software supplier make detailed program documentation available to the user, either directly or by deposit with a third party?

For bespoke systems or modifications to package software it is essential that proper documentation is made available and kept up to date. Include documentation in the contract if necessary and withhold payment until you are satisfied with it. If documentation is not forthcoming when the software is installed it is notoriously difficult to get it later when the supplier's time is concentrated on new sales. For most package software the documentation consists of user manuals. The points raised in questions 1–6 will help to answer question 8.

Sales, purchases and nominal ledgers – general

Menus

> 1. Are programs menu-driven?
>   If YES, can menus be by-passed once the user is familiar with the package?

Most package software is menu-driven. Some packages allow the operator to 'skip through' the menus once they become familiar with the software.

User log

> 2. Does the system maintain a log of usage?

Good systems will maintain a user log which is a record of who did what and when. It is useful for control purposes as it pinpoints unauthorised access, especially if it records unsuccessful attempts. It will also help to track down problems when things go wrong as it shows exactly what was being done at the critical time. If the system does not maintain a user log then this should be done manually using a log book. In it, you should record details of all processing, any unusual messages on the screen and details of daily back-up. Apart from its internal uses, the log book is a valuable source of information for the engineers when they respond to fault calls.

Help messages

> 3. Are informative messages produced on-screen whilst running?

Most packages now provide assistance to the operator by using a set of screen prompts, usually along the foot of the screen. These prompts give alternative courses of action for each stage of the operation.

Error messages

> 4. Are error messages informative and easy to understand?

Error messages should appear on the screen when the program cannot proceed with the next step. If remedial action can be taken by the operator the screen should show a clear instruction, e.g. 'printer not attached', 'non-existent nominal ledger code', which includes the function key to press to re-try the procedure.

Multi-company

> 5. Is the system multi-company?

Most packages can cope with more than one company or more than one department but with many of the cheaper ones it is one or the other and not both. Some of the very cheap packages can still only cope with one company.

Set-up

> 6. Is the original set-up straightforward?

The package will normally be installed by a dealer. From then on the set-up procedures are normally menu-driven and can be easily managed by the user. Some practice with a dummy company, usually included with the software, and a careful study of the manual may be necessary.

Back-up and restore

7. Is there a copy/restore facility in the package?
8. Does the system cover disciplined taking of back-ups?

Many systems have a menu-driven back-up and restore. The better systems can also be set up to enforce back-up on a regular basis. At the very minimum the system should prompt back-up when the 'exit' option is selected from the main or system menu. Unfortunately, too many systems still force the user to rely on the operating system (usually DOS) commands for back-up. For systems where back-up is not enforced or enforceable a regular routine of back-up, done either daily, weekly or at some other suitable time gap, should be set up and followed. Where back-up relies on the operating system you will need to provide a written back-up procedure for the operator to use. The tapes or disks used for back-up should be stored away from the machine, preferably in a fireproof safe or another building.

Sales, purchases and nominal ledgers – documentation

The question on user documentation in the individual checklists cover largely the same points as the general points checklist and the same comments will apply to the individual applications.

Principle 6: Efficiency

It is desirable that good accounting software should make the best practical use of available resources.

This principle is covered in the general points checklist under efficiency, flexibility and software installation and training.

Response times

> 1. Are the various functions of the system menu-driven, or otherwise easy to initiate?
>   Is there a good response time in the initiation of functions?
> 3. Is there a good response time
>   in processing data input?
>   in producing requisite reports?
>   in updating files?
>   in producing back-up files?
>   in deleting redundant information files?

Response time can vary with the configuration and the number of users active on the system. Make your judgement after talking to existing users. Take into account the information in the proposal where the supplier should have indicated the maximum practical (as opposed to possible) volumes of data and number of users that the system can cope with. Unless the demonstration is done under the same conditions and the same configuration as you intend to use it is difficult to make any judgement.

Repeat facility

> 2. Is data entry easily repeated if similar to previous entry?

Automatic repetition of similar or identical data should be available with the better packages and greatly speeds up input of large volumes of data such as invoices.

Record locking

> 4. Does the system prevent access to a record while it is being updated?

Multi-user systems which allow two or more users or progams to have access to the same data at the same time use record or file locking to prevent a second access to the data while it is being updated by the first. The more efficient systems use record locking rather than file locking. This means that two operators can key in invoices to the sales ledger files but will be barred from entering invoices for the same customer at the same instant. One of them will notice a few seconds delay. Period-end procedures would have to lock entire files until they are completed. An unsatisfactory answer to this question is a fundamental weakness in a multi-user system.

System logs and duplicate reports

> 5. Does the system retain a log of file updates until the next occasion on which the relevant information is reported or the relevant file used in a regular control procedure?
> 6. Can regular reports be easily duplicated if required?

Both of these facilities vary with the cost of the software. Logs of file updates are usually only available with more complex systems. If a log is available it should be retained until printed. Most up to date software allows for duplicate reports provided the period end has not been run.

General points checklist – software installation and training

Budget

> 1. Has account been taken in the budget for system development/acquisition of the full costs of
>   initial acquisition?
>   initial training?
>   future training?
> 4. Have requisite consumables (e.g. special stationery, filing facilities, fireproof storage) been provided for?

Make sure that all installation and running costs have been included within the budget. Running costs in particular are likely to be forgotten when setting up the budget for aquisition. They can be substantial.

Siting the equipment

> 2. Is the main equipment to be located in adequate accommodation? Is this such that staff are not seriously affected by the equipment (e.g. noise from the printer)?
> 3. Is there sufficient scope for the installation (if required) of communications equipment?

The supplier will usually make a visit to the site to discuss the physical installation of the equipment, but the contract almost always puts the responsibility for siting and provision of special conditions with the purchaser. Micros do not usually require much in the way of special conditions but they should not be located in a dusty workshop without some protection. A 'clean' line will help protect data from electrical fluctuations caused by having photocopiers, heavy machinery or even kettles on the same circuit. If this is not possible, try to put the computer in the circuit in front of appliances which might cause trouble. Regular back-ups will minimise the inconvenience of recovery in case of this sort of accident. Synthetic carpets can cause problems with static and you may have to use anti-static mats to overcome this. Printers can be noisy, so put them in a room by themselves or use acoustic hoods to cut down the noise.

Supplier support

> 5. Is the supplier capable of giving sufficient initial education, training and other support?

Look at the proposal to make sure the supplier has included a realistic training timetable. Expect a minimum of one day's training per module or application and at least a day of general training for each member of staff who will use the system. Speak to existing users about the quality of training and support, especially responses to telephone calls for help with problems in the early stages.

Demonstration copies

> 6. Are potential users permitted to test the software for a trial period before commitment to acquire it?

It is sometimes possible to get a demonstration copy of the software for a trial period. The packages at the cheaper end of the market are sometimes sent out in demonstration format at minimum cost with the option of converting to a full version, on payment of the balance, after a trial period.

Help with set-up

> 7. If required, does the supplier have sufficient capable personnel to assist users to convert to the new system?
> 8. If required, will the supplier provide machine time to enable users to set up files of input data before installation?

This service is more usual with the larger mini-based systems. It is sometimes possible to get help with set-up for smaller systems at a daily rate. Many dealers in packaged software will not have the resources to help in this way and, in any case, it is a very good way of learning how to use the package.

Principle 7: Flexibility

It is desirable that good accounting software should accommodate limited changes to reflect specific user requirements.

This is covered in the general points checklist under flexibility.

General points checklist – flexibility – reporting

User designed reports

> 1. Can the user easily design additional output reports or displays?
> 2. Is a report generator provided as part of the software or as an option associated with it?
> 3. Can screen layouts, reports and transaction formats be easily adapted to users' requirements?

Most systems have a report generator either as part of each application or as a separate module or both. Report generators vary considerably in their ease of use. Existing users are the best guide as to how much you will gain from this facility.

Screen layouts and transaction formats are usually fixed except for the more expensive and sophisticated packages where the user designs his own system from a basic shell.

Accuracy of user designed reports

> 4. Does the output of the software facilitate proper control to ensure that decisions are not inadvertently taken on the basis of incorrect information?

User defined reports require care on the part of the user to ensure that the information is valid. There are few controls that can be built into package software in this area. Report generators allow the user to pick up information from accounting software and incorporate it in any way he chooses into a free format report. There is usually no possibility of corrupting the original data files but there is no control over data manipulation within the report generator to arrive at the final report.

General points checklist – flexibility – parameters

Parameters, tables and changes

> 1. If the system uses a lot of standing information which changes frequently or regularly, does it allow for such changes to be effected through the use of parameters or tables?

Most packages make use of parameters or tables to set up and alter standing information. You should always be sure that you are aware of the effect of the changes on existing data before making them. Good software will warn you if data will be destroyed as a result of what you are about to do and allow for escape.

> 2. If so, is the use of such parameters or table adequately reported?

There should be a compulsory report (printout) of all parameter changes.

> 3. Is proper control to be exercised over changes to such parameters or tables? If so, how (e.g. through the use of system facilities such as passwords or by inspection of appropriate records)?

Parameter changes should be password protected and only carried out by a senior member of staff who understands the implications of the changes. Printouts of changes should always be taken and reviewed. If parameters are not password protected and printouts are not provided, consider rejecting the software as these parameters or tables affect the fundamental working of the system.

Part III
Reviews and Checklists

Introduction

This section of the book contains detailed information on the leading UK accounting packages which have been subdivided into four categories; three according to price and a fourth, which includes details of software packages that arrived too late for our reviewers to make an independent asessment.

The categories are:

(a) Low price –   suitable for the small business or first time user.

(b) Medium price –   fairly sophisticated, for small to medium size businesses.

(c) High price –   more advanced features suitable for the larger business.

(d) Others –   mixed, without independent review.*

The reviews and checklists in this section have been completed over a period of time. Whilst every effort has been made to keep the checklists updated, some reviews refer to features promised in future releases of the software. In some cases these versions are now available.

Software reviewers and evaluations

Each package was reviewed by a member of our reviews panel – all experienced accountants. Using a standard set of test data, they test all aspects of the package and record the results on our detailed evaluation checklists. Obviously some of the questions can only be answered with reference to a particular user's requirements so these have been left blank.

The reviewers also relate their experiences using the package and summarise its effectiveness and value for money.

* The details of these packages may be of interest to the reader but it should be remembered that the summaries and evaluations were completed wholly by the manufacturers.

The test data and a set of blank checklists are included at the end of the book so that the reader can carry out a similar exercise for themselves and this is strongly recommended both for evaluating a piece of accounting software and for getting a feel for computer-based accounting in general.

The evaluations were carried out on single-user versions of the software. There are severe limitations in simulating the vast variety of conditions which may arise in a multi-user environment and we strongly advise anyone thinking of installing such a system to visit sites which are already operating such a system in conditions similar to those in their own organisation.

We are grateful for the assistance of the software suppliers mentioned in the reviews and also our panel of reviewers.

Alan Beattie	Deloitte Haskins & Sells
Jim Byers	Pannell Kerr Forster
Edward Clack	Scottish College of Textiles
Bernard Cooke	Deloitte Haskins & Sells
Martin Cursue	Peat Marwick McLintock
Colin Hunter	Ernst & Whinney
Colin Kerr	John M. Geoghegan & Co.
Jim McKinnon	Civvals
Steve Malloy	McQueen Systems Ltd
Jeffrey Meek	Primrose McCabe & Co.
Sandy Pratt	Grant Thornton

Low-price packages – MAP, Sagesoft, SNIP and TAS Plus

Reviews	111
Features Rating Table	123
Package Information Table	124
Evaluation Checklists:	
General	126
Performance of Requisite Accounting Functions	126
Reliability – Security and Continuity of Processing	128
Support and Maintenance	128
Ease of Use	128
(a) Interactive Processing	128
(b) User Documentation	130
Efficiency	130
Flexibility	132
(a) Integration Facilities	132
(b) Reporting Flexibility	132
(c) Parameter or Table Facilities	132
Software Installation and Training	132
(a) Financial Resources	132
(b) Other Resources	134
(c) Involvement of Software Supplier	134
(d) Involvement of User Personnel	134
Package Software Acquisition	134
Preliminary Questions Relating to Software Supplies	134
Nominal Ledger	136
General	136
Documentation	136
(a) Manual	136
(b) Help Screens	136

Account Details	136
Transactions	138
Input Controls	138
Integration	140
Output	142
(a) General	142
(b) Trial Balance; P&L and Balance Sheet	144
Year End	146

Sales Ledger 146

General	146
Documentation	146
(a) Manual	146
(b) Help Screens	148
Customer Details	148
Transactions	148
Matching/Allocations	150
(a) Balance Forward	150
(b) Open Item	150
Input Controls	152
Integration	154
Output	154

Purchase Ledger 158

General	158
Documentation	160
(a) Manual	160
(b) Help Screens	160
Supplier Details	160
Transactions	162
Matching/Allocations	162
(a) Balance Forward	162
(b) Open Item	162
Input Controls	164
Integration	166
Output	168
Payments/Cheque Writing	172

Review of MAP Integrated Ledger Package

Anyone acquainted with earlier versions of MAP Business Software should consider the latest version, 6.0. This low-price software comes either as free standing modules, or as a package. Reviewed here is the top of the range 'Complete Accounting' package which consists of ledgers, stock and sales order processing, rounded off with a report generator and data import/export facilities. Job costing and payroll modules make up the full MAP product range. Compared with previous versions, version 6.0 brings a considerable upgrading in capacity, presentation and control features. While its 'budget' nature is occasionally evident, it is good value: this software will fulfil the functions required of record keeping and will provide a satisfactory supply of accounting information. The overall impression of the software is its flexibility: it can be operated with the minimum of controls if desired, it can be expanded at a later date, and there are many user-definable features. Although this flexibility is welcome, it does increase the risk of losing data at particular steps. This may be minimised with attention to frequent backups, and password control if appropriate to the installation. Given a particular configuration, it is easy to use, and comes with a straightforward stepwise guide to operation in the manual.

Although there is a tendency to associate 'low cost' software with small businesses which perhaps lack in-house accounting or computer expertise, other criteria are required to evaluate the long-term adequacy and suitability of a budget package. In the case of MAP, size of business is of rather less importance than complexity of transactions. High volumes can be accommodated given sufficient disk capacity. For applications with complex sales and purchase ledgers however, the limited transaction routines will be found restrictive. The standard financial statements are geared more towards the trading company, but may be adapted to suit a variety of business operations. The user must have, or acquire, a basic awareness of the operating system in order to take backups: the manual gives no guidance on this.

MAP runs on IBM compatibles and Amstrad PC/PCW under MSDOS. It will handle up to 26 companies with a 'database link' facility giving access to consolidation. There is no multi-currency capability. Multiple periods are user-defined. Standard reports through the modules are fixed in format, but are accessed through a variety of selection criteria. In addition the report generator allows user-defined selection of data from all modules in arithmetic calculations thereon, and limited formatting.

Single module applications can be run adequately on a diskette-only machine. For any amount of integration, however, a fixed disk is normally a requirement, at least to hold the program files. For Complete Accounting, these amount to 1.3Mbytes. Writing data to diskette may be found satisfactory: data becomes moveable, and backup simpler through a 'diskcopy' command. As a guide, a single sales or purchase ledger application would hold 250 accounts on a 360kb diskette. Alternatively, the test data was held on a single diskette holding 100 sales and purchase ledger accounts and a nominal ledger set up with 10 cost centres.

Installation is handled simply through a menu selection – and a welcome feature is the facility to expand the data space at a later date without corrupting existing data. Operation is by numbered menu selections, and the manual gives a brief set of 'software standards' which must be adhered to. It is to the writers' credit that so few 'standards' are required: this is just as well, since there are few error messages and no help screens.

Nominal ledger

The nominal ledger comes with a default of 250 accounts numbered 1 to 250. The user can, however, increase the number of accounts to 999, and vary the descriptions under which accounts are subtotalled. The standard format gives up to 20 sales and related purchases and stock accounts, allowing a gross profit by product report to be obtained (incorrectly labelled 'Contribution Report'). The package comes with a suggested list of account names, covering most of the 250 accounts. Inevitably, these will have to be renamed to suit particular applications.

Up to 99 'cost'-centres may be specified on installation. Once specified, the number is fixed for the application, and postings to all revenue and expense accounts must carry a cost-centre suffix, even if required for only a limited range of accounts. Trading, contribution and profit and loss accounts can all be reported by cost-centre. Budgets may be broken down into cost-centre headings. This is a simple facility requiring the input of a period budget which will be carried forward to future periods until changed.

Transaction entry to the nominal is by a standard double entry screen giving up to 6 lines of input. A screen must be accepted for entry before more lines can be added – and errors in previous screens cannot be accessed for amendment. Each transaction carries a sequential number and descriptive text if required. There is provision for both standing entries, accruals and prepayments. Standing entries will be terminated at the year end. Accruals and prepayments may be spread over a number of periods as defined by the operator.

Prior to producing financial statements, closing stocks are entered under a separate menu selection – the software handles the necessary adjustments. Since these can be amended, some users may find this facility to 'what-if' on the monthly accounts a useful, albeit improper, function!

Integration of the nominal ledger with other modules is complete. Unfortunately, the updating process includes an option to request a 'no' to update and a 'yes' to clearing of link files, which could result in loss of data. A period-end on the nominal can be run at will and prior to that on other modules: the software does not guarantee the period-end completeness of the nominal.

Sales and purchase ledgers

The sales and purchase ledgers are almost identical to one another in screen presentation and mechanics of operation. The sales ledger includes a fully integrated invoicing routine and statement print, while the purchase ledger has remittance and cheque printing routines.

Accounts can be specfied as either open item or balance forward; ageing is available in the former only. Sufficient detail can be kept on each account, including credit limits (a warning if exceeded), contacts, and two analysis codes. Separate selections from the main menu are used to post invoices/credits and cash. Contra-transactions between ledgers, write-offs and other non-routine transactions must be adjusted in the nominal ledger. Multiple VAT rate invoices can be handled, and up to 10 nominal analysis categories are provided.

All standard reports are available with particularly flexible selection criteria. However, statements and remittance advices are a source of potential confusion – the limitation in transaction types, and the creation of two 'cash' records to perform the allocation of a non-cash credit against an invoice, both give rise to misleading references being carried.

Within each ledger, system options can be set which cover the imposition of batch control, a mandatory audit trail, automatic updating of nominal ledger link file and, in the sales ledger, unique sequencing of sales invoices. Unfortunately these functions can be set off as well as on! In fairness to the software, this appears to be deliberate policy to allow flexibility of use. If necessary, the option can be password-protected. Moreover, there is a compulsory (and more readily understandable) daybook listing system in addition to the optional audit trail.

Security and control

Throughout the ledgers, entry of transactions must be to valid account codes, and input routines cannot be exited until full double entry has been maintained, if necessary by posting to a designated suspense account. The trial balance will therefore always balance. Completeness of processing is controlled by transaction entry under (optional) batch control. Differences between batch totals can be accepted, but this will be noted on the audit trail. Audit trails can be printed or spooled on the default program drive. By spooling, however, files can later be written to the screen then deleted, without the necessity of printing a hard copy. Within each ledger, audit trails are page numbered sequentially by the system throughout the accounting year.

Password protection is simple but flexible. Each function within a module can be individually assigned a password. Removing and changing of passwords was accomplished successfully, depending on access to the old password.

The onus of taking backups rests entirely with the user via the operating system. The manual mentions this procedure, but gives no detailed guidance.

Maintenance, support and costs

Modules are priced separately at £99 (plus VAT). For any integration, potential users should consider the 'Integrated Accounts' at £175 (sales, purchase and nominal ledgers with stock), or the more flexible 'Complete Accounting' at £299. The equivalent multi-user versions are available at £649.

MAP give telephone support for the first 30 days of use, and their warranty applies to any defects uncovered during this period. Thereafter, an annual nominal sum gives access to help-line support.

Review of Sage Accountant Plus

The cost of reliable computer hardware has gone down considerably over the past year, and software prices have followed suit. One of the good low-cost accounting packages to emerge is Accountant Plus from Sagesoft. Despite a few irritants it is an ideal system for the small client who is computerising accounts for the first time. Accountant Plus is not as powerful as some of its large and more expensive competitors, but the system does offer fully integrated nominal, purchase and sales ledgers, together with sales invoicing, stock control and a report generator. The user is able to design the layout of invoices and the format of credit control letters, and is not restricted to a standard format.

Accountant Plus is a single-user system and it does not offer multi-currency and multi-company features. A more expensive package produced by Sage called Financial Controller does provide these features but this was not the subject under review.

The programs come on a single disk, and the user manual is well laid out and is easy for a first-time user to follow. In common with most accounting packages the system is menu-driven. The main menu gives access to the three ledgers and to stock control, to invoice production, management reports and utility routines. Each of the sub-menus then gives access to specific routines for posting transactions or producing reports.

The authors of the software claim that the system will support five thousand accounts in the sales and purchase ledgers and one thousand in the nominal ledger. While I do not doubt this, I repeat that the system is best suited to the smaller user and suggest that a business with more than a few hundred customers would be well advised to seek a more powerful alternative.

The creation of the ledger accounts is quite simple, the first stage being to set up the nominal ledger accounts. The system demands six control accounts for debtors, creditors, bank, cash, VAT and discount, and thereafter other nominal accounts are established using a six-digit numeric code. I suggest that before embarking on this exercise the user studies the section of the manual which covers 'Monthly Reports'. The reason for this is that in order to aggregate accounts on a particular line of the profit and loss account or balance sheet the account codes have to be within a specific range, and some planning is therefore required when creating accounts. Budgets for each month can be established when setting up the nominal accounts for use with the report generator function; the system does not cater for alternative accounting periods.

Sales and purchase ledger accounts may be established with a six-digit, alphanumeric code of the user's choice. Credit limits can be set for reference purposes for individual customers.

Both ledgers operate on an 'open item' basis. Matching payments against invoices is adequate for a practised user, but this routine is not as helpful as those in some of the more expensive packages.

There is an absence of help screens when inputting data, but the screen layout itself is easy to follow, and the use of the functions keys gives the facility to repeat narrative. There are certain drawbacks in the keying-in process which include the following:

> (a) The input per screen/batch is limited to 12-line entries, and the posting of large batches can be time consuming. This is particularly significant when posting a large journal entry – for example, the opening balances to the nominal ledger – and compensating entries are needed.
>
> (b) When attempting to post a bank payment or receipt to one of the six control accounts, one discovers a feature which at first is quite frustrating: it is only possible by using a journal entry. For example, posting a cheque drawn to reimburse the petty-cash imprest cannot be accomplished through the bank payments routine. The manual suggests that it is possible, but Sage admit that it is not: their Help-Line confirms that such an entry has to be done through the nominal-ledger-journal entry routine. (Version 3, which should now be available, has been amended to allow posting between the bank and petty cash account through the cash receipts routine.) The same applies to the regular payment to or receipt from Customs and Excise for VAT settlement. The reason becomes apparent when using the system to produce a VAT return, where it is suggested that a separate VAT liability account is created.
>
> (c) Errors in posting to the sales and purchase ledgers may be edited

while they are still on the screen. If a mis-posting goes undetected at this stage it can be difficult to correct.

(d) The year-end procedures require the transfer of balances to Retained Profit by journal entry as accounts are not cleared to zero automatically.

Despite these shortcomings, the system is impressive for its price, and the quality of reports and their ease of production is first class. I understand that the latest version includes a bank reconciliation facility and other features designed to help the businessman with his day-to-day affairs.

Security

All the routines within the system can be protected by passwords. The manual does not explain how to amend, create or delete them, but Sage do provide a fact sheet for licensed users which gives chapter and verse.

Without the aid of the fact sheet, tinkering with the passwords can create an amusing exercise. However, I remain cynical about the user of password protection with any accounting package used in the average office environment.

No back-up and restore facilities are included in the software. To take a back-up requires a return to the operating system. The month-end procedures do prompt the user to take two copies of the data files, but I would suggest that this should be done at least once a day.

A full audit-trail exists and this can be printed at any time using the management reports option. Reports can be displayed on screen, printed or spooled; there are no checks to avoid the deletion of spooled reports before they are printed.

Distribution and support

Sage Software distribute their products through dealerships, and there are several in Scotland. Because of its low price there is little profit for the dealer; therefore, depending upon the supplier, a user might not receive the local support which is given with more expensive products. Sage do provide a help-line service from their offices in Newcastle-Upon-Tyne which is prompt in response and attentive in support.

Hardware and costs

The package runs on an IBM PC and other compatible computers, using MS-DOS operating system. It can be run on a twin-floppy, but I suggest that in common with other accounts packages a hard-disk be used whenever integrated ledger systems are involved. The cost of the software is £199, with the option of an additional £75 for Sage-Cover, which entitles the user to all software enhancements and support.

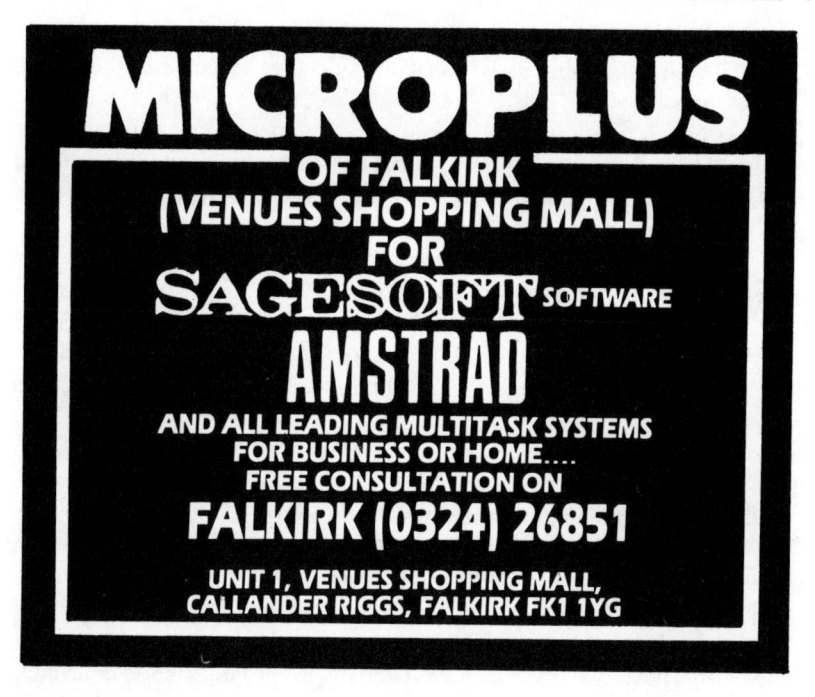

MICROPLUS
OF FALKIRK
(VENUES SHOPPING MALL)
FOR
SAGESOFT SOFTWARE
AMSTRAD
AND ALL LEADING MULTITASK SYSTEMS
FOR BUSINESS OR HOME....
FREE CONSULTATION ON
FALKIRK (0324) 26851
UNIT 1, VENUES SHOPPING MALL,
CALLANDER RIGGS, FALKIRK FK1 1YG

Review of SNIP

This package seems to offer an upward path for the growing business – at a low cost.

The SNIP accounting system is an integrated accounting package, comprising sales ledger, invoicing, purchase ledger, nominal ledger and stock control. Given the low cost of the integrated package it would be worth while purchasing the complete system, even if only certain modules – for example, sales, purchasing and nominal – are used initially. Later the invoicing routine and then the stock control could be developed to provide a comprehensive system at an economical cost.

The basic system would appeal to the first time user of computers and to small businesses in particular. Additional modules for multi-company, multi-department and multi-user systems are available. A job costing routine and sales order processing can also be provided.

The basic system reviewed came on two floppy disks and was run on a PC compatible twin floppy system running under MS-DOS.

Ease of use
Although no index was provided, the manual was clearly laid out, with adequate examples of most routines and entries, and of the many report facilities the

package has to offer. The set-up routines were well documented and the software proved reasonably easy to install. A detailed example of the nominal ledger set up is provided.

The system is menu-driven, and the main menu and sub-menus are adequate. The only major criticism is that the exit from SNIP is through the system utilities rather than through the main menu which would be more logical.

The editing routines were reasonable, but it is unclear at certain points whether the user should use the backspace key, the ESC key or the return key to get the desired result. No use is made of the function keys, available on most PC keyboards, to assist in repeat field entries. (Perhaps this is due to the fact that this system originated on CP/M machines and has only recently re-entered the market place.)

Nominal ledger
This allows for the usual journal entries, cash receipts and payments.

The nominal account codes must be numeric and are allocated over 20 account headings. Account codes for VAT, bank, profit, debtors and creditors control account are requested by the system during set-up, automatically, within the nominal ledger.

The journal posting routine includes accruals, pre-payments and adjustments and allows adjustments to comparative figures. A single journal posting is limited to 49 entries with a balancing figure for the 50th entry so that large journals have to be split down. This was not too much of a limitation in entering, say, 200 nominal account codes. Entries can be made to previous period figures allowing, for example, draft accounts to be altered to include audit adjustments.

Additional account codes can be created during journal processing, and this was a feature of most of the routines in the package.

The system caters for 12 accounting periods only (i.e. monthly) with month-, quarter- and year-end routines.

Sales ledger
The sales ledger allows for either a balance forward or open item basis of accounts. The customer account code is five alphanumeric characters long. The customer details held are comprehensive (20 items in the record) and provide the basis for much of the excellent reporting facility.

The system can enter invoices raised manually, as well as credit notes, cash receipts and discounts. Alternatively the invoicing routine can be invoked to generate invoices and credit notes. Unlike many systems the invoicing system routine can be used without the need for stock control to be set up, allowing invoices to be produced from the sales analysis records of the sales ledger.

When entering invoices one or more VAT rates can be entered for each invoice raised (three rates were used, but the system could cater for five differing VAT rates).

If transactions are batched, no on-screen checking of the batch total is available. The only way of checking the batch total is with the printed control report. There is no restriction on the type of input; transaction invoices, credit notes and adjustments can be intermixed within a batch.

The period-end routine posts all sales analysis code details to one or more nominal ledger accounts and ensures that all sales analysis and control reports are printed before updating the files.

Purchase ledger

The purchase ledger is maintained on an open item basis and the module provides for all the standard posting routines. Supplier account codes are again five alphanumeric characters, with 13 items in total for supplier details within each record. Payments can either be generated automatically using the due date entered for the invoice or selected manually using the remittance posting routine. Transactions can also be marked as held using this routine so that they will not be paid automatically on the due date.

The payment preparation report shows details of transactions due by a specified date, taking into account prompt payment discounts. This can be used to establish the effects of using the automatic payments routine. Remittance advices can be produced as well as a cheque listing.

Stock control

Many users will add this routine at a later date. The stock records are comprehensive, with up to 27 items held on each record. The stock code is ten alphanumeric characters. The program allows for ordering and receiving goods as well as issues, returns, and adjustments. A routine for updating of stock prices is also provided.

Reporting

An excellent range of reports are available from the system. The sales and purchase ledger allows up to nine user-defined reports, in addition to the various control reports. Such reports can be for a range of accounts and can be sorted by account code, name, turnover, category or rep/agent. Age analysis, date of last payment, Y-T-D figures, etc, can all be provided.

My only criticism in this area is the lack of screen based reports for enquiry purposes.

Controls and security

The system allows for password protection on each ledger and in each routine operation. Hence a number of password protection levels are available if required.

Adequate audit trails are produced and control reports are provided by the system, although no sequential numbering of batches – which might assist file reinstatement routines – was available. The back-up and reinstate routines are provided as part of the system utilities, alleviating the need to use the operating system, but no warnings are given to the user when logging off the system about the need for back-ups to be taken.

Summary

This package offers a good number of features and would certainly appeal to the first time user. The basic system costs £250.00; each separate module costs £99.00. Additional modules for multi-company (allowing up to 26 companies) and multi-department (allowing up to 40 departments, with consolidation) are available, also at an extra cost of £99.00 each. The package would seem to offer an upward path for the growing business (although the additional modules were not tested).

This package has around 2,000 users at the moment (1,500 new users in the last 12 months). Support is sparse but growing. The software comes with three months' free support, and costs £75 per annum thereafter (including any updates).

According to the supplier a number of features are due to be added to the basic system, including screen based reports, and the ability to save transaction files in ASCII or DIF format for subsequent use with other packages, such as spreadsheets and free text invoicing.

Review of TAS Plus Financial Accounting Level 2

The introduction to the manual for TAS Plus Financial Accounting Level 2 (Version 4.2), makes the claim that this software is unique. Though I cannot testify that other similar packages do not exist it is certainly different. The package includes TAS Plus, a relational Database, the source code, and the accounting programs all on floppy disks, together with manuals for both the database and the accounting software.

TAS Plus Financial Accounting Level 2 is a comprehensive integrated accounting system consisting of a nominal ledger together with both sales and purchase ledgers. It is written in TAS, a high speed multi-user database application developer or as they call it in their sales literature a Fourth Generation language. A level 3 package is available which includes the specifications of level 2 together with the addition of Sales and Purchase order processing and Stock control. The system can be upgraded to multi-user by the replacement of the TAS Plus single-user version by the multi-user one, which will allow two or more users to share the same data and programs with full record locking. Since the package comes complete with the source code, additional modules could be written for use with it by an enthusiastic user or dealer and it is possible for other packages to be linked to TAS by means of an ASCII editor such as a Sidekick.

This package requires an IBM or compatible microcomputer running on DOS as its operating system with at least 512Kb of RAM and a hard disk. The package takes just over 1Mb of hard disk to store the programmes together. There is a version available for use on machines using concurrent CP/M as its operating system though this has a different specification to the version under review.

Ease of use

The package is user friendly being menu-driven with a logical and easy to follow structure. The entry screens are clear, well laid out and easy to understand. They are supplemented by useful help screens, with online help being available at data entry points. Error correction is relatively simple and can be achieved before completion of data entry.

The manual for the Accounting package is clear in its layout with both set-up and daily processing being covered in a logical manner. Opening balances are entered directly into the respective ledger accounts and adjustments can be made to these balances at a later date. The manual contains specific examples of input processing with explanations being given for each field of information. The product no longer comes supplied with test data, but now includes a tutorial for users to work through and become familiar with the package.

Nominal, sales and purchase ledger

The coding flexibility is good. The nominal ledger accounts are required to follow a standard format of balance sheet followed by first income then expenditure accounts. However, the six digit numeric code length allows for up to 999,999 different nominal accounts and though the system does not allow for sub-accounting of codes the departmental feature of this package with its three digit alphanumeric code would accommodate infinite sub-analysis of nominal accounts as required. The sales and purchase ledger accounts are allocated by way of a ten digit alphanumeric code which allows a potentially unlimited number of accounts. The limiting factor would only be the disk storage capacity of the computer. There is no multi company processing option for this package but the department code could fulfil that requirement if necessary.

The system caters for all of the standard inputs such as invoices, credit notes, cash received, cash paid, refunds, discounts, journal entries and reversing entries. Though the user is restricted to twelve periods per year, journals can be posted to any month in the current year or the previous two years with the effects being carried forward if desired. Up to five separate bank accounts can be reconciled through the system. The input of transactions is individual and not by batch processing. Some of the more interesting features of the input are as follows:

- The nominal distribution of both customers and suppliers is remembered and the system defaults to these accounts on input of an invoice.
- Adjustments for errors in either sales or purchase ledgers can be made leaving both an audit trail and uncluttered ledger account.
- The credit limit of a customer is checked as an invoice is entered and warning given if the preset limit is exceeded.

Reporting
The system comes supplied with some sample formats of reports and these can either be added to or adjusted as required. The reports can either be for individual departments or for the company in total and that includes trial balance reports, balance sheets or any other desired report. The history for sales or purchase ledger accounts can be obtained for any period up to twelve months with this variation being set for individual accounts if required. The database nature of this system facilitates flexible structures in report formats and leads to more than the usual means of accessing data being available to the user.

Security
System security is poor, the only protection against unauthorised use is the restriction on access to the Central Information by means of a six character password. This password can only be changed using the source code. Thus considering the manual lists the file specifications and the various progamme names, including those for the deletion of all data, the user runs the risk of potential data corruption or loss by his staff or unauthorised users. This along with no provision being made within the system for backups by menu option could lead to potential problems with reliability on data. Megatech are aware of the problem of poor security and are currently working on a multi-level password system.

Megatech supply the product either direct or through a dealer network. There are two dealers in Scotland. Support is by way of the dealer or use of a helpline to Megatech. The product has been on the market for over eighteen months and there are over 500 users at present. The cost of level 2 is £499 and the level 3 costing £799. A demonstration version of the package is available at a cost of £30. Updates on the package are made available to existing users at a small charge.

TAS provides a very flexible system which is best used by those who require something outside the standard packages and prefer a tailored package.

Features Rating Table

Package	MAP	SAGESOFT	SNIP	TAS PLUS
	Rating (out of 10)			
Ease of set-up	9	8	8	8
Documentation	7	8	8	8
Performance of accounting functions	7	8	8	8
Ease of use	8	8	7	7
Reporting	8	8	9	10
Security	5	7	7	1
Support (Scotland)	6	7	6	4
Value for money	8	9	9	8
TOTAL (out of 80)	58	63	62	54

Package Information Table

Product Name	MAP
Version Number	6.0.
Dates of Tests	January 1988
Modules Available	Nominal, sales and purchase ledgers, stock control, payroll, job costing, sales order processing and database link.
Cost per Module	£99, database link – £40 Complete Accounting; (ledgers, stock control, sales order processing and database) – £299*
Publisher	MAP Computing (Oldham) Ltd, 99 Windsor Road, Oldham, Lancs OL8 1RP Tel: 061-624 5662
Supplier	As publisher.
What support is available	From MAP dealers and distributors. Helpline support (free for 30 days after purchase).
Operating system	MS-DOS, PC-DOS, CP/M, Novell, Allay, Xen-net, MS-Net, RM Nimbus.
Hardware	Amstrad and IBM compatibles. Amstrad PCW
Network/multi-user version available	Yes – £649.
Hardware used for tests	Olivetti M 24.
Number of UK users	9,000
First operational	1980.
Report generator available?	Yes, with database link module in version 6.0
Links to other packages	Database link translates data files to ASCII format.
Special features	—

* All prices are ex. VAT for version 6.0.

SAGESOFT	SNIP	TAS PLUS
2.1.	3.426.	4.2.
September 1987.	November 1987.	January 1988.
Basic system: nominal, sales and purchase ledgers; Full suite: Nominal, sales and purchase ledgers, sales order processing, purchase order processing, stock control, invoicing and payroll.	Nominal, sales and purchase ledgers, stock control and invoicing. Additional modules for job costing, sales orders and payroll.	Level 2: nominal, sales and purchase ledgers; Level 3: nominal, sales and purchase ledgers, sales order processing, purchase order processing stock control; multi-user.
Basic system – £99 Full Suite – £299. Financial Controller.	£99 (All except additional modules for £250).	Level 2: all modules including database – £499; Level 3: all modules – £799; (database only – £199).
Sagesoft plc, NEI House, Regent Centre, Newcastle upon Tyne, NE3 3DS. Tel: 091-284 7077.	Benchmark Computer Systems Ltd, 8 Leiga Road, Street, Somerset, BA16 0MA. Tel: 0458 43418.	Megatech, 111–113 Wandsworth High Street, London SW18. Tel: 01-870 8541.
As publisher.	As publisher.	As publisher.
Helpline direct from publisher – free for 90 days, thereafter £75 per annum plus third party support.	From supplier – three months free thereafter £75 per annum.	Helpline and dealer support.
MS-DOS.	MS-DOS.	Level 1: CP/M/86, C-DOS, Concurrent CP/M and 16 bit Turbo-DOS; Level 2: DOS.
IBM compatibles.	PC – compatible.	IBM compatible for Level 2.
No (Yes for financial controller).	Is multi-user.	Yes – costs £150 extra.
Compaq II.	Olivetti M 24.	Compaq 286 portable II.
30,000+	2,000	Over 500.
1986.	1980	June 1986.
Yes.	Yes.	Yes.
No.	Yes, additional cost.	Yes.
———	———	Source code available.

Evaluation Checklists

General Points

Performance of Requisite Accounting Functions

		MAP
1	Does the software perform the functions which the user wants performed?	
2	Can the software be used by more than one user at the same time?	yes — Multi-user/networked is apparently available. Single-user system tested.
3	Can the software support groups of companies/departments branches?	yes — 99 branches/cost centres.
	How many such branches or companies can be supported.	26 — Companies coded A–Z.
	Can they be consolidated?	yes
4	Is multi currency processing available?	no
	What are the maximum number of currencies available?	N/A
	Is conversion to sterling automatic?	N/A
5	Are sufficient accounting periods provided by the system?	yes — User specifies number of accounting periods by inputting date of next period end.
	Can these periods be adjusted to suit different user requirements?	yes
6	Are the ends of accounting periods determined by the user rather than being set by the system?	yes
7	Can data from all accounting periods be assessed at any given moment?	no — May be accessed from appropriate backups.
	Can previous months be accessed for enquiries or reports?	no
8	Does the system prevent posting to more than one accounting period at a time?	yes — Affirmative within modules, but may post to different periods between modules.
	Is it impossible to allocate transactions to future periods or to previous closed months?	yes — Safeguards.
9	Does the system permit use of budgets and provide comparisons between budgets and actuals?	yes
10	Is the maximum value of transactions that can be handled by the system sufficient?	yes — Up to £99m per transaction entry.
11	Is the maximum number of accounts on each ledger (e.g. sales ledger, purchase ledger, nominal ledger) sufficient?	Sufficient for sales/purchase ledgers. Maximum of 1000 for nominal ledger may be considered insufficient for some applications.
12	Is the size and format of account numbers adequate and sufficient for analysis purposes?	yes
13	Does the associated hardware incorporate enough memory, disk storage and other peripherals for the software to operate satisfactorily?	Would recommend running package on hard disk machine, particularly if integration required.
14	Does the system offer adequate expansion potential as regards terminals, memory, disk storage capacity and other peripherals?	
15	Are the control features provided by the software adequate to support effective user controls?	yes
16	Are complementary clerical procedures to be imposed and effectively monitored by management?	Essential.

LOW-PRICE PACKAGES

	SAGESOFT		SNIP		TAS
		yes			
yes	Financial controller.	yes	If multi-user version is purchased.	yes	Multi-user version.
yes	Accountant plus financial controller.	yes	Additional cost to the basic system.	yes	Departments.
	No limit.		Up to 26 companies can be set up using multi-company version.		Up to 999 departments.
yes		yes	Multi-department version allows up to 40 departments, with budgets and consolidation.	yes	But only with user modifications.
no		no		no	
				N/A	
				N/A	
	12 monthly periods.		12 monthly periods		12 monthly periods.
no				no	
no	Standard months.	yes	In that user must run period-end routines.	no	
		yes/no	M-T-D, Q-T-D and Y-T-D available.	yes	
yes		no	Only as above.	yes	Unless cleared down by user.
yes	Disk space permitting.	yes		no	Entry by dated batch – posting period taken from batch date.
yes		no	Can allocate to previous period (comparatively through the journal).	no	Period depends on date.
yes		yes	Budget report for nominal accounts P-T-D, Y-T-D, and last year.	yes	
yes		yes	Dependent on disk space.	yes	Limited only by disk space/memory.
yes	Limited only by disk space – set up in initialisation routine.	yes	Must set up in file size routine. 16,000 sales, 16,000 purchase, 999 nominal.		Limited only by disk space.
yes		yes			10 digits alpha-numeric.
		yes	If hard disk system used, considerably more efficient than twin floppy system.		
		yes	Can move up to multi-dept, or multi-company any version and multi-user version (although these not tested).		
yes		yes	Password controls, control reports (batch) and audit trails back-up and recovery.	no	Only access controls are in respect of company set-up info.
yes	Essential.		Manual controls required.		Strict manual controls required.

Reliability – Security and Continuity of Processing

		MAP
1 Does the system facilitate backup storage?	no	Must be done through operating system.
How much time will complete back-up of the system require?		Dependant on system size and back-up medium.
2 Does the system facilitate recovery procedures in the event of system failure?	no	Must be done through operating system.
3 If system failure occurs part way through a batch or transaction, will the operator have to re-input only the batch or transaction being input at the time of the failure?	no	Data input from point of last back-up.
4 Are there any features provided with the software to help track down processing problems?	no	A few very simple messages such as 'disk full' etc. Moreover difficult to exit routine on these events occurring.
5 Are backup procedures provided within each specific software application or within the operating system?		Operating system only.
Are any of these back-up procedures automatic?	no	

Support and Maintenance

1 Will the supplier provide corrections to the program?	yes	Within calendar month of receipt of package, or if on support.
2 Will the supplier provide general enhancements to the programs?	yes	
Will these be provided automatically?	no	} Yes if on support.
Will they be given free of charge?	no	
3 Will the software supplier provide 'hot-line' support to assist with immediate problem solving?	yes	30 days from date of registration.
If so, at what cost?		£40 per module (£60 payroll); £100 Complete Accounting.
4 Is the supplier capable of giving sufficient ongoing education and training and other support?		
5 Can the supplier provide all the hardware, software and maintenance requirements of the user?		
6 Can the supplier provide support in the user's locality?		
7 Is a warranty offered in respect of specification and performance of the system?	yes	30 days.
8 Would there be adequate back-up in the event of hardware or software failure?		Publisher can recover data.
9 Will the software supplier make the program source code available to the user, either directly or by deposit with a third party?	no	
10 If the software is acquired under licence, are there any unduly restrictive conditions in the licence?	no	

The term 'supplier' refers to the supplier of the support and maintenance, whether or not this is the same as the supplier of the software.

Ease of Use

(a) Interactive processing

1 Does the software run under an operating system, which is a commonly accepted standard?	yes	MS-PC-DOS (and CP/M (or M+)).
2 Is the software available concurrently to more than one user?	yes	Multi-user.
3 Can more than one system function be performed concurrently?	no	Not on single-user, but yes on multi-user.
4 Does the software effectively lead the user through the data entry procedures?	yes	But with minimum assistance.
Does the software facilitate immediate error correction?	no	Very few error/help messages.

LOW-PRICE PACKAGES   129

	SAGESOFT		SNIP		TAS
no	Revert to DOS.	yes		no	Back-up relies on DOS.
	2 mins		Depends entirely on size of data files.		5–10 mins. tape drive.
no	Revert to back-up copy. Suggest minimum of daily back-up.	yes	User is informed, if need to reinstate system due to hardware/software failure.	no	
yes		no	Data input from last back-up.		Whole batch.
no	Not really.	no		yes	Individual program and file names identified.
	Operating system.	yes	Provided as part of the integrated package.		Operating system.
no		no	User must initiate the back-up routine.	no	
yes		yes	Must take out maintenance outside 90 day warranty.	yes	
yes	£75 for software support cost.	yes		yes	
no	But see above (2).	yes	Under maintenance agreement.	no	
no			Within 90 day warranty period.	no	
yes		yes		yes	Mon–Fri 10–12, 2–4.
	Free of charge first 3 months.		Maintenance contract £7 per month.		Free.
			A number of dealers who can, but few in Scotland.		
	Minimal profit for dealer, therefore be careful.		Few in Scotland, one in Edinburgh. SNIP Training Centre in Scotland.		Limited in Scotland.
yes		no		no	
no		no		yes	Supplied with software.
no		no		no	
yes	DOS.	yes	MS-DOS.	yes	DOS.
yes	C-DOS or network.	no	Yes for multi-user version.	yes	Multi-user option.
yes	C-DOS or network.	no	Yes for multi-user version.	no	
yes		yes		yes	Menu-driven with input layouts on screen.
no	Few errors/help messages.	yes/no	Reasonable editing routines.	yes	

130 A GUIDE TO ACCOUNTING SOFTWARE

	MAP	
5 Is the software menu-driven?	yes	
Are such menus restricted by password and application?	yes	Password control is optional.
6 Are the user screens adequately titled?	yes	
7 Does the system inform the operator which programs or files are being loaded?	yes	
8 Does the software facilitate file maintenance, back-up and archive copying?	no	

(b) User documentation

	MAP	
1 Is the manual clearly laid out and understandable?	yes	Manual provides understandable overview sufficient for starting up and running simple application. It lacks detail however.
2 Is the manual comprehensive and accurate?	yes	
3 Is there an index to the manual?	yes	
4 Is it easy to locate specific topics in the manual when required?	no	Index is brief, and insufficiently comprehensive.
5 Is it easy to follow through all procedures in the manual?	yes	
6 Are completed examples included in the manual?	no	
7 Are help screens available?	no	
Do they provide detailed on-line instructions on how to use particular features of the software?		
Can they be edited or prepared by the user?		
8 Does the documentation clearly specify the actions to be taken by users at each important stage of processing?	no	For straightforward processing yes. Documentation lacks detail on more complex processing issues.
9 Will the software supplier provide regular updates of documentation in the event of modifications or revisions?	yes	
10 Will the software supplier make the detailed program documentation available to the user, either directly or by deposit with a third party?	no	

Efficiency

	MAP	
1 Are the various functions of the system menu-driven, or otherwise easy to initiate?	yes	
Is there a good response time in the initiation of functions?	yes	
2 Is data entry easily repeated if similar to previous entry?	yes	Commonest default value is previously entered value.
3 Is there a good response time		
(i) in processing data input?	yes	
(ii) in producing requisite reports?	yes	
(iii) in updating files?	yes	
(iv) in producing back-up files?	N/A	
(v) in deleting redundant information files?	N/A	
4 Does the system prevent access to a record while it is being updated?	yes	

SAGESOFT		SNIP		TAS	
yes		yes		yes	
yes			Passwords can be set up for each application, and within each application.	no	With exception of control information file.
yes		yes		yes	Include program names.
yes		yes		yes	
no		yes/no	System utilities routine. Up to user to set up when to make back-ups.	no	Files are easily identified.
yes		yes		yes	Laid out in order and structure of main menu.
yes		yes		no	
yes		no		no	
yes		yes		yes	If subject area is known, e.g. purchase ledger.
yes		yes	Almost all procedures.	no	Some aspects are vague, no general section exists.
yes		yes		yes	
no		no	Only in relation to the file size and program in setting up no. of record.	yes	
				yes	
		no		no	Though use of source code would allow adjustments.
yes		yes	(But not on screen).	yes	
yes	If support contract taken.	yes		yes	
no		no		yes	Source code supplied on disk and names and functions of all programs given in manual.
yes		yes		yes	
yes		yes	Slower on twin floppy. Good on hard disk.	yes	
yes		no	No function keys used.	yes	
yes		yes		yes	
yes		yes	Some can be spooled e.g. statements, invoices.	yes	
yes		yes		yes	
yes	DOS.	yes		N/A	Option system controlled.
yes			Does not occur.	yes	
yes		yes	In multi-user version.	yesd	

132 A GUIDE TO ACCOUNTING SOFTWARE

		MAP
5 Does the system retain a log of file updates until the next occasion on which the relevant information is reported or the relevant file used in a regular control procedure?	no	
6 Can regular reports be easily duplicated if required?	yes	Multiple copies of all reports can be taken prior to further transaction input.
Flexibility		
(a) Integration facilities		
1 Are the different accounting applications integrated?	yes	
Are they integrated on an item by item basis or are they integrated by weekly or monthly end routines?		Item by item.
2 Whichever method is used, can the ledger updating process be satisfactorily controlled?	yes	
3 Does the software run under an operating system which is a commonly-accepted standard?	yes	DOS.
4 Can more than one system function be performed concurrently?	no / yes	Not on single-user system. Multi-user version.
5 Can software be linked to other packages, e.g. word processing, graphics, financial modelling, to provide alternative display and reporting facilities?	yes	Requires database link module.
(b) Reporting flexibility		
1 Can the user easily design additional output reports or displays?	yes	
2 Is a report generator provided as part of the software or as an option associated with it?	yes	Separate module.
3 Can screen layouts, reports and transaction formats be easily adapted to users' requirements?	no	Can be tailored by MAP.
4 Does the output of the software facilitate proper control to ensure that decisions are not inadvertently taken on the basis of incorrect information?	yes	Reports are adequately titled, sequentially numbered and dated, with appropriate totals.
(c) Parameter or table facilities		
1 If the system uses a lot of standing information which changes frequently or regularly, does the system allow for such changes to be effected through the use of parameters or tables?	yes	VAT rates.
2 If so, is the use of such parameters or tables adequately reported?	no	
3 Is proper control to be exercised over changes to such parameters or tables? If so, how (e.g. through the use of system facilities such as passwords or by inspection of appropriate records)?		May be password controlled.
Software Installation and Training		
(a) Financial resources		
1 Has account been taken in the budget for system development/acquisition of the full costs of		
initial acquisition?	N/A	
initial training?	N/A	
future training?	N/A	

LOW-PRICE PACKAGES

SAGESOFT		SNIP		TAS	
no			Amendments to files, e.g. customer accounts not printed, up to user to initiate.	no	
yes		no	Control reports cleared when printed.	yes	
yes		yes		yes	
	Item by item.		As and when user knows the period-end routine or sales/purchases.		Integrated by posting routine – recommended to run daily.
yes		yes	Ensures all sales are analysed and updated to nominal accounts, only.	yes	
yes	DOS.	yes	MS-DOS.	yes	DOS, CP/M.
no	DOS.	no	Unless multi-user version.	no	
yes	C-DOS or network version.				
yes		yes	Additional cost £49.99. Transfer files to ASCII and DIF format, for use with spreadsheet database etc.	yes	Source code available.
yes		yes/no	Report generator allows user flexibility on which items to print and how to sort the report.	yes	
yes		yes	As part of the software.	yes	
yes		no	Screen layouts, report formats, etc, cannot be altered.	no	But source code available.
yes		yes		no	Reports can be set up to give inaccurate information to user.
yes	VAT rates.	no		no	
no				N/A	
no				N/A	
				N/A	
N/A		N/A		N/A	
N/A		N/A		N/A	
N/A		N/A		N/A	

	MAP
(b) Other resources	
2 Is the main equipment to be located in adequate accommodation?	N/A
Is this such that staff are not seriously affected by the equipment (e.g. by noise from the printer).	N/A
3 Is there sufficient scope for the installation, if required, of communications equipment?	N/A
4 Have requisite consumables (e.g. special stationery, filing facilities, fireproof storage) been provided for?	N/A
(c) Involvement of software supplier	
5 Is the supplier capable of giving sufficient initial education and training and other support?	N/A
6 Are potential users permitted to test the software for a trial period before commitment to acquire it?	yes
7 If required, does the supplier have sufficient capable personnel to assist users to convert to the new system?	N/A
8 If required, will the supplier provide machine time to enable users to set up files of input data before installation?	N/A
(d) Involvement of user personnel	
9 Who is to be responsible for running and controlling the system on a regular basis?	N/A
Is this person sufficiently competent?	N/A
10 Who is to be responsible for the installation and implemetation of the system?	N/A
Is the person sufficiently competent?	N/A
11 Which staff will operate the system?	N/A
Do they have sufficient aptitude for computers?	N/A
12 Is there adequate cover for staff in the event of illness and holidays?	N/A

Package Software Acquisition

Preliminary questions relating to software supplier

1. Does the supplier have a good overall reputation as regards experience and reliability?
2. Does the supplier offer a full range of accounting software?
3. Is the supplier's financial status stable?

   Does the supplier demonstrate an adequate capital base, growth and profitability?
4. Does the supplier have sufficient technical resources to modify or tailor software to suit different users' requirements?
5. Does the supplier have a substantial user base?

   Has it shown adequate commitment to existing users and will it provide a list of them?

   Has the supplier sold similar systems to that under consideration?
6. Does the supplier offer adequate contractual terms as regards purchase, installation, delivery, support and maintenance?

   Are all costs clearly indicated?

   Is the date of delivery of all components of the system clearly stated?

SAGESOFT	SNIP	TAS	
N/A	N/A	N/A	
N/A	N/A	N/A	
N/A	N/A	N/A	
N/A	N/A	N/A	
N/A	N/A	N/A	
N/A	yes	yes	Test pack available for £30. (Limited no. of records).
N/A	N/A	N/A	
N/A	N/A	N/A	
N/A	N/A	N/A	
N/A	N/A	N/A	
N/A	N/A	N/A	
N/A	N/A	N/A	
N/A	N/A	N/A	
N/A	N/A	N/A	
N/A	N/A	N/A	

	MAP
7 Is there adequate evidence that the supplier normally meets its contractual obligations?	
8 Will the supplier provide in-depth demonstrations of its software?	

Nominal Ledger

General

1 Are the programs menu-driven?	yes	Single key followed by (enter).
If 'YES' – can menus be by-passed once the user is familiar with the package?		
2 Does the system maintain a log of usage?	no	
3 Are informative messages produced on-screen whilst running?	no	
4 Are error messages informative and easy to understand?	no	Very few error messages – cover operating system problems only.
5 Is the system multi-company?	yes	
6 Is the original set-up straightforward?	yes	
7 Is there a copy/restore facility in the package?	no	
8 Does the system cover disciplined taking of back-ups?	no	Simple procedure for data kept on diskette covered in manual-via operating system. No procedures given for hard disk.

Documentation

(a) Manual

1 Is the manual clearly laid out and understandable?	yes	Manual provides understandable overview sufficient for starting up and running simple application. It lacks detail on dealing with complex and/or problem transactions and issues.
2 Is the manual comprehensive and accurate?	yes	
3 Is there an index?	yes	
4 Is it easy to follow through all procedures?	yes	
5 Is it easy to locate specific points when required?	no	The index is brief and insufficiently comprehensive.
6 Are completed examples included?	no	

(b) Help screens

7 Are help screens available?	no	

If 'YES' –

Do they provide on-line instructions?

Can they be edited or prepared by the user?

Account Details

1 Is the chart of accounts flexible?	no	Limited flexibility within range 1–1000.
2 What is the format of the nominal account code?		Accounts are numbered 1–1000.
3 Is cost centre accounting available?	yes	Number of cost centres must be specified for given company at installation. Once specified, apply to all revenue and expense accounts up to 99 cost centres.
4 What is the maximum number of accounts that can be held?		1000.
5 What is the maximum balance that can be held?		£999,999,999.99.

SAGESOFT		SNIP		TAS	
yes		yes		yes	
no		no		yes	Program names are supplied, and programs can be run from database.
no		no	Other than audit (transaction) trail.	no	
yes		yes		yes	
yes		yes			
no	Financial controller – yes.	no	But is available at an additional £99.	yes	
yes		yes		yes	But slow.
no		yes		no	
no	But manual sets out clear instructions.	no	User must initiate from system utilities routine.	no	
yes		yes		no	
yes		yes	More detail required on editing keys.	no	
yes		no		no	Could do with index and general section.
yes		yes		no	Some are vague.
yes		yes		no	No index, though it is laid out in menu order.
yes		yes	Most examples.	yes	
no		no	Only in relation to the file size and routine for setting-up and amending no. of records.	yes	
				yes	Very good and are available at entry points.
				no	
yes		yes	18 account headings, which can be amended	yes	
	6 digit alphanumeric.		Numeric 00 to range of nominal accounts, set up.		4 digit number followed by 3 digit dept. code.
yes		yes	But only 18 headings are available to which a range of account codes can belong to. Optional dept nominal with up to 20 depts per account.	yes	By department.
	1000.		999.		9999.
	£1M. Single entry £100m balance.		£9,999,999.99 for period to date, QTR-T-D. Y-T-D = £99,999,999.99.		£999,999,999.99.

138 A GUIDE TO ACCOUNTING SOFTWARE

		MAP
6 Can accounts be added/deleted/amended at any time?	yes	Amended only – cannot be deleted at any time.
7 Is file automatically re-sorted when a new account is added?	N/A	
If 'NO' – can a re-sort be initiated?		
8 Is deletion of an account prevented if it has: a non-zero balance.	N/A	Fixed number of accounts once set up. Names can be amended.
a zero balance but postings in the current period.		
a zero balance but postings in the year-to-date?		
9 Is a hard copy of changes in account details automatically produced?	no	
10 Are 12 or 13 (or more) accounting periods available?	more	Operator specifies date of next period end.
11 Can budgets be entered for all revenue accounts?	yes	
12 Can separate budgets be entered for each accounting period?	yes	Changes to monthly budgets must be entered each period.
13 Can this year's results be used to calculate next year's budgets automatically?	no	

Transactions

1 What is the maximum transaction value that can be entered?		£99,999,999.99.
2 Can each journal entry contain an unlimited number of debits and credits?	yes	Journals entered in pages of 13 debits and/or credits. Unlimited number of pages per journal entry.
3 Is each input line numbered?	yes	Lines numbered 1 to 13 on each page.
4 In a long journal entry is it possible to move between screens to view data already input?	no	
5 Can previously entered journal lines be edited before accepting the whole journal?	no	Only those lines on current (last) page.
6 Does each journal entry have a reference number?	yes	
7 Are accruals and prepayments routines, which both reverse automatically at the start of the next accounting period, available?	yes	
8 Can recurring journal entries be provided for automatically?	yes	
9 Is a narrative available for:		
each journal entry	no	
each line of the journal entry?	yes	
10 Can journal entries be posted to future periods?	no	Will not allow dates after current period end to be input.
11 Can journal entries be posted to previous periods?	no	Possible using floppy disk system.
12 Are all transactions retained on file for at least one period?	yes	
13 Can transactions be retained at the period end?	no	Brings b/f total.
14 Can a ledger date pre-date existing transactions?	yes	

Input Controls

1 Is password control used? If 'YES' – give detail.	yes	Password control optional. Each function within module may be protected with 6-character password individually. If all functions protected, whole module is protected from entry.
2 Is a hard copy automatically produced for all input?	yes	Transactions only. Hard copy produced for all transactions input. No copy produced for changes to account details.

LOW-PRICE PACKAGES   139

SAGESOFT		SNIP		TAS	
yes	Except during transactions input.	yes/no yes	Account can be added, by entering*, in nom. code field, in input routines. Account can only be deleted if period, quarter and Y-T-D figures are zero.	no	Not during processing.
yes	Indexed.	no	Must set up account structure carefully, to allow for expansion.	yes	
				N/A	
yes		yes		yes	
yes		yes		no	
yes		yes		no	
no		no	User must use report generator accordingly.	no	
	12		Only 12 account periods are available.		Only 12 accounting periods.
yes		yes	Monthly budgets set for each month.	yes	Monthly.
yes		yes		yes	Monthly.
no		no	But last year figure is held in nominal account, which would simplify this routine.	no	
	£1m.		£9,999,999.99.		£999,999,999.99.
no	12-line entries.	yes		no	7 debits. 7 credits.
no	Not on entry screen, yes on audit trail.	no		no	
no		no	The screen scrolls forward.	N/A	Only one screen.
no		yes	Using the ESC key but erases previous entries on reject batch.	yes	
yes		yes	8 character journal ref.	yes	
no		yes	As part of journal routine.	no	
no		no		yes	
yes		no	But a refrence no. is.	yes	
yes		yes	Description (20 characters in length).	no	
no		no		yes	
no		yes	Comparatives – system produces an audit trail as the comparative postings are accepted.	yes	
yes		yes		yes	
no		no		yes	
no		no		yes	
yes	Each menu can be password protected.	yes	Each option on menu can be password protected (up to 10 characters, in length). Password program may also be password protected.	yes	It only controls access to central info. file. This contains control accounts and company info.
no		yes		no	

	MAP	
3 Are journal entries automatically sequentially numbered?	yes	
4 If integrated, are automatic postings from other modules included in the numbering sequence?	yes	
5 If accruals and prepayments automatically reverse, is the reversal included in the numbering sequence?	no	
6 Are totals, of debit or credit entries, produced for all journal entries?	yes	
If 'YES' – is it necessary that this agrees with a pre-list total?	no	But differences noted on audit trail.
7 Is it necessary that all journal entries balance before posting?	yes	Only possible to alter final screen therefore may have to use a 'balance figure' to find error on previous screens.
8 Is production of an out-of-balance trial balance prevented?	yes	
9 Do all input screens show clearly:		
type of entry	yes	
the distinction between debits and credits?	yes	
10 Can the actual date of posting, or a batch reference, be shown on hard copies of transactions input?	yes	
11 Are the following validated:		
date	yes	
nominal ledger account code	yes	
cost centre code	yes	
If 'NO' – are unidentified/invalid entries posted to a suspense account?		
– how is suspense account treated?		
12 Is a total produced of all debit/credit transactions processed?	yes	
If 'YES' – is a report produced at the end of each processing run to reconcile b/f total, transactions processed and c/f total?	no	
13 Is a reconciliation of numbers of accounts produced after amendment of the accounts detail file?	N/A	Fixed number of accounts, once set up.
14 Does the system prevent the abnormal termination of programs?	yes	

Integration

1 Is integration possible with the following:		
sales ledger	yes	
purchase ledger	yes	
payroll	yes	
2 Can the nominal ledger be updated as often as desired?	yes	
3 Is a hard copy automatically produced at the end of each nominal ledger update?	yes	
4 Is there a sales/purchase ledger print-out of the nominal ledger update?	yes	Print-out for each stage of update: from sales/purchase to link file, and from link file to nominal.

SAGESOFT		SNIP		TAS	
yes		no	Just date and page details.	no	
yes		no		no	
N/A		N/A		N/A	
yes		yes		yes	
no		no		no	
yes		yes	User can reject postings or is prompted to enter another entry.	yes	
yes		yes	Since all journals must balance and all postings must be to valid accounts.	yes	Direct postings can be made to nominal acounts.
yes		yes		yes	
yes		no	Only – minus sign to indicate credit entry. Although audit trail shows 'debits' and 'credits'	yes	
yes		yes	Date of posting, and date of audit listing. No batch reference.	yes	
no		yes	Must be a 'valid' date.	no	Date defines accounting period to which entry is posted.
yes		yes	Must be a previously defined code, or user enters * to create a new one.	yes	Must be valid code.
no		N/A		yes	
no					
yes		yes	The control report routine. Must be run before period-end.	yes	
no				no	
no		no	Up to user to produce a report of account details.	yes	
no		yes	User must log off using the system utilities for proper closing of files.	yes	
yes		yes		yes	
yes		yes		yes	
no		no	Must be entered manually.	N/A	
yes		yes		yes	
no		yes	Control totals.	no	
		yes	1. Sales analysis postings to nominal ledger. 2. Nominal audit trail option CR – control report.	no	

		MAP	
5	Are sales ledger and purchase ledger control accounts agreed to the totals of balances in the individual ledgers?	no	But warning is given when posting directly to control accounts.
6	Is there a check that the nominal ledger cannot be updated twice with the same sales purchases data?	yes	Transactions are deleted on update.
7	Must the nominal ledger be updated from the sales and purchase ledgers before the period-end is run?	no	
8	Must the nominal ledger be in the same period as the sales and purchase ledgers for the update to be carried out?	no	Will update from previous or future periods.
9	Is there any check that all data processed in the sales/purchase ledgers has been posted to the nominal ledger?	no	
10	Are unidentified/invalid entries held in a nominal ledger suspense account?	no	
	If 'YES' – how is this treated?		
11	Can the user select whether to update the nominal ledger with individual sales/purchase ledger entries or in total?	yes	Can specify which module to update from. Once specified, update made in total or, depending on set up, detailing individual transactions on audit trail and transactions listing.
	If 'NO' – is the update made in detail or in total?		
12	Is it impossible to post directly to the sales/purchase ledger control accounts?	no	But a warning is given when doing so.

Output
(a) General

1	Is it necessary to produce an audit trail before the period end procedure is run?	no	Audit trail automatic.
2	Does the audit trail enable all transactions to be traced fully through the system?	yes	
3	Can the actual run date, or batch reference, as well as the current ledger date, be shown on all reports?	yes	Audit reports display system date, an (optional) batch reference, and transaction date, but not period end date. Optional reports display run date and current ledger date.
4	Can the following be seen on screen:–		
	account details	yes	
	account transactions?	yes	
5	Can a print-out of the following be obtained for individual accounts/selected ranges of accounts:–		
	account details	yes	
	account transactions	yes	
6	Do all outputs show clearly the distinction between debit and credit entries?	yes	
7	Are all reports adequately titled?	yes	
8	Do reports provide totals where applicable?	yes	
9	Is the period number shown on reports?	no	Period end date is given.

LOW-PRICE PACKAGES

SAGESOFT		SNIP		TAS
yes		yes	Postings to nominal ledger, is of previously checked sales/purchase transactions. Undertaken by the system as part of the period end.	no
yes	Automatic entry in sales purchase also updates nominal.	yes	Nominal amounts posted are cleared when sales analysis routine is run.	yes
N/A	⎫	no	User must check that sales ledger, purchase ledger reports, have been generated which will update the nominal accounts.	no
	⎬ Update is item-by-item at time of input.			
N/A	⎭	yes		no
N/A		no	User must ensure completion of sales and purchase ledgers routines, period end occurs before nominal period end routine.	no
no	Must be valid nominal account.	no	All must be posted to valid accounts.	yes
no	Individual.	yes	In analysis routine of sales/purchase, user can update in total, or, in detail.	yes	Cleared by journal reported in B/S.
yes		no	Can enter journal entry and post to debtors' control account.	no
no	But advised.	yes	Control report must be run before can proceed to run period end routine.	no	But advised.
yes		yes		yes
yes		no	Only current date and transaction dates shown.	yes
yes		yes	But must enter nominal-maintenance routine, to view.	yes
yes		yes	Using nominal-maintenance routine.	yes
yes		yes	From nominal reports.	yes
yes		yes	From nominal reports.	yes
		yes/no	Debit/credit shown on control reports, other reports show +, − sign.	yes
yes		yes		yes
yes		yes		yes
yes		yes	Date and page number.	yes

		MAP	
10	Can the following be produced:		
	trial balance	yes	
	ledger account detail report	yes	Split into trading account, giving gross profit, and profit and loss account, giving net profit.
	profit and loss account.	yes	
	balance sheet.	yes	
11	Does the ledger account detail report show the source of postings and narrative input?	yes	
12	Does the ledger account detail report show either the full account history or balance b/f together with the current period's transactions?	yes	Balance b/f plus current period's transactions.
13	Are all report pages numbered sequentially, with the end of report identified?		Pages are numbered sequentially, but end of report not identified.
14	Can reports be temporarily retained on file for subsequent printing?	yes	Spooled files written to program drive.
	If 'YES' – are such files protected from deletion?	no	Can be deleted after output to screen however.
15	Is a report generator available for use with the nominal ledger module?	yes	
16	Can transaction files for all previous periods be retained in the system to permit enquiries and reports?	no	Can be copied onto storage medium through operating system.

(b) Trial balance; P & L and balance sheet

1	Does the package provide for flexible formatting of profit and loss account and balance sheet?	no	Yes if report generator used.
2	Can the following be produced for both the current period and the year-to-date:		
	trial balance	yes	
	profit and loss account	yes	
	balance sheet	yes	
	If 'YES' – is it clearly shown whether a report is for the current period or year-to-date?	yes	
3	Can the following show budgets:		
	trial balance	no	
	profit and loss account	no	But actual-v-budget report is in the format of a profit and loss account.
	If 'YES' – can budgets be omitted if wished?		
4	Can the following reports show comparative figures:		
	trial balance	no	But actual-v-budget report is in the format of a profit and loss account.
	profit and loss account	no	
	balance sheet	no	
	If 'YES' – can comparatives be omitted?		
	– can two years' comparatives be shown?		
5	Are budgets worked out from the period number as calculated by the number of period-end procedures run?	yes	

LOW-PRICE PACKAGES

SAGESOFT		SNIP		TAS	
yes		yes		yes	
yes		yes		yes	
yes		yes		yes	
yes		yes		yes	
yes		yes	Type such as cash receipts and description.	yes	
yes	Balance b/f together with the current period's transactions only.	yes	Full account history P-T-D, Q-T-D, Y-T-D and details of this period's transactions.	yes	
yes		yes	By grand totals or analysis totals.	yes	
yes		no		yes	Subsequently printed using operating system.
no				no	
yes		no	Reports are available but mainly pre-defined by the system.	yes	TAS PLUS is a database.
no	Revert to earlier back-ups.	no	Not on this version.	yes	
yes	Semi-flexible – good enough for small business.	yes		yes	Very flexible.
yes	To date only (unless through report generator).	yes		yes	
yes		yes		yes	
yes		yes		yes	
yes		yes		yes	
yes		no	But budget for period (month, and Y-T-D) compared with actual and last year are shown for any (or all) nominal headings/accounts.	yes	
yes		yes		yes	
yes		yes	Separate budget report.		
no		no		yes	
no		yes	Y-T-D and last year.	yes	
no		yes	Y-T-D and last year.	yes	
		no		yes	
		no	Current and previous year only.	yes	
yes		yes	Not by system date, but no. of period end routines processed.	no	Input by user month by month.

		MAP	

6 Are budget variances calculated?
   If 'YES' are they shown as:

value		yes	
percentages		yes	
both		yes	

7 Do budget reports provide for exception reporting? — yes

8 Does the package provide for a trial balance to be produced for each cost centre? — N/A — Multi-user only.

9 Does the package provide for a profit and loss account and balance sheet for each cost centre? — yes — Profit and loss account only. Balance sheet not applicable.

10 Does the package provide for totalling of like items across cost centres? — yes

11 Can trial balance production be varied by:

   printing a range of accounts. — no

   subtotalling on any chosen digit of account code? — no

12 Can vertical percentages be calculated in the profit and loss account? — yes — Can be calculated manually.

13 Can a report be produced to show the breakdown of profit and loss account and balance sheet figures? — yes — In part e.g. report of accruals and prepayments; transaction analysis report, etc.

Year End

1 Can balance sheet items be carried forward and profit and loss account items be cleared automatically at the year-end? — yes

2 Can the destination of individual account balances be specified or are all balances cleared at the year-end transferred into one account only? — no — One account.

Sales Ledger

General

1 Are programs menu-driven? — yes — Single key followed by (enter).
   If 'YES' – can menus be by-passed once the user is familiar with the package? — no

2 Does the system maintain a log of usage? — no

3 Are informative messages produced on-screen whilst running? — no

4 Are error messages informative and easy to understand? — no — Very few error messages – cover operating system problems only.

5 Is the system multi-company? — yes

6 Is the original set-up straightforward? — yes

7 Is there a copy/restore facility in the package? — no

8 Does the system cover disciplined taking of back-ups? — no — Simple procedure for data kept on diskette covered in manual – via operating system. No procedures given for hard disk.

Documentation
(a) Manual

1 Is the manual clearly laid out and understandable? — yes — Manual provides understandable overview sufficient for starting up and running simple application. It lacks detail.

2 Is the manual comprehensive and accurate? — yes

LOW-PRICE PACKAGES 147

SAGESOFT		SNIP		TAS	
yes					
no					
no	Report generator.	yes			
no		yes		yes	
no		no	User selects which nominal accounts, range and account headings to produce.	no	But formats could be re-written or package added.
no		no	Only account headings which represent a range of accounts.	yes	Per department.
no		no	Yes, if optional Departmental Nominal at £99.	yes	Per department.
		no		no	But reports can be re-written to requirements (sample formats in manual).
	Report generator only.				
no		no		yes	
no		no		yes	
		no		yes	
no		no		yes	
no		yes		yes	
N/A		no	One account.	yes	

SAGESOFT		SNIP		TAS	
yes		yes		yes	
no		no		yes	Program names are supplied and programs can be run from database.
no		no	Other than the control reports and transaction trail.	no	
yes		yes		yes	
yes		yes			
yes	Accountant plus – yes financial controller.	no	But is available at an additional £99.	yes	
yes		yes	But manual could be a little more specific about set-ups.	yes	Slow.
no		yes	Part of system utilities routine.	no	
no	But manual sets out clear instructions.	no	User must initiate from system utilities routine.	no	
yes		yes		yes	
yes		yes	More detail required on editing key depressions, backspace etc.	no	Needs index and general section.

		MAP
3 Is there an index?	yes	
4 Is it easy to follow through all procedures?	yes	
5 Is it easy to locate specific points when required?	no	The index is brief and insufficiently comprehensive.
6 Are completed examples included?	no	

(b) *Help screens*

7 Are help screens available?	no	

If 'YES' –

Do they provide on-line instructions?

Can they be edited or prepared by the user?

Customer details

1 What is the format of the customer account code?		Maximum 8 character, alpha-numeric.
2 What other customer details are held?		Name, 4 address lines plus postcode, telephone, contact (25 characters), 6 credit limit, 2 analysis codes, discount % (used by invoicing and sales order processing) and 2 reference lines (for comments).
Do these seem to be sufficient in general?	yes	
3 What is the maximum number of accounts that can be held?		Limited by disk capacity.
4 Can customer details be added/deleted/amended at any time?	yes	Additions and amendments at any time except during transaction input. See below for deletions.
5 Is file re-sorted automatically when a new customer is added?	no	
If 'NO' – can a re-sort be initiated?	yes	
6 Is deletion of a customer prevented if the account has:		
an outstanding balance	yes	Deletion can take place only after a period end, or accounts with zero outstanding balance.
a zero balance but a b/f turnover	no	
7 Is a hard copy of changes in customer details automatically produced?	no	
If 'NO' – can hard copy be taken?	no	May only run off a new (amended) accounts listing.

Transactions

1 Can the system be open item?	yes	
2 Are the following inputs possible:		
invoices	yes	
credit notes	yes	
cash received	yes	
cash refunded	yes	
discounts	yes	
journal entries	no	
write-offs	yes	
3 Can an invoice be analysed to several different sales categories?	yes	
4 Are different VAT codes possible for different items within one invoice.	yes	

LOW-PRICE PACKAGES

SAGESOFT		SNIP		TAS	
yes		no		no	
yes		yes		no	
yes		yes	Reasonable since section for each module.	no	Some are vague.
yes		yes	For most routines.	yes	No index, though laid out in menu order.
no		no	Only in relation to the file size routine for determining records to be set up, and the storage required.	yes	
				yes	Very good and are available at entry points.
				no	
	6 digit alphanumeric.		Alphanumeric 5 character field.		10 digit alphanumeric.
	Address, phone and credit limit. Contact name. Discount details.	yes	Name and address (4 lines), account type – open item or brought forward, customer category, rep./agent, price code, account, prompt payment discount, credit limit, contact name, tel., date last invoice, amount, sales, M-T-D, Y-T-D, balance, 30, 60, 90, 90+ balance.		Address 6 lines, tel., type, contact, salesman, credit limit.
		yes		yes	
	5,000.		4.5 records per 1K of disk space.		Unlimited.
yes	Except during transactions input.	yes	At most times, even during transaction postings, new accounts can be created for example.	yes	
yes	Indexed – always alphabetical.	no		yes	
		yes			
yes		yes		yes	
yes		yes	Must be zero Y-T-D, M-T-D-, in order to delete.	no	
no		no		no	
yes		yes	By setting up the reports routine.	yes	
yes		yes		yes	
yes		yes	Entered through transaction posting, or invoice module.	yes	
yes		yes		yes	
yes		yes		yes	
yes		yes		yes	
yes		yes		yes	
yes		yes		yes	
		yes	Must set up bad debts as a sales analysis code.	no	
yes		yes		yes	
yes		yes	Enter zero on VAT rate in TP, system requests VAT rate for each item.	yes	

		MAP
5 Are all transactions retained on file for at least one period?	yes	Can choose not to delete at period end.
6 Can a ledger date pre-date existing transactions?	yes	

Matching/Allocations
(a) Balance forward

1 Is the balance b/f aged?	no	
2 Can cash be allocated automatically?	no	
If 'YES' – how is the allocation made?		
– can this be over-ridden?		
3 Can cash be allocated manually?	yes	Posted to account balance.
If 'YES' – does the package check that cash allocated = amount received?		
How is any such difference treated?		Not accepted.
4 Can credit notes/journal entries be allocated to previous periods?	yes	
5 Can cash in advance be held and later allocated to subsequent periods?	yes	
6 Can cash be held unallocated?	yes	

(c) Open item

7 Are outstanding transactions displayed for allocation?	yes	
8 Can cash be allocated automatically?	yes	Specify range of transaction line numbers over which allocation to be made. Requests line by line confirmation of allocation.
If 'YES' – how is the allocation made?		
– can this be over-ridden?	yes	
9 Can cash be allocated manually?	yes	
If 'YES' does the package check that cash allocated = cash received?	yes	Requests whether difference to be treated as unallocated cash. Cannot exit routine until all cash either fully allocated and/or labelled 'unallocated'.
How is any difference treated?		
10 Can an over/under-payment of an invoice be recorded?		Only as unallocated cash/outstanding balance respectively.
11 How often are settled items deleted from file?		At period end, on request.
12 Can credit notes be set against the invoices to which they refer?	yes	
13 Can journal entries be set against the invoices/credit notes to which they refer?	N/A	Journals must be posted as IN/CR/CA transaction types.
14 Can cash in advance be held and later allocated to invoice?	yes	Carried as unallocated cash; must be dated at or prior to current period end.
15 Can cash be held unallocated?	yes	
– how is this treated?		Hold as unallocated CR balance forward until allocated.

LOW-PRICE PACKAGES

SAGESOFT		SNIP		TAS	
yes	Current period only.	yes	Cleared at period end, M-T-D, completed transaction.	yes	
yes		no		yes	
N/A		yes		N/A	
N/A		yes	System allocates cash in order to clear the eldest balances first.	N/A	
N/A		yes	Can reject before posting.	N/A	
N/A		yes		N/A	
N/A		yes	User must correct, in case of b/f, i.e. amount received must be allocated (can be in advance).	N/A	
N/A				N/A	
N/A		no	Set off credit note against balance of current period.	N/A	
N/A		yes		N/A	
N/A		yes		N/A	
yes		yes	First nine transactions are displayed (oldest first).	yes	
yes	Within accounts.	no	Must select the transaction (enter line number).	yes	
	First transaction.				Per payment list.
yes				yes	
yes		yes		yes	
yes		yes	If cash allocated not equal to cash received, user can reject it or if accept, enters transaction adjustment, or unallocated cash transaction posted.	yes	
	Paid to account balance.				Suspense account.
yes		yes	If un-allocated noted as a transaction.	yes	
	User choice.		At period end (but cleared transaction is removed from screen display).		Monthly.
yes		yes	Using payment posting.	yes	
yes		yes		yes	
yes		yes	Cash in advance can be held, and allocated to a specific invoice.	yes	
yes		yes		yes	
yes	Shown as such.		Held as unallocated.		Held in customer file as unallocated.

Input Controls

		MAP
1 Is password control used?	yes	Password control optional. Each function within a module may be protected with 6 character password individually. If all functions protected with password whole module is protected from entry. Whole ledger can be protected at main menu.
If 'YES' – give details.		
2 Is a hard copy automatically produced for all input?		Hard copy produced for all transaction input. No copy produced for changes to account details.
3 Are batch totals automatically produced for all transactions input?	yes	
If 'YES' – what is the procedure if this does not agree with a pre-list total?		Requested to accept/reject difference: Accept: noted on audit trail. Reject: return to transactions input.
4 Is it necessary that invoices, cash and adjustments are input in separate batches?	yes	Cash posting separate routine from invoice/credit note posting.
5 Are batches automatically sequentially numbered?	no	Page numbers of audit trail are sequentially numbered for each ledger.
If 'NO' – can they be so numbered?	yes	An optional batch reference can be entered by operator.
6 Is a report produced at the end of each processing run to reconcile b/f total, transactions processed and c/f total?	no	
If 'NO' – is a control balance produced at the end of each posting run?	yes	
7 Are the following validated:		
date	yes	
customer account number	yes	
VAT code	yes	
goods value	yes	
sales analysis code	yes	
8 Is VAT calculated to check figure input?	yes	If VAT amount input disagrees with that calculated using input rate, requests confirmation to accept amount.
9 Is the gross figure agreed to goods+VAT?	yes	
10 Is discount calculated to check the figure input?	no	
11 Can the actual date of posting, or batch reference, be shown on hard copies of transactions input?	yes	
12 Does the screen always indicate that the sales ledger, as opposed to the purchase ledger, is running?	yes	
13 Do all input screens show clearly:		
type of entry	yes	
the distinction between debits and credits	no	
14 Is there any check that the same entry is not input twice?	no	
15 Is there a warning if a customer exceeds the credit limit?	yes	
If 'YES' – what action is required?	none	
16 Is it impossible for new accounts to be created during processing?	yes	

LOW-PRICE PACKAGES

SAGESOFT		SNIP		TAS	
yes	Each menu protected if required.	yes	Each of the options available on SL menu can be password protected (up to 10 characters long), and can be amended. The password program may also be password protected.	no	
no		yes		no	
yes	Running total of input on screen. Edit.	yes	One can enter adjustments through (TP – transaction processing).	no	
yes		no	Manual invoices, credit note and adjustment can be entered in one batch.	yes	
yes		no		no	
		no		yes	
no	Immediate update to all ledgers on input.	yes	Control report – which must be run before the period end.	no	
no				no	
yes		yes		yes	
yes		yes		yes	
yes		yes		yes	
yes		yes		yes	
yes		yes		yes	
yes		yes	Must be written 10% less than true value or £0.05 more.	yes	
yes		no		yes	
yes		no		yes	
yes		yes		yes	
yes		yes		yes	
yes		yes		yes	
yes		yes		yes	
no		no		no	
no		yes		yes	
			Operator confirmation.		Update credit limit or adjust input.
yes		no		no	

154 A GUIDE TO ACCOUNTING SOFTWARE

		MAP
17 Is a reconciliation of numbers of accounts produced after amendment of the customer detail file?	no	
18 Does the system prevent the abnormal termination of programs?	yes	

Integration

		MAP
1 Can the sales ledger be integrated with an invoicing module?		Invoicing facility is part of sales ledger module, and fully integrated.
2 Can the sales ledger be integrated with a nominal ledger module?	yes	
3 Can the nominal ledger be updated as often as desired?	yes	From the sales ledger, prompt to update a nominal link file is given after every processing run.
4 Is a hard copy automatically produced at the end of each nominal ledger update?	yes	
5 Is there a sales ledger print-out (as well as a nominal ledger print-out) of the nominal ledger update?	yes	Printout for each stage of update: from sales ledger to link file, and from link file to nominal ledger.
6 Are the following automatically posted to the appropriate nominal ledger accounts:–		
discount	yes	
discount written back	no	Require to be adjusted through nominal ledger journals.
bad debts written off	no	
contras with purchase ledger	no	
7 Are any invalid/unidentified entries posted to a suspense account?	N/A	Transactions must be given valid nominal code, and must be of type invoice/credit note/cash/discount.
If 'NO' – how are they treated?		
If 'YES' – how is the suspense account treated?		
8 Is the sales ledger control balance agreed to the total of the balances in the sales ledger?	no	But a warning is given when posting directly to the control.
9 Can current and future periods be maintained simultaneously?	no	
10 Is there a check that transactions cannot be posted twice to the nominal ledger?	yes	Transactions are deleted from a link file after update to nominal has taken place.
11 Must the nominal ledger be updated from the sales ledger before the period-end is run?	no	
12 Must the nominal ledger and the sales ledger be in the same period for the update to be carried out?	no	
13 Is there any report/warning that transactions posted to the sales ledger have not yet been posted to the nominal ledger?	yes	Prompt to update nominal link displayed when transactions outstanding. Nominal update can be forced.

Output

		MAP
1 Is it necessary to produce an audit trail before the period-end procedure is run?	no	Audit trail can be set to be automatic on input.

LOW-PRICE PACKAGES

SAGESOFT		SNIP		TAS	
no				no	
yes	Also has a 'crash check' on start up.			yes	
yes		yes	The invoicing module can be initiated either with stock control, or without, in which case, sales analysis must be entered.	yes	Included as standard.
yes		yes	At month-end routine. All sales transactions are posted to nominal ledger, via sales analysis report.	yes	
	Automatic update at the time of input.	yes		yes	
no		yes		yes	
yes		yes	Sales analysis print-out shows which nominal accounts are updated.	no	Can be requested.
yes		yes		yes	
yes		yes		yes	
no		yes		yes	
no		no		yes	
N/A	Can only be coded to valid nominal account.	N/A	Must enter a valid customer account, and/or sales analysis code.	yes	
					Cleared by journal.
yes		yes	Printed on the control.	no	
no		yes		yes	
yes		yes	Can be updated in sales analysis report, posting to nominal only possible once.	yes	
N/A		yes	System will not allow period end to run otherwise.	no	
N/A		yes		no	
N/A		yes	If attempt to run period end, warning to run sales analysis which updates nominal.	no	
yes		yes	Must have print-out of (1) Control report and (2) Sales analysis, which updates nominal.	no	But recommended.

		MAP
2 Does the audit trail enable all transactions to be traced fully through the system?	yes	
3 Can the actual run date, or batch reference, as well as current ledger date, be shown on reports?	yes	Audit reports display system date, an (optional) batch reference, and transaction date, but not period end date. Optional reports display run date and current ledger date.
4 Can the following be produced:–		
list of master file information	yes	
aged debtors report	yes	For open item accounts only.
VAT report	yes	
ledger detail report	yes	
customer statements	yes	
customer name and address labels	yes	
debt collection letters	yes	
5 Does the customer statement show:		
all o/s transactions together with all items settled in the current period	yes	
or all o/s transactions only		
or the balance b/f and the current period's transactions		
or just the current balance		
6 Does the customer statement:–		
show discount separately	no	
show ageing	yes	For open item accounts only.
allow special messages	yes	
allow for suppression of erroneous postings and their corrections?	no	
7 Can the following screens be seen:–		
customer details	yes	
customer transactions	yes	
8 Can hard copies of the following be obtained for individual accounts/selected ranges of accounts:–		
customer details	yes	
customer transactions	yes	
9 Does the ledger account detail report/copy statements show:		
the source of all postings	no	
how part-payments and allocations have been treated	yes	
either the full account history or balance b/f together with the current period's transactions	yes	

LOW-PRICE PACKAGES

SAGESOFT	SNIP		TAS
yes	yes		yes
yes	no	Only current date.	yes
yes	yes		yes
yes	yes		yes
yes	yes	Five VAT rates.	yes
yes	yes	Set-up by user in report maintenance.	yes
yes	yes		yes
yes	yes	User specifies which fields to include.	yes
yes	no		yes
	yes	On open items basis.	yes
yes			
	yes	On brought forward accounts.	
no	yes		
yes	yes	Current, 30, 60, 90, 90+ day	yes
yes	no		yes
no	yes/no	Can produce additional statements, after adjustment.	yes
yes	yes	But only by entering customer maintenance routine.	yes
yes	yes	But must enter payments routine to view (rather awkward) or customer maintenance.	yes
yes	yes		yes
yes	yes	For transactions not yet cleared, prior to period end.	yes
yes	yes	Yes, insofar as, CR, INV, ADJ and transaction detail, but not internal transaction no., SL, PL, etc.	yes
yes	no	Not against specific invoice.	yes
yes	yes	For transactions not yet cleared.	yes

158 A GUIDE TO ACCOUNTING SOFTWARE

		MAP
10 Does the aged analyis show for each customer:		
total balance o/s	yes	
credit limit	yes	
11 Is ageing strictly by transaction date?	yes	May also input a date from which transactions are to be aged.
If 'NO' – how is ageing done?		
12 Does the aged analysis show unallocated cash separately?	yes	
If 'NO' – how is it aged?		
13 Do all outputs show clearly the distinction between debits and credits?	no	e.g. transactions listing: may require to look to cumulative balance movement to determine whether DR/CR.
14 Are all reports adequately titled?	yes	
15 Do reports provide totals where applicable?	yes	
16 Can report production be varied by:		
printing a range of accounts	yes	
printing by e.g. area/rep.	yes	
17 Is the period number shown on reports?	no	Period-end date shown on all optional reports.
18 Are all report pages sequentially numbered with the end of report identified?		Pages numbered but end of report not identified.
19 Is a sales analysis possible?	yes	Specify individual reports by sales analysis category.
20 Can reports be temporarily retained on file for subsequent printing?	yes	
If 'YES' – are such files protected from deletion?	yes	
21 Is a report generator available for use with the sales ledger module?	yes	
22 Can transaction files for previous periods be retained in the system to permit enquiries and reports?	no	Can be copied on to storage medium through operating system.

Purchase Ledger

General

1 Are programs menu-driven?	yes	Single key followed by (enter).
If 'YES' – can menus be by-passed once the user is familiar with the package?	no	
2 Does the system maintain a log of usage?	no	
3 Are informative messages produced on-screen whilst running?	no	
4 Are error messages informative and easy to understand?	no	Very few error messages – cover operating system problems only.

SAGESOFT		SNIP		TAS	
yes		yes		yes	
yes		yes		yes	
yes		yes	Current, 30, 60, 90, 90+ days.	yes	
no		no		no	
	In month paid.		Within period total.		Within the period total.
yes		yes/no	+ debits − credits	yes	
yes		yes		yes	
yes		yes	The report generator allows user to define which field (e.g. rep./agent, to be printed together with which fields to sort on e.g. account no., name, amount outstanding, turnover, category, rep./agent).	yes	
yes		yes		yes	
yes	Using account coding.			yes	
no		no		yes	
yes		yes	Page numbering and grand totals.	yes	
yes		yes	User must set up sales analysis codes.	yes	
yes		no	But user can maintain report structure and print one or more customers according to the report format. Nine report specifications can be set up.	yes	
no	Warning given.			no	
yes		yes	Comes with the sales ledgers.	yes	
yes		no		yes	

SAGESOFT		SNIP		TAS	
yes		yes		yes	
no		no		yes	
no		no	Other than the control reports and transaction trail.	no	
yes		yes		yes	
yes		yes		yes	

A GUIDE TO ACCOUNTING SOFTWARE

		MAP
5	Is the system multi-company?	yes
6	Is the original set-up straightforward?	yes
7	Is there a copy/restore facility in the package?	no
8	Does the system cover disciplined taking of back-ups?	no — Simple procedure for data kept on diskette covered in manual – via operating system. No procedures given for hard disk.

Documentation
(a) Manual

		MAP
1	Is the manual clearly laid out and understandable?	yes
2	Is the manual comprehensive and accurate?	yes — Manual provides understandable overview sufficient for starting up and running simple application. It lacks detail on dealing with complex and/or problem transactions and issues.
3	Is there an index?	yes — The index is brief and insufficiently comprehensive.
4	Is it easy to follow through all procedures?	yes
5	Is it easy to locate specific points when required?	no
6	Are completed examples included?	no

(b) Help screens

		MAP
7	Are help screens available?	no

If 'YES' –

Do they provide on-line instructions?

Can they be edited or prepared by the user?

Supplier Details

		MAP
1	What is the format of the supplier account code?	Maximum 8 character, alphanumeric.
2	What other supplier details are held?	Name, 4 address lines plus postcode, telephone, contact (25 characters), credit limit, 2 analysis codes and 2 reference lines (for comments).
	Do these seem to be sufficient in general?	yes
3	What is the maximum number of accounts that can be held?	Limited by disk capacity.
4	Can supplier details be added/deleted/amended at any time?	yes — Additions and amendments at any time except during transaction processing. See below for deletions.
5	Is file re-sorted automatically when a new supplier is added?	no
	If 'NO' – can a re-sort be initiated?	yes
6	Is deletion of a supplier prevented if the account has:	Deletion can take place only after a period end, for accounts with zero outstanding balance.
	an outstanding balance	yes
	a zero balance but a b/f turnover	no

LOW-PRICE PACKAGES

SAGESOFT		SNIP		TAS	
yes	Financial controller.	no	But is available at an additional £99.	yes	
yes		yes		yes	
no		yes	Part of system utilities routine.	no	
no	But clear instructions in manual.	no	User must initiate from system utilities routine.	no	
yes		yes		yes	
yes		yes	More detail required on editing key depressions, backspace, etc., cancelling entries.	no	Needs index and general section.
yes		no		no	
yes		yes		no	Some are vague.
yes		yes		no	No index, though it is laid out in menu order.
yes		yes	For most routines.	yes	
no		no	Only in relation to the file size routine, for setting-up and amending the number of records.	yes	
				yes	Very good and are available at entry points.
				no	
	6 digit alphanumeric.		Alphanumeric 5 character field.		10 digit alphanumeric.
	Address, phone and credit limit.		Name and address (4 lines), payment type – cheque/transfer, supplier category – 2 chars., prompt payment discount, days for prompt payment, settlement days, contact name, telephone no., date, last invoice, payment, purchases M-T-D, Y-T-D, amount outstanding.		Address 6 lines, tel. no., supplier type, contact, credit limit, terms/discount, salesman.
yes		yes		yes	
	5,000.		16,000, 5.5 records per 1K bytes of disk space.		Unlimited – constrained only by disk size.
yes	Except during transactions input.	yes	At most times, e.g. during transaction posting enter * on supplier acct code to enter supplier maintenance routine.	yes	
no		no		yes	
	Month end.		yes		
yes		yes		yes	
yes		yes	Must be zero Y-T-D, M-T-D-, in order to delete.	no	

		MAP	
7	Is a hard copy of changes in supplier details automatically produced?	no	May only run off a new (amended) accounts listing.
	If 'NO' – can a hard copy be taken?		

Transactions

		MAP	
1	Can the system be open item?	yes	
2	Are the following inputs possible:–		
	invoices	yes	
	credit notes	yes	
	manual payments	yes	
	cash refunded	yes	
	discounts	yes	
3	Can an invoice be analysed to several different expense categories?	yes	
4	Are different VAT codes possible for different items within one invoice.	yes	
5	Are all transactions retained on file for at least one period?	yes	Can choose not to delete at period end.
6	Can a ledger date pre-date existing transactions?	yes	
7	Can 2 references be input for an invoice (own and supplier's reference)?	yes	

Matching/Allocations

(a) Balance forward

		MAP	
1	Is the balance b/f aged?	no	
2	Can cash be allocated automatically?	no	
	If 'YES' – how is the allocation made?		
	– can this be overridden?		
3	Can cash be allocated manually?	yes	Allocated to balance.
	If 'YES' – does the package check that cash allocated = amount received?		
	How is any such difference treated?		Not accepted.
4	Can credit notes/journal entries be allocated to previous periods?	yes	
5	Can cash in advance be held and later allocated to subsequent periods?	yes	

(c) Open item

		MAP	
6	Are outstanding transactions displayed for allocation?	yes	
7	Can cash be allocated automatically?	yes	
	If 'YES' – how is the allocation made?		Specify range transaction line numbers over which allocation to be made. Requests line by line confirmation of allocation.
	– can this be overridden?	yes	

LOW-PRICE REVISIONS 163

SAGESOFT		SNIP		TAS	
no		no	Must set up the reports routine and print off the amended suppliers.	no	
yes				yes	
yes		yes	All purchase accounts held on open item basis.	yes	
yes		yes			
yes		yes		yes	
yes		yes		yes	By journal entry or menu option.
yes		yes		yes	By journal entry.
yes		yes		yes	
yes		yes	Must be analysed over a maximum of 8 purchase analysis codes.	yes	
yes		yes	Enter zero on VAT rate, system requests VAT rate for each item.		
yes		yes		yes	
yes		yes	Own reference, supplier reference.	yes	
yes					
N/A	Open item only.	N/A	System maintains open item only in purchases routine.		
yes		yes	Nine transactions at a time (oldest first).	yes	
yes		yes		yes	
	First item.	yes	By running the automatic payment preparation, marks all transactions due by specified date, for payment, in addition takes account of prompt payment discount.	yes	Payment list in flagged.
yes		yes	Can be over-ridden by running manual remittance posting.	yes	Invoices can be highlighted as disputed.

164 A GUIDE TO ACCOUNTING SOFTWARE

		MAP
8 Can cash be allocated manually?	yes	
If 'YES' does the package check that cash allocated = cash paid?	yes	
How is any difference treated?		Requests whether difference to be treated as unallocated cash. Cannot exit routine until all cash either fully allocated and/or labelled 'unallocated'.
9 Can an over/under-payment of an invoice be recorded?	yes	Only as unallocated cash/outstanding balance respectively.
10 How often are settled items deleted from file?		At period end, on request.
11 Can credit notes be set against the invoices to which they refer?	yes	
12 Can journal entries be set against the invoices/credit notes to which they refer?	N/A	Journals must be posted as IN/CR/CA transaction types.
13 Can cash in advance be held and later allocated to invoice?	yes	Carried as unallocated cash; must be dated at or prior to current period end.
14 Can cash be held unallocated?	yes	
– how is this treated?		Held as unallocated DR balance forward until allocated.

Input Controls

1 Is password control used?	yes	Password control optional. Each function within a module may be protected with 6 character password individually. If all functions protected with same password whole module is protected from entry. Whole ledger can be protected at main menu.
If 'YES' – give details.		
2 Is a hard copy automatically produced for all input?		Hard copy produced for all transactions input. No copy produced for changes to account details.
3 Are batch totals automatically produced for all transactions input?	yes	
If 'YES' – what is the procedure if this does not agree with a pre-list total?		Requested to accept/reject difference: Accept: noted on audit trail. Reject: return to transactions input.
4 Is it necessary that invoices, cash and adjustments are input in separate batches?	yes	Cash posting separate routine from invoice/credit note posting.
5 Are batches automatically sequentially numbered?	no	Page numbers of audit trail are sequentially numbered for each ledger?
If 'NO' – can they be so numbered?	yes	An optional batch reference can be entered by operator.
6 Is a report produced at the end of each processing run to reconcile b/f total, transactions processed and c/f total?	no	
If 'NO' – is a control balance produced at the end of each posting run?	yes	

LOW-PRICE PACKAGES

SAGESOFT		SNIP		TAS	
yes		yes		yes	Menu option.
yes		no		yes	
	Paid to account balance.				Suspense account.
yes		yes	Affects actual amount outstanding, can be negative figure.	yes	
	User choice.		At period end (but cleared transaction is removed from the screen display of remittance posting).		Monthly.
yes		yes	Manual posting.	yes	
yes		yes	Using remittance posting.	yes	
yes		yes	Must re-enter, cash payment.	yes	
yes		yes		yes	
	Shown as such.		Debit balance, negative amount outstanding.		Shown as unallocated on supplier record.
yes	Each menu protected if required.	yes	Each option on PL menu can be password protected (up to 10 characters long), and can be amended. The password program may also be password protected.	no	
no		yes		no	
yes	Running total of input on screen.	yes	But only on printed output not on most screens.	yes	
	Edit.		One must enter adjustments through transaction posting, or remittance posting.		Operator to adjust input.
yes		no	Transaction posting allows for invoices, credit notes and adjustments, in same batch.	yes	
yes		no		no	
		no		yes	
no	Immediate update to all ledgers on input.	yes	Control report which must be run before the period end.	no	
no				no	

		MAP
7 Are the following validated:–		
date	yes	
supplier account number	yes	
VAT code	yes	
goods value	yes	
analysis code	yes	
8 Is VAT calculated to check figure input?	yes	If VAT amount input disagrees with that calculated using input rate, requests confirmation to accept amount.
9 Is the gross figure agreed to goods+VAT?	yes	
10 Is discount calculated to check the figure input?	no	
11 Can the actual date of posting, or batch reference, be shown on hard copies of transactions input?	yes	
12 Does the screen always indicate that the purchase ledger, as opposed to the sales ledger, is running?	yes	
13 Do all input screens show clearly:		
type of entry	yes	
the distinction between debits and credits	no	Purchase ledger follows sales ledger in labelling transaction types as either invoices or credit notes.
14 Is there any check that the same entry is not input twice?	no	
15 Is there a warning if a supplier is overpaid?	no	
16 Is it impossible for new accounts to be created during processing?	yes	
17 Is a reconciliation of numbers of accounts produced after amendment of the customer detail file?	no	
18 Does the system prevent the abnormal termination of programs?	yes	

Integration

1 Can the sales ledger be integrated with a job costing module?	yes	
2 Can the purchase ledger be integrated with a nominal ledger module?	yes	
3 Can the nominal ledger be updated as often as desired?	yes	From the purchase ledger, prompt to update a nominal link file is given after every processing run.
4 Is a hard copy automatically produced at the end of each nominal ledger update?	yes	
5 Is there a purchase ledger print-out (as well as a nominal ledger printout) of the nominal ledger update?	yes	Print-out for each stage of update: from purchase ledger to link file, and from link file to nominal ledger.

SAGESOFT		SNIP		TAS	
yes		yes	Only that it is a valid date, 'past date' allowable.	yes	
yes		yes	Name displayed on screen.	yes	
yes		yes	Must be one of five defined VAT codes.	yes	
yes		yes	Total goods amount must reconcile with that analysed to purchase analysis of individual items.	yes	
yes		yes		yes	
yes		yes	VAT value must be 90–100% of true value, or not in excess of £0.05 of true value.	yes	
yes		yes		yes	
yes		yes	In remittance payments posting routine.	yes	
yes		yes	All dates of posting show on control report, and date of control report.	yes	
yes		no	But supplier appears on remittance posting.	yes	
yes		yes		yes	
yes		yes	Only insofar as, i.e., a −ve indicates credit note and +ve indicates credit balance.	yes	
no		no		no	
no		no		yes	Not possible.
yes		no	One enters an * in supplier account code and supplier maintenance routine is entered.	no	If account not found system asks if it is to be set up.
no		no		no	
yes	Also has a 'crash check' on start-up.	yes	But user must remember to log off – using the system utilities for proper closing of files.	no	
no		yes	Additional cost £99.	no	
yes		yes	At month-end, all purchase transactions are posted to nominal ledger, via purchase analysis report.	yes	
	Automatic update at the time of input.	yes		yes	
no		yes	As part of purchase analysis report.	yes	
yes		yes	Purchase analysis report shows which nominal accounts are updated.	no	But can be taken.

		MAP
6 Are the following automatically posted to the appropriate nominal ledger accounts:–		
discount	yes	
discount written back	no	Require to be adjusted through nominal ledger journals.
contras with sales ledger	no	
7 Are any invalid/unidentified entries posted to a suspense account?	N/A	Transactions must be given valid nominal code, and must be of type invoice/credit note/cash/discount.
If 'NO' – how are they treated?		
If 'YES' – how is the suspense account treated?		
8 Is the purchase ledger control balance agreed to the total of the balances in the purchase ledger?	no	But a warning is given when posting directly to the control.
9 Can current and future periods be maintained simultaneously?	no	
10 Is there a check that transactions cannot be posted twice to the nominal ledger?	yes	Transactions are deleted from a link file after update to nominal has taken place.
11 Must the nominal ledger be updated from the purchase ledger before the period-end is run?	no	
12 Must the nominal ledger and the purchase ledger be in the same period for the update to be carried out?	no	
13 Is there any report/warning that transactions posted to the purchase ledger have not yet been posted to the nominal ledger?	yes	Prompt to update nominal link displayed when transactions outstanding.

Output

1 Is it necessary to produce an audit trail before the period-end procedure is run?	no	Audit trail automatic on input.
2 Does the audit trail enable all transactions to be traced fully through the system?	yes	
3 Can the actual run date, or batch reference, as well as current ledger date, be shown on reports?	yes	Audit reports display system date, an (optional) batch reference, and transaction date, but not period-end date. Optional reports display run date and current ledger date.
4 Can the following be produced:		
list of master file information	yes	
aged creditors report	yes	For open item accounts only.
VAT report	yes	
ledger detail report	yes	
remittance advices	yes	
supplier name and address labels	yes	
suggested payments		A 'date due by' report, for open item accounts only.
cheques	yes	

LOW-PRICE PACKAGES

SAGESOFT		SNIP		TAS	
yes		yes		yes	
yes		yes		yes	
N/A		no	But transfer payments listing is available.	yes	
N/A	Can only be coded to valid nominal account.	N/A	Must enter a valid supplier account, and/or purchase analysis code.	yes	
					Cleared by journal, uncleared included in B/S.
yes		yes	Printed on the control of report.	no	
no		yes		yes	
yes		yes	Can be updated in purchase analysis report, posting to nominal only possible once.	yes	
N/A	Automatic on input.	yes	System will not allow period end to run otherwise.	no	
N/A		yes		no	
N/A		yes	If attempt to run period end, warning to run purchase analysis which updates the nominal.	no	
yes		yes	Must have print-out of (1) Control report (2) Purchase analysis, which updates the nominal.	no	
yes		yes		yes	
yes		no	Only current date.	yes	
yes		yes		yes	
yes		yes		yes	
yes		yes		yes	
yes		yes		yes	
yes		yes		yes	
yes		yes		yes	
no		yes	Payment preparation report will list all due invoices.	yes	
no		no	But a cheque listing for remittances can be produced.	yes	

	MAP
5 Can remittance advices show:	
individual invoices	yes
discount	yes
supplier's reference	yes
6 Can the following screens be seen:–	
supplier details	yes
supplier transactions	yes
7 Can hard copies of the following be obtained for individual accounts/selected range of accounts:–	
supplier details	yes
supplier transactions	yes
8 Does the ledger account detail report show:–	
the source of all postings	no
how part payments and allocations have been treated	yes
either the full account history or balance b/f together with the current period's transactions	yes
9 Is ageing strictly by transaction date?	yes May also input a date from which transactions are to be aged.
If 'NO' – how is ageing done?	
10 Does the aged analysis show unallocated cash separately?	yes
If 'NO' – how is it aged?	
11 Do all outputs show clearly the distinction between debits and credits?	no Require to look for movement in cumulative balance, and/or transaction type, for distinction in remittance advices and transaction listing.
12 Are all reports adequately titled?	yes
13 Do reports provide totals where applicable?	yes
14 Can report production be varied by:–	
printing a range of accounts	yes
printing by e.g. area	yes
15 Is the period number shown on reports?	no Period end date shown on all optional reports.
16 Are all report pages sequentially numbered with the end of report identified?	Pages numbered, but end of report not identified.
17 Is a purchase analysis possible?	yes Specify individual reports by analysis category.
18 Can reports be temporarily retained on file for subsequent printing?	yes Spooled files written to program drive.
If 'YES' – are such files protected from deletion?	yes
19 Is a report generator available for use with the purchase ledger module?	yes

LOW-PRICE PACKAGES 171

SAGESOFT		SNIP		TAS
yes		yes	Each transaction	yes
yes		yes	Shown separately.	yes
yes		yes	Own reference and supplier reference, where one has been input.	yes
yes		yes	But only by entering supplier maintenance routine.	yes
yes		yes	But must enter remittance posting routine to view.	yes
yes		yes		yes
yes		yes	For transactions in current period, not yet cleared.	yes
yes		yes	Only as invoice etc.	yes
yes		yes	Shows balance outstanding against a specific invoice.	yes
yes		yes	For transactions not yet cleared.	yes
yes		yes	30, 60, 90, 90+ days.	yes
no	In month paid.	yes		yes
yes		no	Plus and minus signs shown not debit/credit.	yes
yes		yes		yes
yes		yes		yes
yes	.	yes	The report generating allows up to nine report formats to be set up, with a number of sort fields.	yes
yes	Using account code.	yes	Supplier category.	yes
yes		no	Only the system date when report is generated.	yes
yes		yes	Page numbering and grand totals.	yes
yes		yes	User must set up purchase analysis cones, in purchase maintenance.	yes
yes		no	But user can maintain report structure and print one or more suppliers, according to report format.	yes
no				no
yes		yes	Included with purchase ledger.	yes

		MAP	
20	Can transaction files for previous periods be retained in the system to permit enquiries and reports?	no	Can be copied onto storage medium through operating system.

Payments/Cheque Writing

		MAP	
1	Can the system write cheques?	yes	
	If 'YES' – is the payment posted automatically to the purchase ledger?	N/A	Cheque writing routine uses cash postings already made to purchase ledger since remittance file last cleared down.
2	Is there an automatic cheque writing facility? If 'YES':		
	is a list of suggested payments printed in advance of the cheques?	no	A 'due date by' report is available.
	is the total cash requirement printed in advance of the cheques?	no	
	can the automatic payment routine be aborted if either of the above is not satisfactory?	N/A	Cheques will only be written after the following steps have been taken: 1. Cash to be paid has been posted to purchase ledger. 2. A remittance advice has been printed. 3. The remittance advice file has been cleared down (i.e. transactions appearing in current remittance will not be reproduced in subsequent remittances).
3	Can the following payment/report options be selected:		
	individual invoice selection	no	
	supplier selection	yes	
	pay all invoices of a certain age	no	
	pay according to due date	no	
	pay all invoices except those marked not to be paid	no	
	other (specify)		
4	Is discount automatically calculated by the payment routine?	no	
5	Can invoices be held as disputed?	yes	If not paid via cash postings no cheque will be printed.
	If 'YES' – can a report of disputed invoices be produced?	no	

LOW-PRICE PACKAGES

SAGESOFT	SNIP		TAS	
yes	no		yes	
no	no	Optional extra.	yes	
			yes	
no	no		yes	But not standard option.
			yes	
			yes	
			yes	
N/A	yes	Mark for remit.	yes	
N/A			yes	
N/A	yes	Allow automatic preparation of due date invoices, for remittance.	yes	
N/A	yes	Can manually mark invoices for remit, or hold.	yes	
N/A	yes		yes	
		Take account of prompt payment discount (part of automatic payment preparation).		
no	yes		yes	
N/A	yes	Mark as held.	yes	
	no		yes	

Medium-price packages – Finax, Multifacts, Multisoft and Pegasus Senior

Reviews	**176**
Features Rating Table	**193**
Package Information Table	**194**
Evaluation Checklists:	
General	**196**
Performance of Requisite Accounting Functions	196
Reliability – Security and Continuity of Processing	198
Support and Maintenance	198
Ease of Use	198
(a) Interactive Processing	198
(b) User Documentation	200
Efficiency	200
Flexibility	202
(a) Integration Facilities	202
(b) Reporting Flexibility	202
(c) Parameter or Table Facilities	202
Software Installation and Training	202
(a) Financial Resources	202
(b) Other Resources	202
(c) Involvement of Software Supplier	204
(d) Involvement of User Personnel	204
Package Software Acquisition	204
Preliminary Questions Relating to Software Supplies	204
Nominal Ledger	**206**
General	206
Documentation	206
(a) Manual	206
(b) Help Screens	206

Account Details	206
Transactions	208
Input Controls	208
Integration	210
Output	212
(a) General	212
(b) Trial Balance; P&L and Balance Sheet	212
Year End	214

Sales Ledger 216

General	216
Documentation	216
(a) Manual	216
(b) Help screens	216
Customer Details	216
Transactions	216
Matching/Allocations	218
(a) Balance Forward	218
(b) Open Item	218
Input Controls	220
Integration	222
Output	222

Purchase Ledger 226

General	226
Documentation	226
(a) Manual	226
(b) Help screens	226
Supplier Details	226
Transactions	228
Matching/Allocations	228
(a) Balance Forward	228
(b) Open Item	230
Input Controls	230
Integration	232
Output	234
Payments/Cheque Writing	236

Review of Finax

Introduction

Finax is a range of fully integrated accounting and management systems designed for use in both the accounting profession and business. The system is built round the cash book and can be made into a conventional three ledger system by adding a purchase ledger and sales ledger module. Invoicing and stock control are available as additional modules. Because the system was designed for accountants to use in practice, the accounts preparation facilities come as a separate module rather than as basic reports built into a nominal ledger module. Reports can be entirely user-defined which gives maximum flexibility in experienced hands.

The system can run as a single-company system for business use or as a multi-company system for professional offices and larger companies. Because of its dual role, Finax is one of the packages which allows data prepared on the client's system to be passed to his accountant for the preparation of management or final accounts.

The flexibility of this package makes it very powerful but it also means that it is not to be recommended for inexperienced users unless they are prepared to allocate time and a realistic amount of cash to training and support in the initial stages.

Setting-up

Setting-up is very straightforward and all that is required initially is the company name, accounting period and proposed nominal coding structure. In a multi-company system, each company can either use default nominal ledger codes supplied by Orchard, a completely new user defined format or take all or part of a nominal coding structure already set up for an existing company. The detail for the separate ledgers is set up using parameters and the required responses to the various prompts are clearly explained in the manual.

Up to 960 nominal accounts are available using a 3–8 digit alphanumeric code. An extra digit is available (regardless of code length) on all transaction screens to be used for cost centre analysis.

There are no specific month-end close-off routines and all transactions are available at all times during the year to allow full reporting of previous months. Reports are produced by specifying the date or date range required. Because dates are so important there is a facility to re-enter a transaction and change an erroneous date so that the transaction will be included in the correct period.

Security

In common with the majority of accounting packages the normal exit from the system is by stepping back through the menus until the exit point. Abnormal termination due to power failure should not normally cause problems and missing data can usually be re-entered without difficulty. On entry or re-entry to the system the software will check that all files are usable and correspond to the correct date. There are no back up or restore routines within the software and no enforced back up of data files. The user has to rely upon the operating system for back up. The manual stresses the need for back up, explains why it is necessary and suggests possible routines to be followed.

Password protection is available within each company to protect sensitive areas. Each operation can have a separate password but there is no facility to allocate personal passwords.

Manuals and support

At first glance the manual looks fairly daunting as it has no comprehensive index. However, it has been designed so that the page references correspond to the main and sub-menus on the screen, which makes it very easy to go straight from the screen to the right page to get help.

Entry screens are reasonably straightforward and show the response expected at each stage during the entry. Each line of an entry is accepted individully and errors can be corrected simply by stepping back along the line to the error and re-keying.

The 'hot-line' response to problems was efficient and helpful and Orchard lays emphasis on the need for proper training sessions before the client is let loose on his own.

Nominal ledger

Direct entry to the nominal ledger is through the bank and cash routines or by journal. Journals can be either straightforward two-sided entry where the account code for each side of the entry is keyed in and the amount is only entered once or a multiple entry where codes and amounts are entered until the journal balances. For both types of entry the balance on each account is shown before and after the values are entered so that the operator can see the result of the entry before accepting it. In addition, the multiple journal entry screen shows the running total, and exit from the screen is only possible if the total is zero. During input it is possible to look at transactions and balances, display the trial balance and set up missing accounts. One useful but slightly alarming facility is the *change journals* option which allows alterations to amounts and posting accounts. Though any alteration to amounts must be balanced in the same way as an ordinary journal the potential for disaster is still there, especially as printouts are user-defined, depend on dates for accuracy and are far from compulsory. The option can be password protected but this is a prime example of a facility ideal for client accounting which requires maximum flexibility but, for business use, gives cause for unease from a control point of view.

Period-end journals are entered using the bank and cash routines and re-setting the default account, which is normally the main bank account, to accruals, prepayments or stock account. It is also possible to use more than one bank account by re-setting the default before a batch of entries. The screen always shows which account is in use as the default account during posting, but using these facilities successfully entails using a methodical approach.

Recurring journals and bank reconciliation are both available and VAT return information can be easily prepared by using the VAT return option which allows input of over/under declarations and import/export information before picking up the VAT for the period from the data files.

Sales and purchase ledgers

Up to five purchase and sales ledgers can be set up for each company. The system comes with standard reports but all reports, statements and remittance advices can be user-defined giving maximum flexibility. There is no account code structure as such: the first account set up is number 1, the second 2, and so on. However, the system uses not the code but the surname or company name to sort and search. An account may be accessed using the code, part of the name or by asking for a search. The *part name* is case sensitive and set up instructions should be read carefully before entering the account names. Selective customer or supplier reporting can be done by setting up user-defined categories within the database incorporated within the package. Up to 90 fields of database information can be set up for each customer. This data can be printed out in the form of user-defined reports, including labels.

Both ledgers allow invoices to be entered as paid and the payment then goes automatically to the default bank account. It is also possible to cater for one-off, cash with order transactions by specifying the transaction as a non-account transaction. This is the best way of processing cash purchases and sales as only transactions processed through the sales and purchase ledger are included in the automatic VAT return.

There is no separate routine for credit notes which are entered as negative invoices and are shown as credit notes on the printout. There is no journal adjustment facility within the sales and purchase ledger and adjustments for contras, discount taken in error, etc., need a fair knowledge of the system and accounting techniques if they are to be done successfully. A misposting to the wrong account can be directed to the correct account by using the change entries routine, which allows alterations to the analysis, the date and the account but not the invoice amount.

Each supplier and customer is linked to a default nominal expense or sales code, but sub-analysis of an invoice is available during input so that an invoice can be analysed over several nominal codes or the default can be simply over-ridden by a single alternative code. The sales ledger can be set to cope with a settlement discount but it is either on or off and it has to be over-ridden for non-discount customers. Both ledgers can be set up to allow a trade discount to be given to individual customers or to reflect discounts allowed by individual suppliers.

Transaction reports are not compulsory but a listing of invoices (credit notes) and aged debtors/creditors reports are available either on the screen or as printouts at any time.

As all transactions update the nominal ledger at the time of input the nominal is always up to date and there is no danger of a transaction being left unposted.

Cash can be allocated to specific invoices or left unallocated for subsequent posting; and discount can be posted during the cash posting and allocation.

Invoices in the purchase ledger can be selected for automatic payment by month or by age in days.

Hardware and costs

The package runs on IBM and compatible machines using MS-DOS operating system. The programs require up to 2Mb of disk space and a machine with 512K of RAM is required so this package cannot realistically run on a twin floppy machine. The software costs between £1300 (single-company) and £3000 (multi-company) for the complete accounting suite including the sales and purchase ledger.

Review of MULTIFACTS

Introduction

Multifacts software is a multi-user version of a middle-of-the-range accounting system called FACTS which can run on several popular microcomputer network systems. For this review the software was tested on a variety of IBM and IBM-compatible microcomputers.

The software arrived on several 5¼ inch floppy disks. The documentation does not properly explain what commands to type or other actions to take to start up the system. However, by resorting to the facilities of the computer's operating system, I eventually found a small file containing documentation for start up.

Having achieved that, I was astonished to find an error message which said 'The previous run did not end correctly' and immediately the system halted. Eventually, and again resorting to the operating system, I found an undocumented utility program had been supplied which seemed to clear the problem. The moral is, of course, that you should get your dealer to install and configure the system for you!

Documentation
The user manual runs to approximately 450 pages, 16 chapters and 8 appendices. The first five chapters or so describe the principal features of the system including installation, security, starting up the system and setting up ledgers. The narrative is sometimes confused and misleading and I would advise any first-time micro-computer user intending to use this system, to have the dealer *hold your hand* as you set up the various ledgers and systems.

The rest of the manual is given over to a separate chapter for each of the system modules. In most cases, the information and description about each system is complete and reasonably well laid out. Multifacts provide information fields in ledgers for additional analysis and extraction purposes. Although this is a nice idea, the documentation rarely provides adequate explanations or examples of the purposes to which these information fields might be put.

Overview information
Multifacts has been specially designed for the small- to medium-sized business. It will run on a range of micro-computers which operate under the MS-DOS, Unix and Xenix operating systems. Although it will run on floppy disk, hard disk or local area networks, from bitter experience during the review testing, I would not recommend using a twin floppy disk microcomputer.

The software has the following modules available:

   Sales order processing
   Sale invoice preparation
   Point of sale invoice preparation
   Sales ledger
   Purchase ledger
   Nominal ledger
   Management accounts including nominal report generator
   Job costing
   Stock control and purchase order processing
   Payroll
   Interface to other software packages

All of these modules are fully integrated. Up to 20 separate companies can be incorporated within the system – each company having different period and year end dates. Within any company the system will support up to nine different sales and/or purchase ledgers.

You can have twelve or thirteen accounting period years. Each ledger maintains a period number and these can be moved out of step if required.

Nominal ledger

Setting up the nominal ledger is a conventional process – create the chart of accounts, post budgets, and post opening trial balances. The nominal ledger uses a six-character alphanumeric code. Each account can be designated as a profit and loss account or a balance sheet account. Printed trial balances are structured according to the level of analysis required by the accounts codes. Accounts codes can be designated as narrative only. These accounts cannot have transactions posted to them and exist only to print narrative on reports.

The documentation does not, in my view, emphasise adequately the great care and planning which must be given to setting up the chart of accounts.

The system allows you to retain transactions for the current period only or for the year to date and also to attach a budget to any account. Budgets are maintained for each accounting period and a useful facility is provided, when *tuning* a budget for an account, to adjust the budget for a range of periods by a percentage or absolute amount.

A nice feature to be found in all the system modules is a facility known as *Nudge*. This allows you to display account numbers and the narratives in sequential order, starting from any known part of the number, by pressing a single key. For example, if you know that all income accounts are within the range 100,000–100,999 you can fill in the account number of 1000 – and press the nudge key (i.e. function key number 2). Each of the sales income accounts will be displayed in order until you come to the one you want.

Another nice feature is recurring journals, of which there may be three types – journal, depreciation or cash book. Recurring journals are set up once, designating the range of periods they should operate. Separate audit trails are provided for each of the three journal types. The cash book recurring journal is particularly welcome enabling you to identify standing order payments. The conventional journal postings program provides a good variety of journal types – accruals and prepayments journals auto-reverse at each month end.

The enquiry and reporting facilities of the nominal ledger system are good. Reports can be printed directly or can be held temporarily on the computer disk for separate printing. This useful facility should allow for better use of an operator's time as all printing can be left until the end of the day.

A report-generating module can create user-defined management reports including consolidation of nominal ledgers from different companies and using different currencies. Users will require significant amounts of training and practice before they can hope to get the best from this facility. However, the module is very powerful and has considerable potential if used properly.

One of the most frustrating features of the system is that you can delete neither a company nor a subsidiary ledger for a company. I found to my cost that company '1' is not the same as company '01' nor company ' 1'. This is because, throughout the system, all key fields are defined as alphanumeric. As a result, I ended up having three companies all company number one and all totally different. The only way I found to get rid of these companies was to delete all the data files from my computer's hard disk. Surprisingly, the system does not provide any means of restoring data from back-up floppy diskettes without resorting to the operating system.

A serious fault with the system is that all transactions, master records, narratives and system control records for every company are held in a single file. This is probably due to limitations in MS-DOS and networking but it is a serious drawback.

The consequence of this approach is that if one user out of several all posting concurrently to different companies makes a mistake in processing, resulting in a restoration of data from back-up, all users must be restored. I should not like to be responsible for controlling that situation!

Sales and purchase ledgers

The sales and purchases ledgers use an alphanumeric account code. The manual advises users to create customer or supplier account codes with at least the first (i.e. leftmost) character as an alphanumeric character and the rest as numbers.

Both the sales and purchases ledgers allow individual accounts to be either open item or brought forward. A nice feature is that each customer or supplier account is given a default nominal code which means that the system will automatically prompt the operator with the nominal ledger analysis for any invoices being posted to that ledger account.

The sales ledger system allows up to four bands of settlement terms (i.e. percentage discount for settlement within X days) and up to eight bands for trade discount on invoice lines.

The operators' input screens for posting invoices, credit notes and cash are reasonably well laid out. The nudge facility for finding customer account numbers is particularly suited to efficient posting operations.

Invoices and credit notes cannot be batched together and a maximum of 30 items per invoice is permitted. Each invoice can have a reference and a comment but neither of these fields is very big.

Multifacts sales ledger provides both automatic and manual cash allocation. Automatic allocation attempts to match cash against the oldest invoice first and is fairly rudimentary. The process stops if the remaining cash to be allocated is less than the next oldest unmatched invoice – despite the fact that there may be a more recent invoice exactly matching, the cash remaining, further ahead. When using manual cash matching, the sytem displays only the allocated balance of adjustments and invoices. Whenever payments to account are allocated against invoices the system displays only the remaining unallocated value. This makes the process of manually allocating cash very difficult.

Other problems are that an operator cannot reverse cash allocations and that a returned cheque is normally treated as a negative 'on account' payment because the original matched invoice and cash will no longer be displayed.

The enquiries and reporting facilities of the sales ledger are good. Multifacts is designed to use preprinted invoice and statement stationery and there is a reasonable degree of flexibility in the layout design for invoices.

The purchase ledger system looks and operates in a very similar way to the sales ledger system and uses the same type of routines for cash input and matching as the sales ledger system.

I was impressed with the facilities for automatic supplier payment selection. The options provided selection by account number range, supplier type, payment frequency or individual supplier and for each of these options the operator can choose to pay individual invoices by reference to transaction date, due date or individual items. A nice touch is the opportunity to calculate and display the total ledger outstanding balances and the total value of items selected for payment.

Control and security

All the conventional printed audit trails for transactions, postings and reporting are provided. For some strange reason, however, the system does not use any batch numbering and batch input control could be improved.

The system provides good access security. Each log on password can be linked to any combination of menu options. However, there is no printed log to indicate who did what and when. I would also have expected the system to provide some evidence at least of the date and time of security data back up onto floppy disk or streamer tape. These are unusual omissions.

Accounts in the purchase or sales ledger cannot be deleted unless the outstanding balance is zero. Accounts in the nominal ledger can only be removed if the balance is zero and there are no transactions in the account. The month-end and year-end procedures are very simple and will not operate until key audit reports have been printed, for example transactions day books.

Distribution and support

The software is distributed through a dealer network. The authors claim to have 250–300 dealers throughout the UK of whom approximately 50–75 dealers actively sell this package. Most of the authorised dealers are located in the South East of England. There are 4 or 5 dealers based in Edinburgh and Glasgow.

Conclusions

Generally, Multifacts is an average system which is easy to use with logical screen and menu layouts. A useful enhancement to the system would be an on-line help facility.

The package has some good features, several irritating or poor design features, moderate documentation. Each module of the system costs £300 for a single user version and £600 for a multi-user version for up to four or five users. A larger network will incur a larger software cost but this has not yet been determined.

Review of MULTISOFT

Accounting systems for microcomputers range from simple, basic and usually cheap packages to complex and flexible multi-user packages which supply a basic shell for the user to tailor to his own requirements and are aimed at businesses which are large enough to employ an accountant and have fairly complex requirements.

There is a middle range of packages which can be tailored to some extent by the user but which keep the accounting functions standard and menu-controlled. These packages can have quite sophisticated built-in features and controls and they cover the widest market for accounting software. Multisoft is one of the better packages in this middle range.

The Multisoft accounting system comprises a set of modules (e.g. nominal ledger, payroll, etc.) based on the Multisoft Operating System Supervisor (MOSS) module. The modules are integrated and can be purchased separately, as and when required, so that a basic computerised accounting system can be established initially, and additional modules, such as stock control and invoicing, added later. The software is available in either single- or multi-user versions and it runs under MS-DOS, Xenix and Unix. It will run on a twin floppy disk system, but for serious use a hard disk system is recommended. The software reviewed here ran under MS-DOS on a hard disk machine.

The software arrives with a practice company set up and with no access restrictions to systems or programs. The only limiting factor on the number of companies which can be set up is the size of the computer system used.

The manual provided is comprehensive and reasonably easy to use, although no index is included. A system of menus and sub-menus is used throughout the software to guide the user, and these are all adequately explained in the manual. There are no help screens as such, but each input/processing screen includes user instructions along the foot of the screen and some functions also have a *look up* facility to help with data selection.

Security

Security and back-up controls within Multisoft are fairly comprehensive. Each operator can be allocated a user password which allows access to certain routines only. Passwords can be set up at company level (access to certain companies only), system level – e.g. to give access to only the purchase ledger – and program level, e.g. to restrict access to posting data within the purchase ledger.

The MOSS program retains a log of all work carried out, referenced by computer allocated, consecutive, batch numbers. The system will only operate if either the printer is active or printout is directed to the spooler. These features ensure that a full audit trail is always taken.

Back-up and restore procedures are menu driven and the normal exit from the system is via back-up. In addition, the system can be set to enforce a back-up of data after a pre-determined period of use.

Nominal ledger

A standard nominal ledger is provided with the system and this can be amended and extended as required. The account codes are four alpha or numeric characters, but they cannot be random as they dictate the order in which account totals are set out in nominal ledger reports. The first character of the code can be used to indicate the ledger section (e.g. fixed assets) and the remainder the nominal account and, if applicable, the department.

The number of accounting periods in a year can be either 12 or 13 and the system can retain a full record of transactions for all these until the final year-end routine is run. A *draft* year-end routine can be carried out so that entries can be made for the new accounting year, but final adjustments can also be made to the old year's accounts. When all the adjustments have been made, the final routine is run, and this locks the old figures.

Four standard reports are provided and more can be added very simply, but the structure of all reports is rather basic and, as stated above, dependent on the nominal account coding. It is worth mentioning, however, that a Financial Management module is available which allows the user to format complex reports. In addition, there is a Lotus/Multiplan Link module which enables the transfer of balances, account numbers, etc., from the nominal, purchase and sales ledgers across to a Lotus 123 or Multiplan spreadsheet.

Data entry is straightforward and accruals/prepayments and standard periodic entries (e.g. depreciation) are handled by the system. Posting is done in batches and when each has been entered the system asks for the batch total; if this does not agree with the total actually entered an explanation is automatically requested for audit trail purposes.

Data can be posted to any period of the year so that amendments can be made to earlier periods and there is no problem with sales and purchases being in different periods. Budgets can be set up individually for each period, calculated from pre-set percentage tables or based on a percentage of last year's budget or actual. Comparative figures for the previous year are also retained.

Purchase ledger

It is not difficult to set up the ledger initially as the procedure is comprehensively and clearly explained in the manual. The complexity of the system created is at the discretion of the user; the options available would adequately meet the needs of the vast majority of businesses.

The number of accounting periods in a year can be set as 12, 13 or 52 and a history of invoices per account can be retained for up to a year even if these have been paid.

Each ledger account can be operated on either an open item or balance forward basis as wished. Temporary accounts can be set up for *one-off* suppliers and these will be automatically deleted at the end of the period in which the balance becomes zero. Each account is given a six alpha character *short* name and this can be used to access the account as an alternative to the account codes.

Data input is, as with the nominal ledger, straightforward, and the system can handle payments on account as well as specifically allocated items. Although there is currently no need, the system is able to deal with up to ten rates of VAT. New purchase ledger accounts can be set up while data is being posted, which is a useful facility.

Other points worth mentioning are that remittance advices, cheques and bank giros can be automatically produced and, by using the optional purchase analysis module, analysis reports can be obtained independently of the nominal ledger.

The ledger can be integrated with the nominal ledger or can be operated on a *stand-alone* basis. Six standard reports are supplied with the system and more can be created using the report generator.

Sales ledger

The sales ledger is very similar in set up and mode of operation to the purchase ledger and is, again, a very adequate piece of software.

Points to note are that user-defined messages can be printed automatically on selected customer statements, and user-defined letters can also be produced for mailshots or credit control purposes.

Distribution and support

Multisoft programs are available through a dealer network and the current cost per module of the single-user version is in the region of £390. Software support is provided by the dealer network, backed up by Multisoft by telephone. There is a three-month software warranty.

Conclusion

Multisoft is a competent and well thought out accounting system which is worth investigation by anyone who is either considering computerisation for the first time or else upgrading from a more basic system. Although only the nominal, purchase and sales ledger modules have been considered here a variety of other modules are available (e.g. costing, stock control, sub-contractors' ledger) so that a fairly complex system can be built up.

Review of PEGASUS Senior

Introduction

The Pegasus product was originally a very basic, single-user accounting package comprising sales, invoicing, purchases, payroll, stock control, bill of materials, nominal ledger, and job costing. The modules can be used stand-alone or can be linked to provide a fully integrated management information system. In addition, the modules can be linked to other software packages, such as Lotus, MultiPlan and Dbase, by using the Report Generator which comes as an integral part of each of the Pegasus modules.

A revamped version of the original product, comprising many additional features, is now available, in either single-user or networked forms, called Pegasus Senior. Pegasus are also currently working on a true multi-user Unix version of the product.

This review is based on the single-user version of Pegasus Senior. The modules reviewed were the sales, purchase and nominal ledgers, which were run on a Compaq portable III with 640K RAM and a 40 megabyte hard disk.

Setting up the system

The process of actually copying your program files onto your hard disk would normally be done by your supplier. However, if you do have to do this yourself you will find plenty of helpful information in the user manuals. This covers such things as how to create a new directory on the hard disk for the Pegasus system and data (note that the programs and data must reside in the same

PEGASUS·BUSINESS·SOFTWARE

AND

MicroAge
BUSINESS CENTRES

Providing you with complete Accounting solutions:

Pegasus Senior Version 3

Advanced software with many powerful new features for single and multi-user environments. Upgrades available for existing users.

Pegasus System Builder

To tailor your every accounting need to your specification.

Pegasus Elite

To provide database facilities directly with Pegasus Version 3.

MicroAge Support

To give you peace of mind. - Consult MicroAge.

MicroAge
BUSINESS CENTRES

Prospect House, Technology Park, DUNDEE DD2 1TY
Telephone: (0382) 561501

directory), how to run the install program and how to reconfigure your CONFIG.SYS file to allow Pegasus to run successfully.

Having successfully installed the programs, the next step is to set up the Company Parameter file which contains your own company's name, address, telephone number, VAT number, etc. This file also contains the master password, which allows access to all parts of the system including the company parameter file. An individual logging on to Pegasus with the access password also has to enter another password on entering each module which determines the functions he/she can access.

Pegasus can handle up to 36 companies, denoted by A to Z or 0 to 9, and a company parameter file must be set up for each company which is to be processed on the system. Therefore you can set up different access passwords for each company.

Parameters must also be set up within each module which determine how data is to be processed, how reports are to be formatted and how the module is to interface to other modules. Pegasus can also handle up to 26 foreign exchange rates, which are also set up in the parameters. The parameters section also holds details concerning passwords to allow access to individual areas within the module.

Each module can have up to four levels of password security. Level 1 allows the user access to all parts of the module apart from the parameters section (which can only be accessed by someone logging onto the system using the master password). Level 2 allows access to everything other than parameters and the facility to create reports using the Report Generator. Level 3 prevents access to the period-end routine and Level 4 only allows the user to make enquiries on ledger accounts.

Processing data

The Pegasus system is menu-driven, with functions being logically grouped together under hierarchical menu options. Ledger Processing contains functions to create or amend accounts, post transactions and make ledger enquiries.

All modules offer an alpha search facility so that you don't have to memorise account codes. The maximum length of account code for each module is 8 alphanumeric characters. The nominal ledger also has a facility for departmental analysis, the department code being up to four characters long, again alphanumeric. The nominal ledger account titles can be up to 30 characters long, while the sales and purchase ledgers offer six lines of 30 characters for names and addresses. Each account in the sales and purchase ledgers can be designated as either open item or balance forward, and two quantity discount terms and two settlement discount terms can be set up for sales ledger accounts. Purchase ledger accounts can have two payment discount rates set up as well as a standard payment period.

Sales and purchase ledger transactions can be identified by two fields, both of up to 10 alphanumeric characters, for the usual *our reference* and *their reference*. In the nominal ledger, manual postings numbers are automatically generated but can also be identified by a three-character field for recording the initials of the individual responsible for entering the transaction (this must be entered), and a 58-character narrative field. Nominal ledger transactions generated from within the sales and purchase ledgers are identified by a three character *source* identifier (S/L for sales ledger, P/L for purchase ledger, etc.). In addition, the customer or supplier account name can be recorded against the nominal ledger transaction.

Sales and purchase ledger transactions can be up to a maximum value of £99,999,999.99 while nominal ledger transactions can be up to a maximum value of £999,999,999.99 if desired.

The sales and purchase ledgers can each cater for up to 10 different types of receipt/payment and 10 different types of adjustment transactions, which are defined by the user in the parameters section.

All of the posting programs have the usual error-checking facilities to ensure that VAT is posted correctly, that journals balance and that analysis of invoices is complete before being written to the data files, etc. Screen prompts are helpful and relevant throughout the system, and each program is fully described in the user manual should any great problems be encountered (which is unlikely because the system as a whole, if set up correctly, is very easy to use). As an ex-programmer I always find it interesting to see how well various packages cope with the problem of posting receipts, particularly in catering for the various permutations of under-payment, over-payment, cash on account, matching receipts to individual invoices and coping with payment discount, etc. This, as I know only too well, is something of a nightmare to care for comprehensively while still keeping the program easy to follow for the user. Pegasus have handled this area particularly well, which is indicative of the overall quality of the product.

The sales ledger provides a warning if an invoice is posted to an account which will take that account over its credit limit, but the warning can be ignored. In both the sales and purchase ledgers transactions can be forward posted, so that the ledger may be held open for late invoices at the period end while still allowing processing to begin for the following period.

Getting information out
All of the modules have a range of standard reports which provide most of the information an average company might require from the system. Reports can be printed to any of up to three printers, to the screen, to Multiplan files, to spool

files to be printed later or to CSV files which can be picked up by other packages such as Lotus and Dbase. There is nothing to prevent spooled reports not being printed out to provide hard copy, although the period-end routine does give a warning that all reports should be run first.

The sales and purchase ledgers allow the user to define how information should be analysed for reporting purposes within the parameters. This gives a fairly comprehensive method of analysing sales and cost information without using a nominal ledger. Up to six methods of analysis can be created in this way for both ledgers. Also determined by the parameters are the ageing period for credit control reports. Three ageing periods are allowed so that, for instance, you can have debts aged 30, 60 and 90+ days.

Statement, remittance advice and cheque and debtors letter formats are set up in the parameters section to allow the package to suit almost any pre-printed stationery. The set-up of these items is quite simple, involving the user filling out a grid on the screen defining the character position and length of each field to be printed, and the number of blank lines to be printed after it. For this purpose a list of all the fields that can be printed is given in the user manual. The manual also contains a grid on which you can write out all the items you want to appear on your pre-printed forms in the position in which you want them to appear before filling in the screen form. The manual also helpfully suggests that you photocopy the form before you use it and use the photocopies in case you don't get it right first time!

Perhaps the best part of the Pegasus package is its report generator, which allows you to pick out which items you want to have printed, define the order in which they will appear on the line, and to insert your own fields which can be calculated from other fields on the line. The data can also be sorted before being printed, and sub-totals and page breaks can be set up to occur on a change in any of the fields printed or on a change in any character position in the field. Reports defined in this way can be printed to a printer, to the screen, to a Multiplan file or to a CSV file. In my experience many companies use one of the last two options to produce their management accounts rather than the nominal ledger special reports formatting facilities provided by Pegasus. This allows information to be drawn into a pre-defined spreadsheet so that what-if analysis can be carried out or so that other calculations can be made automatically by the spreadsheet based on the information produced by Pegasus.

The special reports facility contained in the nominal ledger allows the user to define the balance sheet and Profit and Loss account formats. Each nominal ledger account is given a special report code when it is created. The Balance Sheet and Profit and Loss account formats are defined in such a way that the user is given total flexibility as to the format of these reports. Some suppliers do provide assistance in defining these reports but, in fact, a semi-computer-literate accountant should have little trouble doing this himself with the help of the manual. Balance Sheets and Profit and Loss accounts can be produced either for each department individually (if the nominal ledger has been set up to have accounts split into departments) or for the entire ledger. Actual values can also be compared against previous year figures and/or budgets, if required.

Security and control
The password features are fairly basic compared with other similar packages, but are probably adequate for most companies in its target market, i.e. fairly small companies with perhaps half a dozen accounts staff. Control over the completeness, accuracy and integrity of data is more a matter of user discipline rather than being imposed by the software. For instance, Pegasus does not provide any batch control facilities, although the system does force transaction input audit trails to be printed to a printer or to a spool file. There is nothing to prevent spooled reports not being printed so that important reports could quite easily be forgotten, or deliberately not printed, although a reminder is given each time you run a period end. In addition, Pegasus does not force data copies to be taken at any time although, again, a reminder to do this is given every time a period end is run.

Despite all this, Pegasus can be used very successfully provided that a suitable set of operational procedures is drawn up and followed by everybody using the system.

There is a facility to print out an access log that details which users have accessed the system at various dates and times.

Opinion
Pegasus is an ideal package for the small company which is probably computerising for the first time and wants something easy to use while allowing potential for future expansion. Pegasus Senior comes in both single-user and network versions. Since the data file structures are the same for both versions it is relatively easy to upgrade from single-user, involving only the purchase of the network version of the software at an extra £200 per module and, of course, networking software.

More sophisticated users may find that, although Pegasus provides all the reporting functions they require, the security levels and control features built in to the software leave something to be desired.

Further information
Pegasus is sold through a network of authorised dealers who are able to provide advice on setting up the system and who also run regular Pegasus training courses or will provide training for individual customers.

Pegasus Senior costs around £550 per module for the single-user version, and £750 per module for the network version. Costs of training will vary from supplier to supplier, but it would be reasonable to budget for up to two days' training per module at approximately £250 to £350 per day.

Pegasus runs on IBM-compatible machines under MS-DOS.

Features Rating Table

Package	FINAX	MULTI-FACTS	MULTI-SOFT	PEGASUS Senior
	Rating (out of 10)			
Ease of set-up	9	5	7	9
Documentation	8	4	7	7
Performance of accounting functions	7	7	8	8
Ease of use	7	7	8	8
Reporting	9	8	6	8
Security	6	8	8	8
Support (Scotland)	8	4	7	7
Value for money	7	4	7	7
TOTAL (out of 80)	61	47	58	62

Package Information Table

Product Name	FINAX
Version Number	787.0.
Date of Test	February 1988.
Modules Available	Nominal, sales and purchase ledgers, stock control and invoicing.
Cost per Module	Complete system: single-user – £1300 multi-user – £3000.
Publisher	Orchard Business Systems, 168 Crawley Road, Horsham, Sussex RH12 4EU. Tel: 0403 210625.
Supplier	As publisher.
What support is available	Hotline support from Orchard as well as support from dealer.
Operating system	PC-DOS and MS-DOS.
Hardware	Apricot and IBM compatibles.
Network/multi-user version available	Yes – network.
Hardware used for tests	Zenith 286.
Number of UK users	1,200.
First operational	1982.
Report generator available?	Yes.
Links to other packages	Yes.

MULTIFACTS	MULTISOFT	PEGASUS Senior
3.05.	3 release 4.5.	7HS.
December 1987. Nominal sales and purchase ledgers, sales order processing, invoicing, point of sale invoice preparation, management accounts, job costing, stock control, payroll and external systems link.	September 1987. Nominal, sales and purchase ledgers, stock control, invoicing, financial management, costing and sub-contractor's ledger.	December 1987. Nominal sales and purchase ledgers, stock control, job costing, invoicing, bill of materials, sales order processing and payroll.
Single-user – £300, multi-user (2–5) – £600. Facts Software Ltd, Ketwell House, 75–9 Tavistock Street, Bedford MK40 2RR. Tel: 0234 218191.	Single-user – £390, multi-user – £590. Multisoft Systems Ltd, Cross & Pillory House, Cross & Pillory Lane, Alton, Hampshire GU34 1HL. Tel: 0420 85572	Single-user – £550, multi-user – £750. Pegasus Software Ltd, Brikat House, 35–41 Montague Street, Kettering, Northants NN16 8XG. Tel: 0536 410044.
As publisher. Authorised dealer.	As publisher. Via dealer network, backed by supplier.	As publisher. Through dealer.
MS-DOS, PC-DPS, UNIX and XENIX. Any that support operating systems with 256Kb of RAM and a hard disk.	MS-DOS, UNIX and XENIX. Micros that run on operating systems.	MS-DOS, IBM compatibles.
Yes. Compaq IBM PC and XT AT.	Yes. Compaq Deskpro.	Yes. Compaq portable II.
5,000.	3,000+.	300 (1130).
1982.	1983.	1986.
Yes – nominal ledger only.	Yes – within each module.	Yes.
Yes – using external link module.	Yes.	Yes.

Evaluation Checklists

General Points

Performance of Requisite Accounting Functions		FINAX
1 Does the software perform the functions which the user wants performed?		
2 Can software be used by more than one user at the same time?	yes	
3 Can the software support groups of companies/departments branches?	yes	
How many such branches or companies can be supported.	36	
Can they be consolidated?	yes	
4 Is multi-currency processing available?	no	Currently under development.
What are the maximum number of currencies available?		
Is conversion to sterling automatic?		
5 Are sufficient accounting periods provided by the system?	N/A	Accounting data remains open throughout the year.
Can these periods be adjusted to suit different user requirements?	N/A	
6 Are the ends of accounting periods determined by the user rather than being set by the system?	N/A	
7 Can data from all accounting periods be accessed at any given moment?	yes	
Can previous months be accessed for enquiries or reports?	yes	
8 Does the system prevent posting to more than one accounting period at a time?	yes	
Is it impossible to allocate transactions to future periods or to previous closed months?	no	
9 Does the system permit use of budgets and provide comparisons between budgets and actuals?	yes	
10 Is the maximum value of transactions that can be handled by the system sufficient?		99,999,999.99.
11 Is the maximum number of accounts on each ledger (e.g. sales ledger, purchase ledger, nominal ledger) sufficient?		16,000 sales and purchases. 960 nominal ledger.
12 Is the size and format of account numbers adequate and sufficient for analysis purposes?		3–8 alphanumeric for nominal analysis categories set up for sales and purchases.
13 Does the associated hardware incorporate enough memory, disk storage and other peripherals for the software to operate satisfactorily?		512K RAM needed.
14 Does the system offer adequate expansion potential as regards terminals, memory, disk storage capacity and other peripherals?		
15 Are the control features provided by the software adequate to support effective user controls?	yes	User controls essential.

MEDIUM-PRICE PACKAGES

MULTIFACTS		MULTISOFT	PEGASUS Senior	
yes	MULTIFACTS version running on LAN and LAN-based products.	yes	yes	If multi-user upgrade is acquired.
yes		yes	yes	
20		Disk size limitation.	35	
yes	Version 3 (Oct./Nov. '86) will allow nominal consolidation.	yes	yes	
no	Version 3 will allow nominal reports to be produced with currency conversion against exchange rate table.	yes	yes	
		99	26	
		yes	yes	
	12 or 13 periods if ledgers linked to nominal ledger otherwise 1–99.	Allow 12/13/52.	yes	
yes		yes	yes	
yes		yes	yes	
no		yes	In nominal/transactions in all other systems.	no
no	Only via back-up history.	yes	no	
yes		yes	In Sales/Purchase Ledgers. Allows costing/nominal flexibility, i.e. nominal allows posting to future and past period. Accruals/ Journals/Prev. Year adjs.	Posting to future period only.
yes		Yes – sales and purchase ledgers. No – nominal ledgers.	no	Posting and future period only.
yes	Budgets allocated to period, rather than annual figure split across periods.	yes	yes	
yes		Operating system restriction in DOS.	Up to 99,999,999.99.	
	Limited by disk size.	See 3 and 10.	65,000.	
	6 digit alphanumeric.	6 alphanumeric sale/purch/cost 22 alphanumeric stock 4+4 alphanumeric nominal	8 alphanumeric.	
	256K recommended.	DOS requires minimum 256K RAM. Varies in XENIX/UNIX.	yes	256K recommended.
yes		yes	yes	Although really only suitable for a small accounts dept.

16 Are complementary clerical procedures to be imposed and effectively monitored by management?

Reliability – Security and Continuity of Processing

		FINAX
1 Does the system facilitate back-up storage?	no	Depends on operating system.
How much time will complete back-up of the system require?		Varies with data size.
2 Does the system facilitate recovery procedures in the event of system failure?	yes	
3 If a system failure occurs part way through a batch or transaction, will the operator have to re-input only the batch or transaction being input at the time of the failure?	yes	
4 Are there any features provided with the software to help track down processing problems?	yes	
5 Are back-up procedures provided within each specific software application or within the operating system?		Operating system.
Are any of these back-up procedures automatic?	no	

Support and Maintenance

1 Will the supplier provide corrections to the program?	yes	
2 Will the supplier provide general enhancements to the programs?	yes	
Will these be provided automatically?	yes	
Will they be given free of charge?	no	Small charge to cover cost.
3 Will the software supplier provide 'hot-line' support to assist with immediate problem solving?	yes	
If so, at what cost?		
4 Is the supplier capable of giving sufficient ongoing education and training and other support?		
5 Can the supplier provide all the hardware, software and maintenance requirements of the user?		
6 Can the supplier provide support in the user's locality?		
7 Is a warranty offered in respect of specification and performance of the system?	no	
8 Would there be adequate back-up in the event of hardware or software failure?		
9 Will the software supplier make the program source code available to the user, either directly or by deposit with a third party?	no	
10 If the software is acquired under licence, are there any unduly restrictive conditions in the licence?	no	

The term 'supplier' refers to the supplier of the support and maintenance, whether or not this is the same as the supplier of the software.

Ease of Use
(a) Interactive processing

1 Does the software run under an operating system, which is a commonly accepted standard?	yes	DOS.
2 Is the software available concurrently to more than one user?	yes	

MEDIUM-PRICE PACKAGES

MULTIFACTS		MULTISOFT		PEGASUS Senior	
yes		yes	Automatic – can be enforced on time basis.	no	Depends on operating system.
			Depends on media and disk base/file sizes.		Depends on size of files, but on average 20–30 minutes.
yes	Data verification program checks data files and allows system to be re-entered if no corruption.	yes	Auto-restore.	no	
yes		no	Failure forces, in updating mode, restore from back-up.	no	
yes	Data verification program highlights corruption.		Logging system within system.	yes	File checker utility.
yes	Routine written by Facts, with standard layout of menu, etc.		Within application software.		Within operating system.
no	User is prompted to back-up on entry and exit from system.	yes	User option for automatic back-up.	no	
yes		yes		yes	On payroll for legislative changes.
yes		yes		yes	
no		yes		yes	
no		no		yes	
yes	Dealer only.	yes			
	FOC to dealers.		Confidential between us/dealer.		
no		yes	Software is standard, warranty is three months.		
no		no		no	
no		no		no	
yes	DOS.	yes	DOS/XENIX V/UNIX V.	yes	MS-DOS/PC-DOS/XENIX.
yes		yes	Networked or multi-user.	yes	If multi-user version used.

	FINAX	
3 Can more than one system function be performed concurrently?	yes	
4 Does the software effectively lead the user through the data entry procedures?	yes	
Does the software facilitate immediate error correction?	yes	
5 Is the software menu-driven?	yes	
Are such menus restricted by password and application?	yes	
6 Are the user screens adequately titled?	yes	
7 Does the system inform the operator which programs or files are being loaded?	no	
8 Does the software facilitate file maintenance, back-up and archive copying?	no	

(b) User documentation

	FINAX	
1 Is the manual clearly laid out and understandable?	yes	
2 Is the manual comprehensive and accurate?	yes	
3 Is there an index to the manual?	no	Cross reference to menu.
4 Is it easy to locate specific topics in the manual when required?	yes	Cross reference to menu.
5 Is it easy to follow through all procedures in the manual?	yes	
6 Are completed examples included in the manual?	no	
7 Are help screens available?	yes	
Do they provide detailed on-line instructions on how to use particular features of the software?	yes	
Can they be edited or prepared by the user?	no	
8 Does the documentation clearly specify the actions to be taken by users at each important stage of processing?	yes	
9 Will the software supplier provide regular updates of documentation in the event of modifications or revisions?	yes	
10 Will the software supplier make the detailed program documentation available to the user, either directly or by deposit with a third party?	yes	NCC ESCROW

Efficiency

	FINAX
1 Are the various functions of the system menu-driven, or otherwise easy to initiate?	yes
Is there a good response time in the initiation of functions?	yes
2 Is data entry easily repeated if similar to previous entry?	yes
3 Is there a good response time:	
(i) in processing data input?	yes
(i) in producing requisite reports?	yes
(iii) in updating files?	yes
(iv) in producing back-up files?	yes
(v) in deleting redundant information files?	yes
4 Does the system prevent access to a record while it is being updated?	yes
5 Does the system retain a log of file updates until the next occasion on which the relevant information is reported or the relevant file used in a regular control procedure?	no

MEDIUM-PRICE PACKAGES 201

MULTIFACTS	MULTISOFT		PEGASUS Senior	
no	yes	Networked or multi-user.	no	
yes	yes		yes	
yes			yes	
yes	yes		yes	
yes	yes		yes	
yes	yes		yes	
no	yes	From menu.	yes	
yes	yes		yes	
yes	yes		yes	
yes	yes		yes	
no	no	Good contents listings.	no	Comprehensive contents page.
yes	yes		yes	
yes	yes		yes	
no	nos		yes	
no	yes	All input instructions give user prompts.	yes	All input screens give user prompts.
	yes		yes	
	no		no	
yes	yes		yes	
yes	yes		yes	
no	no		no	
yes	yes		yes	
yes	yes		yes	
yes	yes	In many cases previous entry is re-displayed.	yes	
yes	yes		yes	
yes	yes	.	yes	
yes	yes		yes	
yes	yes		yes	
yes	yes	Auto by system.	yes	
yes	yes	In systems where appropriate, i.e. multi-user/update mode.	yes	
no	yes		yes	

	FINAX	
6 Can regular reports be easily duplicated if required?	yes	

Flexibility
(a) Integration facilities

	FINAX	
1 Are the different accounting applications integrated?	yes	
Are they integrated on an item by item basis or are they integrated by weekly or monthly end routines.		Item by item.
2 Whichever method is used, can the ledger updating process be satisfactorily controlled?	yes	
3 Does the software run under an operating system which is a commonly-accepted standard?	yes	
4 Can more than one system function be performed concurrently?	yes	Networked.
5 Can software be linked to other packages, e.g. word processing, graphics, financial modelling, to provide alternative display and reporting facilities?	yes	

(b) Reporting flexibility

	FINAX	
1 Can the user easily design additional output reports or displays?	yes	
2 Is a report generator provided as part of the software or as an option associated with it?	yes	Part of software.
3 Can screen layouts, reports and transaction formats be easily adapted to users' requirements?	yes	
4 Does the output of the software facilitate proper control to ensure that decisions are not inadvertently taken on the basis of incorrect information?	yes	

(c) Parameter or table facilities

	FINAX	
1 If the system uses a lot of standing information which changes frequently or regularly, does the system allow for such changes to be effected through the use of parameters or tables.	yes	
2 If so, is the use of such parameters or tables adequately reported?	no	No compulsory printouts.
3 Is proper control to be exercised over changes to such parameters or tables?	yes	
If so, how? (e.g. through the use of system facilities such as passwords or by inspection of appropriate records)		Passwords.

Software Installation and Training
(a) Financial resources
1 Has account been taken in the budget for system development/acquisition of the full costs of

   initial acquisition?

   initial training?

   future training?

(b) Other resources
2 Is the main equipment to be located in adequate accommodation?

   Is this such that staff are not seriously affected by the equipment (e.g. by noise from the printer).

MEDIUM-PRICE PACKAGES

MULTIFACTS		MULTISOFT		PEGASUS Senior	
yes		yes		yes	
yes		yes		yes	
	Daybooks can be run at any time, to update nominal and job costing, etc.		Batch file updates to nominal/costing/analysis.		Optional user can specify which method to be used when running the integration program.
yes		yes		yes	
yes		yes		yes	MS-DOS/PC-DOS.
no		yes	Networked or multi-user.	no	
yes	Factslink.	yes	Lotus/multiplan.	yes	Lotus, etc.
no		yes	Not displays.	yes	Using report generator.
yes	Report generator is option for nominal ledger.	yes	Within each sub-system.	yes	Provided as standard part of each module.
no		yes	Some fixed printed data. Content is variable.	no	Although additional reporting is possible through the report generator.
yes		yes		yes	
yes		yes	e.g. Payroll tables, discount tables, descriptor tables.	yes	
no		yes		yes	
yes		yes		yes	
	Password control can lock people out of system controls if applicable.		Passwording.		Can only be changed by holder of master access password.
		N/A			
		N/A			

	FINAX

3 Is there sufficient scope for the installation if required, of communications equipment?

4 Have requisite consumables (e.g. special stationery, filing facilities, fireproof storage) been provided for?

(c) Involvement of software supplier

5 Is the supplier capable of giving sufficient initial education and training and other support?

6 Are potential users permitted to test the software for a trial period before commitment to acquire it?

7 If required, does the supplier have sufficient capable personnel to assist users to convert to the new system?

8 If required, will the supplier provide machine time to enable users to set up files of input data before installation?

(d) Involvement of user personnel

9 Who is to be responsible for running and controlling the system on a regular basis?

Is this person sufficiently competent?

10 Who is to be responsible for the installation and implementation of the system?

Is this person sufficiently competent?

11 Which staff will operate the system?

Do they have sufficient aptitude for computers?

12 Is there adequate cover for staff in the event of illness and holidays?

Package Software Acquisition

Preliminary questions relating to software supplier

1 Does the supplier have a good overall reputation as regards experience and reliability?

2 Does the supplier offer a full range of accounting software?

3 Is the supplier's financial status stable?

Does the supplier demonstrate an adequate capital base, growth and profitability?

4 Does the supplier have sufficient technical resources to modify or tailor software to suit different users' requirements?

5 Does the supplier have a substantial user base?

Has it shown adequate commitment to existing users and will it provide a list of them?

Has the supplier sold similar systems to that under consideration?

6 Does the supplier offer adequate contractual terms as regards purchase, installation, delivery, support and maintenance?

Are all costs clearly indicated?

Is the date of delivery of all components of the system clearly stated?

7 Is there adequate evidence that the supplier normally meets its contractual obligations?

8 Will the supplier provide in-depth demonstrations of its software?

MULTIFACTS	MULTISOFT	PEGASUS Senior

Nominal Ledger

	FINAX	
General		
1 Are programs menu-driven?	yes	
If 'YES' – can menus be by-passed once the user is familiar with the package?	yes	
2 Does the system maintain a log of usage?	no	
3 Are informative messages produced on-screen whilst running?	yes	
4 Are error messages informative and easy to understand?	yes	
5 Is the system multi-company?	yes	Single- and multi-company version.
6 Is the original set-up straightforward?	yes	
7 Is there a copy/restore facility in the package?	no	
8 Does the system cover disciplined taking of back-ups?	no	
Documentation		
(a) Manual		
1 Is the manual clearly laid out and understandable?	yes	
2 Is the manual comprehensive and accurate?	yes	
3 Is there an index?	no	Cross-reference to menu on-screen.
4 Is it easy to follow through all procedures?	yes	
5 Is it easy to locate specific points when required?	yes	See 3 above.
6 Are completed examples included?	yes	
(b) Help screens		
7 Are help screens available?	yes	
If 'YES' –		
Do they provide on-line instructions?	yes	
Can they be edited or prepared by the user?	no	In general no, but some can.
Account Details		
1 Is the chart of accounts flexible?	yes	
2 What is the format of the nominal account code?		3–8 alphanumeric digits.
3 Is cost centre accounting available?	yes	
4 What is the maximum number of accounts that can be held?		960.
5 What is the maximum balance that can be held?		9,999,999,999.99.
6 Can accounts be added/amended at any time?		Yes – added. No – deleted.
7 Is file automatically re-sorted when a new account is added?	yes	
If 'NO' – can re-sort be initiated?		
8 Is deletion of an account prevented if it has: a non-zero balance a zero balance but postings in the current period a zero balance but postings in the year-to-date	N/A	No deletion available.
9 Is a hard copy of changes in account details automatically produced?	no	

MEDIUM-PRICE PACKAGES 207

MULTIFACTS		MULTISOFT		PEGASUS Senior	
yes		yes		yes	
no		yes	Only in Xenix/Unix.	no	
no		yes		yes	Print-out via utilities.
yes		yes		yes	
yes	Usually, but not always.	yes		yes	
yes	But all details and transactions are held in a *single* data file!	yes		yes	
no	Dealer set up recommended	yes		yes	
yes		yes		no	Back-up/restore option on menu refers to DOS.
no		yes	Back-up can be enforced.	no	Back-up/restore option on menu refers to DOS.
yes	Chapters on set-up and initialisation are very poor and confused.	yes		yes	
yes		yes		yes	
no		no	Good contents listing.	no	Comprehensive contents list.
no		yes		yes	
yes		yes		yes	
no		no		yes	
no		yes	All input instructions give user prompts.	yes	Help with posting/errors at foot of screen.
		yes		yes	
		no		no	
yes		yes		yes	
	6 alphanumeric.		4 alphanumeric nom. code. 4 alphanumeric dept. codes.		8 character, alphanumeric.
yes	By using structured nominal accounts numbers only.	yes		yes	4 character cost-centre code.
	Disk limit. 99,999,999.99.		Disk limit.		65,000. 999,999,999.99.
	Yes – added and amended. No – deleted.	yes	Deletion protection with balances on accounts or historic data.	yes	Except during transactions posting.
yes		N/A	Indexed files.	no	
				yes	Done automatically by the system at period end.
yes		yes		yes	
yes		yes		yes	
yes		yes		yes	
no		no		no	

		FINAX
10 Are 12 or 13 (or more) accounting periods available?	N/A	No periods as such, all data remains available for year.
11 Can budgets be entered for all revenue accounts?	yes	
12 Can separate budgets be entered for each accounting period?	yes	
13 Can this year's results be used to calculate next year's budgets automatically?	yes	

Transactions

1 What is the maximum transaction value that can be entered?		99,999,999.99.
2 Can each journal entry contain an unlimited number of debits and credits?	yes	Using multiple entry journals.
3 Is each input line numbered?	yes	
4 In a long journal entry is it possible to move between screens to view data already input?	yes	Plus previous journals.
5 Can previously entered journal lines be edited before accepting the whole journal?	no	But can be edited subsequently.
6 Does each journal entry have a reference number?	yes	
7 Are accruals and prepayments routines, which both reverse automatically at the start of the next accounting period, available?	yes	
8 Can recurring journal entries be provided for automatically?	yes	
9 Is a narrative available for:		
each journal entry	yes	
each line of the journal entry	yes	
10 Can journal entries be posted to future periods?	no	But can be held for automatic posting by data date.
11 Can journal entries be posted to previous periods?	yes	
12 Are all transactions retained on file for at least one period?	yes	1 year.
13 Can transactions be retained at the period-end?	yes	1 year.
14 Can a ledger date pre-date existing transactions?	no	

Input Controls

1 Is password control used?	yes	
If 'YES' – give detail		By function only.
2 Is a hard copy automatically produced for all input?	no	
3 Are journal entries automatically sequentially numbered?	yes	
4 If integrated, are automatic postings from other modules included in the numbering sequence?	yes	
5 If accruals and prepayments automatically reverse, is the reversal included in the numbering sequence?	yes	
6 Are totals, of debit or credit entries, produced for all journal entries?		Running total shown.
If 'YES' – is it necessary that this agrees with a pre-list total?	no	
7 Is it necessary that all journal entries balance before posting?	yes	
8 Is production of an out-of-balance trial balance prevented?	yes	

MEDIUM-PRICE PACKAGES 209

MULTIFACTS		MULTISOFT		PEGASUS Senior	
yes		yes		yes	13.
yes		yes		yes	
yes		yes		yes	
no	The manual says YES, but I cannot work out how!	yes		yes	
no	99,999,999.99. Maximum 999 entries in a journal.	yes	999,999,999.99.	no	999,999,999.99. Up to 50 per journal sheet.
yes		yes		yes	On screen.
yes		no		yes	
yes		no		yes	
yes		yes		yes	
yes		yes	Can be set to reverse over several periods.	yes	
yes		yes		yes	
yes	16 characters.	yes		yes	58 characters.
yes	16 characters.	yes		yes	20 characters.
no		yes		yes	
no		yes		no	
yes		yes		yes	
yes		yes	Up to 1 year.	yes	Optional.
yes		yes		no	
yes		yes		yes	
	Each menu option can be linked to each operators access log on password.		3-level security passwords+overall system.		4 levels of control available, including MASTER.
yes		yes		yes	Optional to printer or spooler.
yes		yes		yes	
yes		yes		yes	
no		yes		yes	
	Net balance only is reported.	yes		yes	
no		yes	Over-ride requests reason for difference and includes in audit trail.	no	
yes		yes		yes	
yes		yes		yes	

		FINAX
9 Do all input screens show clearly:		
type of entry	yes	
the distinction between debits and credits	yes	
10 Can the actual date of posting, or a batch reference, be shown on hard copies of transactions input?	yes	
11 Are the following validated:		
date	yes	
nominal ledger account code	yes	
cost centre code	yes	
If 'NO' – are unidentified/invalid entries posted to a suspense account?		
– how is suspense account treated?		
12 Is a total produced of all debit/credit transactions processed?	no	
If 'YES' – is a report produced at the end of each processing run to reconcile b/f total, transactions processed and c/f total?		
13 Is a reconciliation of numbers of accounts produced after amendment of the accounts detail file?	no	
14 Does the system prevent the abnormal termination of programs?	yes	

Integration

1 Is integration possible with the following:		
sales ledger	yes	
purchase ledger	yes	
payroll	no	
2 Can the nominal ledger be updated as often as desired?	N/A	Automatic update of each individual transaction.
3 Is a hard copy automatically produced at the end of each nominal ledger update?	N/A	
4 Is there a sales/purchase ledger printout of the nominal ledger update?	N/A	
5 Are sales ledger and purchase ledger control accounts agreed to the totals of balances in the individual ledgers?	no	
6 Is there a check that the nominal ledger cannot be updated twice with the same sales/purchases data?	N/A	
7 Must the nominal ledger be updated from the sales and purchases ledgers before the period-end is run?	N/A	
8 Must the nominal ledger be in the same period as the sales and purchases ledgers for the update to be carried out?	N/A	
9 Is there any check that all data processed in the sales/purchase ledgers has been posted to the nominal ledger?	yes	
10 Are unidentified/invalid entries held in a nominal ledger suspense account?	N/A	All entries validated at time of input.
If 'YES' – how is this treated?		

MEDIUM PRICE PACKAGES

MULTIFACTS		MULTISOFT		PEGASUS Senior	
yes		yes		yes	
no	Credits are input as 'minus' values.	yes		yes	
yes		yes		no	One date and batch reference.
yes		yes		yes	
yes		yes		yes	
yes		yes		yes	
no		yes		yes	
		yes		no	
no		no		no	
yes		yes		yes	
yes		yes		yes	
yes		yes		yes	
yes		yes		yes	
no	Only at period end.	yes		yes	
yes		yes		yes	
yes		yes		yes	
no		no		no	
yes		yes		yes	
	This is done automatically by systems at period end.	no	Transactions will not be lost.	no	Can be forced by setting an option.
yes		no		yes	Though over-ride possible.
yes		yes	Logging system/update reports.	yes	Warning is given within sales/ purchase ledger at period end.
N/A	All postings in subsidiary ledgers are validated against nominal ledger codes at time of entry.	yes		yes	
			Cleared by journal.		Cleared by journal.

212 A GUIDE TO ACCOUNTING SOFTWARE

	FINAX
11 Can the user select whether to update the nominal ledger with individual sales/purchases ledger entries or in total?	no
If 'NO' – is the update made in detail or in total?	Detail.
12 Is it impossible to post directly to the sales/purchase ledger control accounts?	no

Output
(a) General

	FINAX
1 Is it necessary to produce an audit trail before the period-end procedure is run?	no No period-end.
2 Does the audit trail enable all transactions to be traced fully through the system?	yes
3 Can the actual run date, or batch reference, as well as the current ledger date, be shown on all reports?	yes
4 Can the following be seen on screen:	
account details	yes
account transactions	yes
5 Can a print-out of the following be obtained for individual accounts/selected ranges of accounts:	
account details	yes
account transactions	yes
6 Do all outputs show clearly the distinction between debit and credit entries?	yes
7 Are all reports adequately titled?	yes
8 Do reports provide totals where applicable?	yes
9 Is the period number shown on reports?	N/A
10 Can the following be produced:	
trial balance	yes
ledger account detail report	yes
profit and loss account	yes
balance sheet	yes
11 Does the ledger account detail report show the source of postings and narrative input?	yes
12 Does the ledger account detail report show either the full account history or balance b/f together with the current period's transactions?	Full history.
13 Are all report pages numbered sequentially, with the end of report identified?	yes
14 Can reports be temporarily retained on file for subsequent printing?	yes
If 'YES' – are such files protected from deletion?	no But data available for whole year.
15 Is a report generator available for use with the nominal ledger module?	yes
16 Can transaction files for all previous periods be retained in the system to permit enquiries and reports?	yes

(b) Trial balance; P&L and balance sheet

	FINAX
1 Does the package provide for flexible formatting of profit and loss account and balance sheet?	yes All reports can be user-defined/modified.

MEDIUM-PRICE PACKAGES 213

MULTIFACTS		MULTISOFT		PEGASUS Senior	
yes		no		yes	
no		no	Total.	no	
yes		no	Audit trail mandatory during posting. Deletion is listed at period-end routine.	no	System reminder.
yes		yes		yes	
yes		yes		no	Yes for some reports.
yes		yes		yes	
yes		yes		yes	
yes		yes		yes	
yes		yes		yes	
yes		yes		yes	
yes		yes		yes	
yes		yes		yes	
yes		yes	Where applicable.	yes	Where applicable.
yes		yes		yes	
yes		yes		yes	
yes		yes		yes	
yes		yes		yes	
yes		yes		yes	
	Full account history.	yes	Full account history.		B/f and current transaction.
yes		yes			End of report not identified.
yes		yes		yes	
yes		yes	From within Multisoft.	yes	From within Pegasus.
no	Separate module must be purchased.	yes		yes	
yes	For enquiry only.	yes		yes	Optional.
yes	Using nominal ledger account number structuring.	yes	4 formats allowed.	yes	

	FINAX	
2 Can the following be produced for both the current period and the year-to-date:		
trial balance	yes	
profit and loss account	yes	
balance sheet	yes	
If 'YES' – is it clearly shown whether a report is for the current period or year-to-date?	yes	
3 Can the following show budgets:		
trial balance	yes	
profit and loss account	yes	
If 'YES' – can budgets be omitted if wished?	yes	
4 Can the following reports show comparative figures:		
trial balance	yes	
profit and loss account	yes	
balance sheet	yes	
If 'YES' – can comparatives be omitted?	yes	
– can two years' comparatives be shown?	yes	
5 Are budgets worked out from the period number as calculated by the number of period-end procedures run?	N/A	No periods as such.
6 Are budget variances calculated?	yes	
If 'YES' are they shown as:	yes	
value	yes	
percentages	yes	
both	yes	Either or both.
7 Do budget reports provide for exception reporting?	yes	
8 Does the package provide for a trial balance to be produced for each Cost Centre?	yes	
9 Does the package provide for a profit and loss account and balance sheet for each cost centre?	yes	
10 Does the package provide for totalling of like items across cost centres?	yes	
11 Can trial balance production be varied by:		
printing a range of accounts	yes	} User-defined reports.
subtotalling on any chosen digit of account code	yes	
12 Can vertical percentages be calculated in the profit and loss account?	yes	User-defined reports.
13 Can a report be produced to show the breakdown of profit and loss account and balance sheet figures?	yes	

Year End

1 Can balance sheet items be carried forward and profit and loss account items be cleared automatically at the year-end?	yes	
2 Can the destination of individual account balances be specified or are all balances cleared at the year-end transferred into one account only?		Balance sheets – yes. Profit and loss all to one account.

MEDIUM-PRICE PACKAGES 215

MULTIFACTS		MULTISOFT		PEGASUS Senior	
yes		yes		yes	
yes		yes		yes	
yes		yes		yes	
		yes		yes	
yes		yes		yes	
yes		yes		yes	
yes		yes		yes	
no		yes		yes	
no		yes		yes	
no		yes		yes	
				yes	
		no	This and last only.	no	
no		no		yes	Number of options – user-defined.
yes		yes		yes	
yes		yes		yes	
yes		yes		yes	
yes		yes		yes	
no		yes		no	
no		yes		yes	Via report generator.
no		yes		yes	
yes		yes		yes	Via report generator.
no		yes		yes	
yes		no	Separate field code.	yes	Using report generator.
no	Yes if using report generator.	yes		no	
no		yes		no	
yes		yes		yes	
	Into one account only.		One account.		One account.

Sales Ledger

	FINAX
General	
1 Are programs menu driven?	yes
If 'YES' – can menus be by-passed once the user is familiar with the package?	yes
2 Does the system maintain a log of usage?	no
3 Are informative messages produced on-screen whilst running?	yes
4 Are error messages informative and easy to understand?	yes
5 Is the system multi-company?	yes — Single- and multi-company version.
6 Is the original set-up straightforward?	yes
7 Is there a copy/restore facility in the package?	no
8 Does the system cover disciplined taking of back-ups?	no
Documentation	
(a) Manual	
1 Is the manual clearly laid out and understandable?	yes
2 Is the manual comprehensive and accurate?	yes
3 Is there an index?	no — Cross-reference to menu on-screen.
4 Is it easy to follow through all procedures?	yes
5 Is it easy to locate specific points when required?	yes — See 3 above.
6 Are completed examples included?	yes
(b) Help screens	
7 Are help screens available?	yes
If 'YES' –	
Do they provide on-line instructions?	yes
Can they be edited or prepared by the user?	no — In general no, but some can.
Customer Details	
1 What is the format of the customer account code?	Sequential: assigned by system, sort/access, etc. By name or part name.
2 What other customer details are held?	Name, address, salutation, credit limit, discount rate, invoice address and user-defined fields.
Do these seem to be sufficient in general?	
3 What is the maximum number of accounts that can be held?	16,000.
4 Can customer details be added/deleted/amended at any time?	yes — Deletion only possible if no I/V on file for customer.
5 Is file re-sorted automatically when a new customer is added?	yes
If 'NO' – can a re-sort be initiated?	
6 Is deletion of a customer prevented if the account has:	
an outstanding balance	yes
a zero balance but a b/f turnover?	yes
7 Is a hard copy of changes in customer details automatically produced?	no
If 'NO' – can a hard copy be taken?	yes
Transactions	
1 Can the system be open item?	yes

MEDIUM-PRICE PACKAGES

MULTIFACTS		MULTISOFT		PEGASUS Senior	
yes		yes		yes	
no		yes	In Xenix/Unix only.	no	
no		yes		yes	Printout via utilities.
yes		yes		yes	
yes	Usually, but not always.	yes		yes	
yes		yes		yes	
yes		yes		yes	
yes		yes		no	} Copy restore at present relies on DOS.
no		yes	Backup can be enforced.	yes	
yes		yes		yes	
yes		yes		yes	
no		yes	User created.	no	Comprehensive contents list.
yes		yes		yes	
yes		yes		yes	
no		no		yes	
no		yes	All input screens give user prompts.	yes	Help at foot of screens.
		yes		yes	
		no		no	
	6 alphanumeric.		6 alphanumeric.		8-character, alphanumeric.
	Name, address, delivery address, account type, default nominal analysis code, credit limit, stopped account (Y/N) settlement, trade and invoice discounts.		Name and address, short name, contact, statement address, category, credit limits and discounts.		Name and address, short name, comment, tel. no., ledger account code, credit limit, currency quantity discounts, settlement discounts.
yes		yes		yes	
	No limit.		None. Disk consideration only.		65,000.
yes	Except during transactions posting.	yes		yes	Except during transactions posting.
yes			Not necessary, indexation is automatic.	no	
					This is done automatically by the system at each period end.
yes		yes		yes	
no		yes		no	
no		no		no	
no		yes		yes	Via account enquiry option.
yes		yes	Cash account can be either open item or balance forward.	yes	Each account can be either open item or balance forward.

218 A GUIDE TO ACCOUNTING SOFTWARE

	FINAX	
2 Are the following inputs possible:		
invoices	yes	
credit notes	yes	
cash received	yes	
cash refunded	yes	
discounts	yes	
journal entries	no	Erroneous entries can be edited.
write-offs?	yes	
3 Can an invoice be analysed to several different sales categories?	yes	
4 Are different VAT codes possible for different items within one invoice?	yes	
5 Are all transactions retained on file for at least one period?	yes	1 year.
6 Can a ledger date pre-date existing transactions?	no	

Matching/Allocations
(a) Balance forward

1 Is the balance b/f aged?	N/A	System is open item but statements can be produced in b/f format.
2 Can cash be allocated automatically?		
If 'YES' – how is the allocation made?		
– can this be over-ridden?		
3 Can cash be allocated manually?		
If 'YES' – does the package check that cash allocated = amount received?		
How is any such difference treated?		
4 Can credit notes/journal entries be allocated to previous periods?		
5 Can cash in advance be held and later allocated to subsequent periods?		
6 Can cash be held unallocated?		

(b) Open item

7 Are outstanding transactions displayed for allocation?	yes	
8 Can cash be allocated automatically?	yes	
If 'YES' – how is the allocation made?		From listing, oldest invoice first.
– can this be over-ridden?	yes	
9 Can cash be allocated manually?	yes	
If 'YES' – does the package check that cash allocated = cash received?	yes	
How is any difference treated?		User controlled.
10 Can an over/underpayment of an invoice be recorded?	yes	
11 How often are settled items deleted from file?		User controlled.
12 Can credit notes be set against the invoices to which they refer?	yes	Using cash routine.

MEDIUM-PRICE PACKAGES 219

MULTIFACTS		MULTISOFT		PEGASUS Senior	
yes		yes		yes	
yes		yes		yes	
yes		yes		yes	
yes		yes		yes	
yes		yes		yes	
yes		no		yes	
yes		yes		yes	
yes		yes		yes	
yes		yes		yes	
yes		yes	Option for up to 12 months.	yes	
yes		yes		yes	System gives a warning if this occurs.
no		yes		yes	
yes		yes		yes	
	Oldest transaction first.		Oldest transaction first.		Allocation made to oldest oustanding balance.
yes				yes	
yes		yes		yes	To specified period number.
yes		yes		yes	
	Either discount or cash on account.		Partial allocation of cash or invoices.	N/A	Total amount posted to period.
yes		yes	All ageing is transaction date calculated.	no	
no		yes	See 4.	no	
yes		yes		yes	
yes		yes		yes	
yes		yes	Oldest transaction first.	no	
	Oldest invoice first until remaining unallocated cash is less than next oldest invoice.				
yes					
yes		yes		yes	
yes		yes		yes	
	Either discount or payment on account.		Partial allocations of cash or invoices.	yes	Rejected if cash allocated>cash received. Posted to unallocated cash if cash received>cash allocated.
yes	Underpayment.	yes		yes	
no	Overpayment.				
	Month end.		Can be returned for up to 1 year.		Monthly (at period end).
yes		yes		yes	

220 A GUIDE TO ACCOUNTING SOFTWARE

		FINAX
13 Can journal entries be set against the invoices/credit notes to which they refer?	N/A	No journals.
14 Can cash in advance be held and later allocated to invoice?	yes	
15 Can cash be held unallocated?	yes	
– how is this treated?		As unallocated cash.

Input Controls

1 Is password control used?	yes	
If 'YES' – give detail		By function.
2 Is a hard copy automatically produced for all input?	no	
3 Are batch totals automatically produced for all transactions input?	no	
If 'YES' – what is the procedure if this does not agree with a pre-list total?		
4 Is it necessary that invoices, cash and adjustments are input in separate batches?	no	
5 Are batches automatically sequentially numbered?	yes	
If 'NO' – can they be so numbered?		
6 Is a report produced at the end of each processing run to reconcile b/f total, transactions processed and c/f total?	no	
If 'NO' - is a control balance produced at the end of each posting run?	no	
7 Are the following validated:		
date	yes	
customer account number	yes	
VAT code	yes	
goods value	no	
sales analysis code	yes	
8 Is VAT calculated to check figure input?	yes	System calculation.
9 Is the gross figure agreed to goods+VAT?	yes	See above.
10 Is discount calculated to check the figure input?	no	
11 Can the actual date of posting, or batch reference, be shown on hard copies of transactions input?	yes	
12 Does the screen always indicate that the sales ledger, as opposed to the purchase ledger, is running?	yes	
13 Do all input screens show clearly:		
type of entry	yes	
the distinction between debits and credits	yes	
14 Is there any check that the same entry is not input twice?	no	
15 Is there a warning if a customer exceeds the credit limit?	no	Credit limit and current balance displayed on input screens.
If 'YES' – what action is required?		
16 Is it impossible for new accounts to be created during processing?	no	

MEDIUM-PRICE PACKAGES 221

MULTIFACTS		MULTISOFT		PEGASUS Senior	
yes		N/A	No journals.	yes	
yes		yes		yes	
yes		yes		yes	
yes	System reports unallocated cash as a unique transaction type.		As outstanding, unallocated cash.		Posted to ledger on account and allocated using separate routine.
yes		yes		yes	
	Linked menu systems and access log on passwords.		3 level security passwords and overall system.		4 levels of control, restricting the functions available to each level.
yes		yes		no	Hard copy can be sent to screen, spool file, or printer.
no		yes		no	
			Continue input or log reason.		
yes		yes		no	
no		yes	Plus manual – cross reference if required.	no	
no				no	
no		yes		no	
no				no	
yes		yes		yes	Warning if date out of sequence.
yes		yes		yes	
yes		yes	Allows user to enter self-determined code. Range 1–10.	yes	
yes		no		yes	
yes		yes		yes	
yes		yes		yes	Reasonableness check.
yes		yes		yes	
yes				no	
yes		yes		no	Posting date and batch reference.
yes		yes		yes	
yes		yes		yes	
yes		yes		yes	
no		no		no	
no	But sales invoicing modules or sales order processing module are more likely to have this check.	yes		yes	
			Operator option.		Operator option.
yes		no		yes	

	FINAX

17 Is a reconciliation of numbers of accounts produced after amendment of the customer detail file? — no

18 Does the system prevent the abnormal termination of programs? — yes

Integration

1 Can the sales ledger be integrated with an invoicing module? — yes

2 Can the sales ledger be integrated with a nominal ledger module? — yes

3 Can the nominal ledger be updated as often as desired? — Automatic update on input.

4 Is a hard copy automatically produced at the end of each nominal ledger update? — no

5 Is there a sales ledger print-out (as well as a nominal ledger print-out) of the nominal ledger update? — no

6 Are the following automatically posted to the appropriate nominal ledger accounts:

    discount — yes

    discount written back — yes

    bad debts written off — no. Requires user intervention.

    contras with purchase ledger? — no

7 Are any invalid/unidentified entries posted to a suspense account? — N/A. Validated on input.

    If 'NO' – how are they treated?

    If 'YES' – how is the suspense account treated?

8 Is the sales ledger control balance agreed to the total of the balances in the sales ledger? — no

9 Can current and future periods be maintained simultaneously? — yes

10 Is there a check that transactions cannot be posted twice to the nominal ledger. — N/A

11 Must the nominal ledger be updated from the sales ledger before the period-end is run? — N/A

12 Must the nominal ledger and the sales ledger be in the same period for the update to be carried out? — N/A

13 Is there any report/warning that transactions posted to the sales ledger have not yet been posted to the nominal ledger? — N/A

Output

1 Is it necessary to produce an audit trail before the period-end procedure is run? — No period end as such.

2 Does the audit trail enable all transactions to be traced fully through the system? — yes

3 Can the actual run date, or batch reference, as well as current ledger date, be shown on reports? — yes

MEDIUM-PRICE PACKAGES 223

MULTIFACTS		MULTISOFT		PEGASUS Senior	
no		yes	If maint. list taken.	no	
yes		yes	Forces restore if updating.	no	
yes		yes		yes	
yes		yes		yes	
no		yes		yes	
yes		yes		yes	
yes		yes		yes	
yes		yes		yes	
yes	Program provides all 4 types of adjustment – posting to any account in nominal ledger.	yes		no	Posted to suspense and labelled for re-posting.
yes		yes		no	
yes		no		no	
no		yes		yes	
no	All entries are validated against nominal ledger accounts at time of entry.				
			Error is highlighted on update of nominal. Sales/invoicing is validated on-line.		By journal.
no		no		no	
no		no		yes	Advance postings.
no		yes		yes	
yes		no	All nominal is automatically batch updated and copes with mult. period numbers in other systems.	yes	
yes		no		yes	
yes			Not necessary.	yes	
yes		no	Depends on transaction retention requirements.	no	There is a warning given, but this can be ignored – can be made compulsory.
yes		yes		yes	
yes		yes		no	Run date and batch reference or ledger date and batch reference.

224 A GUIDE TO ACCOUNTING SOFTWARE

		FINAX	
4	Can the following be produced:		
	list of master file information	yes	
	aged debtors report	yes	
	VAT report	yes	Automatic VAT report.
	ledger detail report	yes	User-defined if printed, screen enquiry standard.
	customer statements	yes	
	customer name and address labels	yes	
	debt collection letters	yes	
5	Does the customer statement show:		
	all o/s transactions together with all items settled in the current period		
	or all o/s transactions only		Format defined by user.
	or the balance b/f and the current period's transactions		
	or just the current balance		
6	Does the customer statement:		
	show discount separately	yes	
	show ageing	yes	Format can be user-defined.
	allow special messages	yes	
	allow for suppression of erroneous postings and their corrections	yes	
7	Can the following screens be seen:		
	customer details	yes	
	customer transactions	yes	
8	Can hard copies of the following be obtained from individual accounts/selected ranges of accounts:		
	customer details	yes	
	customer transactions	yes	User-defined report.
9	Does the ledger account detail report/copy statements show:		
	the source of all postings	yes	
	how part payments and allocations have been treated	yes	
	either the full account history or balance b/f together with the current period's transaction?		Full account history
10	Does the Aged Analysis show for each customer:		
	total balance o/s	yes	
	credit limit	no	
11	Is ageing strictly by transaction date?	yes	
	If 'NO' – how is ageing done?		
12	Does the aged analysis show unallocated cash separately?	yes	
	If 'NO' – how it is it aged?		

MEDIUM-PRICE PACKAGES 225

MULTIFACTS		MULTISOFT		PEGASUS Senior	
yes		yes		yes	
yes		yes		yes	
yes		yes		yes	
yes		yes		yes	
yes		yes		yes	
yes		yes		yes	
no		yes	3 levels.	yes	User-defined.
yes		yes	Optional o/s only.	yes	
		yes	Option.		
yes		yes	Option.		
		yes	Option.		
yes		yes	Option.	no	
yes		yes	Option.	yes	
yes		yes	Option.	yes	
no		yes	If * selected.	no	
yes		yes		yes	
yes		yes	Plus archived data.	yes	
yes		yes		yes	
yes		yes		yes	
yes		yes		yes	
no		yes		yes	
yes		yes		yes	
yes		yes		yes	
yes		yes		yes	
no		no		no	
yes	Either by transaction date or due date		Option for tax point date or anticipated payment date		Can be either by date, or aged 1 period at each period end
no	According to transaction date	yes		yes	

226 A GUIDE TO ACCOUNTING SOFTWARE

		FINAX
13 Do all outputs show clearly the distinction between debits and credits?	yes	
14 Are all reports adequately titled?	yes	
15 Do reports provide totals where applicable?	yes	
16 Can report production be varied by:		
printing a range of accounts	yes	
printing by e.g. area/rep?	yes	
17 Is the period number shown on reports?	n/a	Date shown
18 Are all report pages sequentially numbered with the end of report identified	yes	
19 Is a sale analysis possible?	yes	
20 Can reports be temporarily retained on file for subsequent printing?	yes	
If 'YES' – are such files protected from deletion	no	Can be recreated – all data retained for year
21 Is a report generator available for use with the sales ledger module?	yes	
22 Can transaction files for previous periods be retained in the system to permit enquiries and reports?	yes	

Purchase Ledger

General

1 Are the programs menu-driven?	yes	
If 'YES' – can menus be by-passed once the user is familiar with the package?	yes	
2 Does the system maintain a log of usage?	no	
3 Are informative messages produced on-screen whilst running?	yes	
4 Are errors messages informative and easy to understand?	yes	
5 Is the system multi-company?	yes	Single- and multi-company versions
6 Is the original set-up straightforward?	yes	
7 Is there a copy/restore facility in the package?	no	
8 Does the system cover disciplined taking of back-ups?	no	

Documentation

(a) Manual

1 Is the manual clearly laid out and understandable?	yes	
2 Is the manual comprehensive and accurate?	yes	
3 Is there an index?	no	Cross-reference to menu on-screen
4 Is it easy to follow through all procedures?	yes	
5 Is it easy to locate specific points when required?	yes	See 3 above
6 Are completed examples included?	yes	

(b) Help screens

7 Are help screens available?	yes	
If 'YES' –		
Do they provide on-line instructions?	yes	
Can they be edited or prepared by the user?	no	In general no, but some can

Supplier Details

1 What is the format of the supplier account code?		Sequential – assigned by system, sort/access by name or part name.

MEDIUM-PRICE PACKAGES 227

MULTIFACTS		MULTISOFT		PEGASUS Senior	
yes		yes		yes	
yes		yes		yes	
yes		yes		yes	
yes		yes		yes	
yes		yes		no	Yes if using report generator
yes		yes		no	
yes		yes			Pages numbered, but last page not identified
yes		yes		yes	
yes		yes		yes	
yes		yes	From within Multisoft.	yes	From within Pegasus.
no		yes		yes	
no		yes		no	
yes		yes		yes	
no		yes	In Xenix/Unix	no	
no		yes		yes	Printout via utilities.
yes		yes		yes	
yes	Usually but not always	yes		yes	
yes		yes		yes	
yes		yes		yes	
yes		yes		no	Relies on DOS.
no		yes	Can be enforced.	no	
yes		yes		yes	
yes		yes		yes	
no		no	Good contents list.	no	Comprehensive contents list.
yes		yes		yes	
yes		yes		yes	
no		no		yes	
no		yes	Input prompts.	yes	Input prompts.
		yes		yes	
		no		no	
	6 alphanumeric		6 alphanumeric.		8-character, alphanumeric.

		FINAX
2 What other supplier details are held?		Name, address, salutation, credit limit, discount rate, etc., user defined fields
Do these seem to be sufficient in general?	yes	
3 What is the maximum number of accounts that can be held?		16,000
4 Can supplier details be added/deleted/amended at any time?	yes	
5 Is file re-sorted automatically when a new supplier is added?	yes	
If 'NO' – can a re-sort be initiated?		
6 Is deletion of a supplier prevented if account has:		
an outstanding balance?	yes	
a zero balance but a b/f turnover?	yes	Deletion possible if no invoices on file for supplier.
7 Is a hard copy of changes in supplier details automatically produced?	no	
If 'NO' – can a hard copy be taken?	yes	

Transactions

1 Can the system be open item?	yes	
2 Are the following inputs possible?		
invoices?	yes	
credit notes?	yes	
manual payments?	yes	
cash refunds?	yes	
discounts?	yes	
3 Can an invoice be analysed to several different expense categories?	yes	
4 Are different VAT codes possible for different items within one invoice?	yes	
5 Are all transactions retained on file for at least one period?	yes	
6 Can a ledger date pre-date existing transactions?	no	
7 Can two references be input for each invoice (own and supplier's reference)?		Extra space for user reference or additional narrative available.

Matching/Allocations
(a) Balance forward

1 Is the balance b/f aged?	N/A	System open item but statements can be produced in bal fwd format.
2 Can cash be allocated automatically?	N/A	
If 'YES' – how is the allocation made?	N/A	
– can this be over-ridden?	N/A	
3 Can cash be allocated manually?	N/A	
If 'YES' – does the package check that cash allocated = amount paid?	N/A	
How is any such difference treated?	N/A	
4 Can credit notes/journal entries be allocated to previous periods?	N/A	
5 Can cash in advance be held and later allocated to subsequent periods?	N/A	

MEDIUM PRICE PACKAGES 229

MULTIFACTS		MULTISOFT		PEGASUS Senior	
	Name, address, contact name, payment frequency, account type, default nominal code, stopped a/c (Y/N), settlement discount terms.		Name, address, short name, contact, category, payment method, bank code etc.		Name, address, short name, cheque payee name, tel. no., comment, credit limit, payment days, bank code, settlement discount, currency code.
yes		yes		yes	
	Unlimited.		Disk consideration.		65,000
yes	Except during transaction posting.	yes		yes	Except during transaction posting.
yes		N/A	Not necessary, indexation automatic.	no	
				yes	Done at period end.
yes		yes		yes	
no		yes		no	
no		no		no	
no		yes		yes	Using ledger enquiries.
yes		yes		yes	
yes		yes		yes	
yes		yes		yes	
yes		yes		yes	
yes		yes		yes	
yes		yes		yes	
yes		yes		yes	
yes		yes		yes	
yes		yes	Option for up to 12 months.	yes	
yes				yes	
no		yes		yes	System warning if this occurs.
no		yes	Ageing is by transaction dates.	yes	
yes		yes		yes	
	Oldest invoice first.		By due date/balance total.		Oldest outstanding balance.
yes		yes		yes	
yes		yes		yes	To specified period no.
yes		yes		no	
	Either discount or payment on account.		Partial payments/allocations.		
yes		yes		no	
no		yes		no	

	FINAX

(b) Open item

6 Are outstanding transactions displayed for allocation?	yes	
7 Can cash be allocated automatically?	yes	
If 'YES' – how is the allocation made?		Oldest invoice first.
– can this be over-ridden?	yes	
8 Can cash be allocated manually?	yes	
If 'YES' – does the package check that cash allocated = cash paid?	yes	
How is any difference treated?		User controlled.
9 Can an over/underpayment of an invoice be recorded?	yes	
10 How often are settled items deleted from file?		User controlled.
11 Can credit notes be set against the invoices to which they refer?	yes	Using cash routine.
12 Can journal entries be set against the invoices/credit notes to which they refer?	N/A	No journals.
13 Can cash in advance be held and later allocated to invoice?	yes	
14 Can cash be held unallocated?	yes	
– how is this treated?		As unallocated cash.

Input Controls

1 Is password control used?	yes	
If 'YES' – give detail		Passwords assigned to individual functions.
2 Is a hard copy automatically produced for all transactions input?	no	
3 Are batch totals automatically produced for all transactions input?	no	
If 'YES' – what is the procedure if this does not agree with a pre-list total?		
4 Is it necessary that invoices, cash and adjustments are input in separate batches?	no	
5 Are batches automatically sequentially numbered?	yes	
If 'NO' – can they be so numbered?		
6 Is a report produced at the end of each processing run to reconcile b/f total, transactions processed and c/f total?	no	
If 'NO' – is a control balance produced at the end of each posting run?	no	
7 Are the following validated:		
date	yes	
supplier account number	yes	
VAT code	yes	
goods value	no	
analysis code	yes	
8 Is VAT calculated to check figure input?		Calculated by system.
9 Is the gross figure agreed to goods+VAT?	yes	See above.

MEDIUM-PRICE PACKAGES 231

MULTIFACTS		MULTISOFT		PEGASUS Senior	
yes		yes		yes	
yes		yes		no	
	Oldest invoice first until remaining unallocated cash is less than next oldest invoice.		Automatic payment accounts.		
yes		yes			
yes		yes		yes	
yes		yes		yes	
	Either discount or payment on account.		Partial payments/allocations.		Puts into cash on account if less. Does not accept if more.
yes	Underpayment.	yes		yes	
no	Overpayment.				
	Month-end.		System option up to yearly.		At period end.
yes		yes	Mandatory.	yes	
yes		N/A	No journals.	yes	
yes		yes		yes	
yes		yes		yes	
	System reports unallocated cash as a unique transactions type.		Outstanding unallocated cash.		As posting to the ledger that may be allocated manually at a later date.
yes		yes	3 level security passwords and overall system.	yes	
	Linked menu options and access log on passwords.				4 levels of password control.
yes		yes		no	May be directed to spooler or screen.
no		yes		no	
			Either re-enter batch or record reason.		
yes		yes		no	
no		yes		no	
no					
no		yes		no	
no				no	
yes		yes		yes	
yes		yes		yes	
yes		yes	In range.	yes	
yes		no		yes	
yes		yes		yes	
yes		yes		yes	
yes		yes		yes	

		FINAX	
10	Is discount calculated to check the figure input?	no	
11	Can the actual date of posting, or batch reference, be shown on hard copies of transactions input?	yes	
12	Does the screen always indicate that the purchase ledger, as opposed to the sales ledger, is running?	yes	
13	Do all input screens show clearly:		
	type of entry	yes	
	the distinction between debits and credits	yes	
14	Is there any check that the same entry is not input twice?	no	
15	Is there a warning if a supplier is overpaid?	no	But it is apparent from screen.
16	Is it impossible for new accounts to be created during processing?	no	
17	Is a reconciliation of numbers of accounts produced after amendment of the customer detail file?	no	
18	Does the system prevent the abnormal termination of programs?	yes	

Integration

		FINAX	
1	Can the purchase ledger be integrated with a job-costing module?	no	Not at present.
2	Can the purchase ledger be integrated with a nominal ledger module?	yes	
3	Can the nominal ledger be updated as often as desired?		Updated at time of input.
4	Is a hard copy automatically produced at the end of each nominal ledger update?	N/A	
5	Is there a purchase ledger printout (as well as a nominal ledger printout) of the nominal ledger update?	N/A	
6	Are the following automatically posted to the appropriate nominal ledger accounts:		
	discount	yes	
	discount written back	no	Requires user intervention.
	contras with sales ledger	no	
7	Are any invalid/unidentified entries posted to a suspense account?	N/A	Validated on input.
	If 'NO' – how are they treated?		
	If 'YES' – how is the suspense account treated?		
8	Is the purchase ledger control balance agreed to the total of the balances in the purchase ledger?	no	
9	Can current and future periods be maintained simultaneously?	yes	
10	Is there a check that transactions cannot be posted twice to the nominal ledger?	N/A	
11	Must the nominal ledger be updated from the purchase ledger before the period-end is run?	N/A	

MEDIUM-PRICE PACKAGES 233

MULTIFACTS		MULTISOFT		PEGASUS Senior	
no		yes		yes	
yes		yes		no	Posting date and batch reference.
yes		yes		yes	
yes		yes		yes	
yes		yes		yes	
no		no		no	
no		no		yes	
yes		no		yes	
no		yes	If maint. report taken.	no	
yes		yes		yes	
yes		yes		yes	
yes		yes		yes	
no		yes		yes	
yes		yes		yes	
yes		yes		yes	
		yes		yes	
yes	Program permits all 3 types of adjustment – posting to any account in nominal ledger.	yes		no	To suspense and totalled separately.
yes		no		no	
no		yes	In nominal where auto-posting is expected but this would only occur if incorrectly set-up nominal ledger.	yes	
	All entries are validated against nominal ledger accounts at time of entry.				Cleared manually from various totals.
no		no	Cleared by journal.	no	
no		no		yes	
no		yes		yes	
yes		no	Transactions will not be lost.	yes	

234 A GUIDE TO ACCOUNTING SOFTWARE

		FINAX
12 Must the nominal ledger and the purchase ledger be in the same period for the update to be carried out?	N/A	
13 Is there any report/warning that transactions posted to the purchase ledger have not yet been posted to the nominal ledger?	N/A	

Output

		FINAX
1 Is it necessary to produce an audit trail before the period-end procedure is run?	no	No period end as such.
2 Does the audit trail enable all transactions to be traced fully through the system?	yes	
3 Can the actual run date, or batch reference, as well as current ledger date, be shown on reports?	yes	
4 Can the following be produced:		
list of master file information	yes	
aged creditors report	yes	
VAT report	yes	Automatic VAT report.
ledger detail report.	yes	User-defined report if printed, screen enquiry STD.
remittance advices	yes	
supplier name and address labels	yes	
suggested payments	no	
cheques	yes	With remittance advice.
5 Can remittance advices show:		
individual invoices	yes	
discount	no	
supplier's reference	yes	
6 Can the following screens be seen:		
supplier details	yes	
supplier transactions	yes	
7 Can hard copies of the following be obtained for individual accounts/selected ranges of accounts:		
supplier details	yes	
supplier transactions	yes	User-defined report.
8 Does the ledger account detail report show:		
the source of all postings	yes	
how part-payments and allocations have been treated	yes	
either the full account history or balance b/f together with the current period's transactions		Full account history.
9 Is ageing strictly by transaction date?	yes	
If 'NO' – how is ageing done?		
10 Does the aged analysis show unallocated cash separately?	yes	
If 'NO' – how is it aged?		

MEDIUM-PRICE PACKAGES

MULTIFACTS		MULTISOFT		PEGASUS Senior	
yes		no		yes	Over-ride with caution.
yes		no	Not necessary.	yes	
yes		no	Depends on transaction retention option taken.	no	Warning is given to do this.
yes		yes		yes	
yes		yes			Yes – batch reference run date. No to separate dates.
yes		yes		yes	
yes		yes		yes	
yes		yes		yes	
yes		yes		yes	
yes		yes		yes	
yes		no		yes	
yes		yes		yes	
yes		yes	+Giro+BACS+Auto Pay+Block Clearing House Payments.	yes	
yes		yes		yes	
yes		yes		yes	
yes		yes		yes	
yes		yes		yes	
yes		yes		yes	
yes		yes		yes	
yes		yes		yes	
yes		yes		yes	
no		yes		yes	
yes		yes		yes	
no		yes		no	Optional either by date or aged one period at period end.
	Can be either transaction date or due date.				
no		yes		yes	
	According to date of transaction.				

236 A GUIDE TO ACCOUNTING SOFTWARE

		FINAX	
11	Do all outputs show clearly the distinction between debits and credits?	yes	
12	Are all reports adequately titled?	yes	
13	Do reports provide totals where applicable?	yes	
14	Can report production be varied by:		
	printing a range of accounts	yes	
	printing by, e.g., area	yes	
15	Is the period number shown on reports?	no	Period date.
16	Are all report pages sequentially numbered with the end of report identified?	yes	
17	Is a purchase analysis possible?	yes	
18	Can reports be temporarily retained on file for subsequent printing?	yes	All data available until year end.
	If 'YES' – are such files protected from deletion?	no	But see above.
19	Is a report generator available for use with the purchase ledger module?	yes	
20	Can transaction files for previous periods be retained in the sytem to permit enquiries and reports?	yes	

Payments/Cheque Writing

1	Can the system write cheques?	yes	Not a standard option.
	If 'YES' – is the payment posted automatically to the purchase ledger?	yes	
2	Is there an automatic cheque writing facility? If 'YES':	no	
	is a list of suggested payments printed in advance of the cheques?		
	is the total cash requirement printed in advance of the cheques?		
	can the automatic payment routine be aborted if either of the above is not satisfactory?		
3	Can the following payment/report options be selected:		
	individual invoice selection	yes	
	supplier section	yes	Each account brought up in turn for individual selection.
	pay all invoices of a certain age	yes	
	pay according to due date	no	
	pay all invoices except those marked not to be paid	no	
	other (specify)		
4	Is discount automatically calculated by the payment routine?	no	Unallocated amount suggested as discount.
5	Can invoices be held as disputed?	no	
	If 'YES' – can a report of disputed invoices be produced?		

MEDIUM-PRICE PACKAGES 237

MULTIFACTS		MULTISOFT		PEGASUS Senior	
yes		yes		yes	
yes		yes		yes	
yes		yes		yes	
yes		yes		yes	
yes		yes		yes	Using analysis.
yes		yes		no	
yes		yes			Pages are numbered but end of report not identified.
yes		yes		yes	
yes		yes		yes	
yes		yes	From within Multisoft.	yes	From within Pegasus.
no		yes		yes	
no		yes	Up to 12 months.	yes	
yes		yes		yes	
yes		yes	From cash input.	yes	
yes		yes		yes	
yes		yes		yes	
yes		no	But see reports.	yes	Total on suggested payments list.
yes		no	Not mid-processing.	yes	
yes		yes		yes	Using invoice numbers not very satisfactory.
yes		yes		yes	
yes		yes		yes	
yes		yes		yes	
no	Supplier type payment frequency.	yes		yes	
yes		yes	and on input of invoice.	yes	
no		yes		yes	
		yes		yes	

High-price Packages

Reviews	**240**
Features Rating Table	**253**
Package Information Table	**254**
Evaluation Checklists:	
General Points	**256**
Performance of Requisite Accounting Functions	256
Reliability – Security and Continuity of Processing	258
Support and Maintenance	258
Ease of Use	260
(a) Interactive Processing	260
(b) User Documentation	260
Efficiency	260
Flexibility	262
(a) Integration Facilities	262
(b) Reporting Flexibility	262
(c) Parameter or Table Facilities	262
Software Installation and Training	264
(a) Financial Resources	264
(b) Other Resources	264
(c) Involvement of Software Supplier	264
(d) Involvement of User Personnel	264
Package Software Acquisition	264
Preliminary Questions Relating to Software Supplier	264
Nominal Ledger	**266**
General	266
Documentation	266
(a) Manual	266
(b) Help Screens	268
Account Details	268

Transactions	268
Input Controls	270
Integration	272
Output	272
(a) General	272
(b) Trial Balance; P&L and Balance Sheet	274
Year End	276

Sales Ledger   278

General	278
Documentation	278
(a) Manual	278
(b) Help screens	278
Customer Details	278
Transactions	280
Matching/Allocations	280
(a) Balance Forward	280
(b) Open Item	280
Input Controls	282
Integration	284
Output	286

Purchase Ledger   288

General	288
Documentation	290
(a) Manual	290
(b) Help screens	290
Supplier Details	290
Transactions	292
Matching/Allocations	292
(a) Balance Forward	292
(b) Open Item	292
Input Controls	294
Integration	296
Output	296
Payments/Cheque Writing	300

240 A GUIDE TO ACCOUNTING SOFTWARE

Review of OMICRON PowerSystems

Overall impressions
Omicron PowerSystems are thoroughly professional but lacking in artistic impression – a rough diamond. A review of the three ledgers (sales, purchases and nominal) discloses a flexible and versatile system with a particular strength in its ability to allocate income and expenditure to complex cost centre structures.

Installation
The manual contains no instructions on how to load the software or configure the system. A file is provided on disk which, if listed, provides this information. Obviously a job for the aficionado rather than the average user. The local supplier is, of course, expected to set up the system and train user staff.

Leaping into the system to set up the various parameter files is an exasperating experience. The old adage that if you want to set up a flexible package you have to know how to exercise the flexibility applies here. However, if you follow the manual, blow by blow, reading up the detail of each option on the installation menus, the options become clear even if the decisions on how you wish to exercise them become more difficult.

Useful options were:

(1) The nominal ledger account code and cost centre can be defined up to a maximum of seven characters each, provided that the aggregate does not exceed eight.

(2) Fourteen posting documents can be defined and allocated user defined names that mean something to the operator. The order in which data is called for can be defined for each document as can the suppression of unused fields.

(3) A hierarchical structure of cost centres for income and expenditure can be set up to a maximum of 10 levels – you need a complex structure indeed to stretch that. The set up is easily accomplished by starting at the company level and defining each centre and how it relates to the ones further up the structure.

Day-to-day processing
The main menus are user definable and, as mentioned above, so are the individual posting elements, so the friendliness of the system is to a great extent in the user's hands.

The screen handling I found irritating in that you have to 'go round the block' to amend any field which has been miskeyed. Most packages allow the *up cursor* to go backwards to enable the amendment of previous fields within a document during the keying process. With this package you have to wait until you have keyed all the fields and then select by line number the one you wish to amend. This all looks old fashioned. Omicron say that experienced operators prefer to deal with prompts and supply data at the same position on the screen for all items. Certainly the automatic repetition of the data from the previous posting, unless changed before hitting the carriage return, makes for very quick entry of similar items with the same narrative, to, for example, different cost centres.

The concept of keying a document and leaving it unbalanced if necessary is a very useful facility in a busy accounts office. This means that you can store a half keyed document on the machine and pick it up later without having to balance it or post it. Naturally there are safeguards which remind you of the existence of the incomplete document and posting is, of course, not possible until the balance is achieved. The usual facilities are available for automatically reversing month-end accruals and for formats of regularly used documents.

Reporting

The choice of preset reports is fairly ordinary but the report generator allows the user to set up a report much as he chooses. Getting the report generator to work I found somewhat daunting on first sight but when the report came out roughly as I planned it on the first attempt, I decided it was easier than it looked. Comparisons with previous year-end budgets are easily achieved and a nice touch is the two versions of budget, namely *original* and *revised*, which can be supported by the system.

There was one aspect to the pre-set reports which I found helpful and this was the ability to produce a cost centre income and expenditure statement automatically for nominated cost centres. The format may not be wonderful but as a document on which to base a monthly financial commentary, it would be most useful.

Integration with word processing is available in the report generator but the Power Link facility not only allows data to be supplied to a spreadsheet but also allows budgets to be loaded in the reverse direction.

Security

There are the usual two levels of password – one for the operator and one for the administrator who can change parameter files. On the multi-user versions there is also a log of who has used the system. Omicron tell me that they have enhanced these facilities in the most recent shipments.

I found it impossible to unbalance the ledgers and powering down in the middle of a posting resulted in a complete denial of access on power up. Resort to the back-up is then essential.

The program suite contains no back-up or restore utilities and though reminders are issued to take security copies before major updates, the discipline of backing-up has to be done direct through the operating system.

The validation of data at input is generally good except for one glaring omission which Omicron tell me has been rectified in the latest version. In the sales and purchase ledgers there is no validation of the nominal account and cost centre codes. The double entry for invalid codes is achieved by dumping entries to a suspense account for manual correction.

Manual and user documentation
The manual is clear and easy to use for following through a set of procedures but it is poorly indexed and consequently not easy to use as a reference document.

There are no *help* screens. The errors messages are, in my view, too brief and jargon based and merely report the invalidity rather than give advice on how to remedy the situation. For example, in my view, an error message 'ACCOUNT CODE INVALID LENGTH' should read 'ACCOUNT CODE MUST BE 4 CHARACTERS'.

Support
According to Omicron, of the 3,000 or so users in the UK, only about 150 are in Scotland and support in Scotland is through three dealers in Glasgow and two in Dundee. Omicron policy is to charge about 15% of the purchase price each year for a support and enhancement contract. This gives the user the latest updates of software together with telephone support. Training is advised and dealers have been instructed in how to provide this.

Hardware and costs
The package will run on MS-DOS or UNIX and each system can support 999 separate ledgers if disk space allows. The minimum sensible configuration on an IBM-PC compatible is 256K and 10Mb of disk storage.

Costs, I thought, are at the upper end of the scale for single user ranging from £900 for a single currency sales ledger to £1,250 for the multi-currency version. The single user nominal ledger is £900. The multi-user equivalents are about £1,500 per module.

Review of SMB Plus (Version 3.5)

The SMB accounting system is a fairly typical example of a recent phenomenon in the computerised accounting market – powerful multi-user programs which have traditionally been developed and supplied on mini computer systems, being brought down to cater for an additional demand in the micro marketplace. Such software is able to take advantage of the new found speed and dramatically increased data storage capabilities of the new breed of micros.

SMB is comparatively expensive in this arena however (£795 per module for a PC-DOS version), and potential users at this end of the market are likely to be part of a larger operation running the software as corporate policy or be needy of some of the more powerful features available. Generally the software is targetted at larger operations, with typically up to 10 screens running simultaneously. The company sees Distribution-type organisations as a strong market area for their product.

The system consists of a suite of 13 modules – strangely, weekly and monthly payroll are separate modules – covering the full range of accounting and management reporting needs although the average user will find between 4 and 6 modules meet the majority of his requirements. As noted above, the software has its origins in the minicomputer marketplace and operates over a range of operating systems from DOS, CP/M and networks at the lower end through XENIX and UNIX and up to the IBM System 36 range of minis. I tested the basic ledgers on a Compaq Portable III with a hard disk under DOS and found it acceptably fast and easy to use.

Detailed and heavily cross referenced manuals are supplied for all modules, and these include clear step by step guides on setting up the ledgers. The ease of setting up such powerful software is a major feature of the system and I was not surprised to be told by the suppliers that most users require only 1 or 2 days operational instruction before setting about their own implementation. My only criticism would be the lack of friendliness of the system once the user is halfway through completing a screen of information. There is no easy method of aborting from a screen, rather the screen of information must be completed and then amended at a final 'Accept Y/N?' prompt.

The password security system in the package is as powerful as one would expect in the multi-user environment. There are master passwords for the system as well as the ability to provide users with log-on names which permit access only to certain modules. This is applied on an exception basis i.e. access to routines which should typically be protected, such as payroll, is granted only to specified users. There are no in-built back up and recovery routines, this being dependent on the relevant hardware and operating system combination.

Nominal ledger
The nominal ledger system incorporates a powerful management reporting system which serves to complement rather than replace the standard reporting procedures. Much thought must be given to the coding structure of the nominal, as a choice of 7 standard coding schemes are provided in the standard package.

No alpha characters are allowed, but a maximum of 10 digits spread over up to 4 sub categories is available with the categories being used to determine department and expense type. A useful feature is the ability to replicate the final coding structure and nominal ledger over as many companies as are being run, with full consolidation facilities also provided. Budgeting routines, covering budgets and forecasts for this and next year, are comprehensive and include the facility to set up a number of standard *spreading* factors.

Either 12 or 13 accounting periods are permitted, and the user can decide to retain up to 12 months of detailed information. As information is passed from subsidiary ledgers in detail this option should be used with care where disk space is at a premium. Helpfully, the user can determine the cleardown frequency of nominal accounts as monthly, quarterly or yearly. Journal entry input includes automatically reversing accruals and prepayments as well as the ability to incorporate standing journals. Audit trails are generated during input but can be spooled for later printing, and the full audit trails for the system are extremely comprehensive.

The major standard report in the nominal is the detailed trial balance which the user can print from a set of 6 options each of which produce detailed variances. The set up of profit and loss and balance sheet reporting is left to the user custom building his own from the report generator section of the nominal.

Links to the nominal ledger are available from the usual payroll and sales and purchase ledgers as well as from the fixed assets and stock modules.

Purchase ledger

The ease of set up of the system continues in the purchase ledger. Supplier account codes can be from 4 to 8 digits with any mix of alpha and numeric characters, and a combination of open-item and balance forward accounts is acceptable. Individual payment terms for suppliers can be determined by the user calculating on a number of days or months after the invoice date, or even a particular date in the following month.

For each transaction posted, both the supplier's reference and an internal reference can be held and space is available to apply a short narrative against each posting line. This information is retained against the transaction when the details are passed to the appropriate nominal account. A feature of these postings which many users of traditional PC based accounting software would appreciate is the immediate update of both the supplier's account and the nominal account once the input line has been completed. Thus, at all times the nominal is completely up to date. However, on occasions this can be a mixed blessing since there is no opportunity to review a batch of invoice postings for obvious errors before passing them through to the nominal ledger. Thus, strict *ad hoc* review of nominal reports is necessary to ensure that mispostings are kept to a minimum.

A feature worthy of mention is the invoice authorisation routine which permits the recording of an invoice awaiting authorisation, provides reporting facilities on such invoices and will allow posting to take place automatically once the appropriate authorisation has been received.

The system has a high level of functionality in the automatic payments routines, necessary in a typical company environment where the purchase ledger may stretch to several thousand accounts. As well a producing cheques and bank giros as one might expect, the system is also capable of producing a BACS file for processing supplier payments through the central Banks Automated Clearing Service. This latter feature is one which some suppliers of accounting software seek to sell as a module in its own right.

Reporting facilities are strong including the feature of retaining a 99 period supplier history, and ageing of supplier accounts over 6 periods.

In addition to the nominal ledger link, the system provides an automatic link to the SMB job/contract costing and will interface with the purchase order processing module.

Sales ledger

Typically, the sales ledger mirrors the operation of the purchase ledger and is as comprehensive a system as I have seen.

An area of particular note is the emphasis placed on reporting the credit status of customer accounts to monitor potential bad debt situations. The user can quickly produce reports showing only those accounts where balances exceed a pre-determined value, age exceeds a particular number of months, credit limit is exceeded by a minimum value or where cash has not been received since a set date.

The system is also strong in its treatment of foreign currency accounts, an important consideration for larger companies selling into a number of foreign markets (up to 1,296 different currencies are allowed!) In addition, retentions can be applied to invoices, thereby allowing the user to set a separate due date for part of the invoice and report this accurately when checking on overdue transactions.

Automatic links are available to the order entry and invoicing modules as well as to the nominal and job/contract costing systems.

Distribution and support

The majority of sales of SMB software are made through the dealer network, some also coming direct from Datasolve, a subsidiary of the giant Thorn EMI organisation. Generally support is provided direct from the supplier. Prices range from £795 for the single user product up to £2,500 for the System 36 version inclusive of the, albeit limited, training assistance. Support is provided at an annual charge per module of between £175 and £300.

Conclusion

The SMB suite of programs is certainly comprehensive and proved to be robust during my testing procedures. It is clearly aimed at the multi-user market place with features such as BACS, multicurrency and consolidations and budgetting clearly designed to appeal in such environments. At all levels links are also available to external packages such as spreadsheets and databases and this combined with the report generator module serves to enhance its appeal.

Review of TETRAPLAN

In the age of the Amstrad, Tetraplan may seem quite expensive (two modules cost the same as a hard disk Amstrad 1512). It is, however, a proper accounting package rather than a computerised back-of-an-envelope system and, in my opinion, you get what you pay for with Tetraplan.

It is available on a wide range of machines and has modules covering practically every aspect of a normal business. The modules on offer are:

- Nominal ledger
- Sales ledger
- Purchase ledger
- Order entry
- Invoicing/sales analysis
- Purchase order processing
- Stock control
- Job costing
- Payroll/SSP
- Bill of materials
- Fixed assets
- Report writer
- Cash book
- BACS
- SMP (Statutory Maternity Pay)

If a particular aspect of your business is not covered by any of these, or you need to analyse the output further, then links are available to wordprocessing, database and spreadsheet packages.

At the lowest level, this takes the form of merely producing a file that can be read into another package such as Lotus 1–2–3. At a higher level the UNIX/XENIX version has the same file structure as many other packages such as the Informix database package. This means that any custom-made application created by the user or a supplier can treat Tetraplan files as if they were its own. I would not recommend that novices should create their own sales order procesing systems, but it does open up possibilities.

Nominal ledger

Nominal ledger codes can be up to 16 alphanumeric characters in length. They can be divided up into a maximum of five sections (each split takes up one character). Reports can be produced using the five levels in any order as sort keys. This is how Tetraplan handles departments and cost centres.

Multiple companies can be catered for by using the first digit as a company code. Individual company reporting is performed by specifying that only accounts beginning with A, for example, are to be reported. The system will check that journals relate to only one company or that sales and purchase invoices are posted to the correct company. Alternatively, another user licence can be purchased and the companies kept completely separate.

Tetraplan will allow up to 13 periods in a year and lets the user specify when the period ends occur. Transactions, which may be up to £999,999,999.99, are retained for the full year.

A variety of journal types are available: opening balance, reversing and recurring are all catered for, and they can be posted to current, future and prior periods.

A report writer facility is provided as part of the nominal ledger package, and reports showing actual against budget, variance and percentage variance can be produced.

Sales and purchase ledgers

If you deal with some of your suppliers and customers in foreign currency then you can set up accounts for them in that currency. Foreign currency invoices and cash can then be posted to the account. Any exchange difference is worked out and posted to the appropriate nominal ledger account automatically.

Alpha search is available in both modules (so that you can find the account even if you have forgotten the number). Due dates are calculated automatically by the system from the terms of trade given to customers and suppliers, but they can be over-ridden. Credit limits can be set on sales ledger accounts, although the operator is only told when they are breached if the Order Entry or Invoicing module is being used.

In the purchase ledger, invoices can be flagged as *Do not pay*. This can be used either for disputed invoices or for all invoices until they have been authorised.

Reliability and security

Security on micros is essentially no different from that on larger systems. The problem with most microcomputer installations is the fact that the machine is usually accessible to the users, who may know the operating system sufficiently well to get around any controls in the programs – i.e., segregation of duties is unenforceable.

That said, Tetraplan has very good controls indeed. Individual menus and programs can be password protected or even removed from a user's list of options. The system keeps a log of all activity, and audit trails are mandatory, but like all reports they are spooled to disk. On the one hand, this speeds up processing because the computer does not have to wait for the slow printer, but, on the other, the reports can be deleted without being printed.

Backing up data to floppy disk or tape streamer is automated in the UNIX version of the package, which requires only that the back-up option is selected from the System Manager's menu. The DOS version merely reminds you that you should back up your data when you exit Tetraplan.

Ease of use and documentation

Setting up the system to work the way you want (*configuration*) is relatively easy. Each module has a number of switches covering each option available. These are set when the module is installed. They can be changed at any time, but are best left alone by the inexperienced user. To avoid wading through the manual for a one-off exercise, however, it might be better to get your supplier or consultant to set them for you.

Each module is consistent in the way it asks for data and is readily understandable by the novice user. One thing I personally find confusing is all the different operations that can be performed with the function keys. Their use is, however, explained on a permanently displayed menu on the bottom of the screen.

There is a manual for each module containing an overview of its functions, how to set it up and how it interacts with the other modules. Each process is then explained in detail with examples.

Support

Tetraplan is distributed by a large number of dealers and resellers throughout the UK, of which 22 are based in Edinburgh, Glasgow, Aberdeen and Dundee.

Conclusion

Tetraplan offers a comprehensive accounting system which covers the areas most businesses need. The software is available on a wide variety of machines so that as your business grows you probably will not need to buy a new system (you will probably need to buy Tetraplan again though!)

There are a few annoying details about the system, such as no separate picking list in the Stock Control module, but on the whole the package is flexible, high in functionality, and has a large number of users.

Hardware and costs

Tetraplan is available in single-user (MS-DOS), networked (MS-DOS) and muilti-user (XENIX and UNIX) versions. The single-user version requires a hard disk PC with 512K.

Costs start at £490 a module for the single-user system, rising to £1,790 a module for the 32-user licence version.

Review of SunAccount

The majority of computerised accounting systems, while differing considerably in the facilities which they offer, tend to follow a familiar pattern as regards structure and presentation. The authors of SunAccount either were not familiar with this pattern or made a conscious decision to design the system in a quite different and original way.

The first and most obvious difference is the fact that there are no separate sales and purchase ledgers. Debtor and creditor accounts are simply included in the nominal ledger and, with certain exceptions, can be treated in exactly the same way as all other nominal ledger accounts. This concept may not be difficult for any accountant to grasp, but it is nevertheless a considerable break from tradition.

The second most striking difference is that there is no simple series of menus and sub-menus to guide the user easily through the system. However, on-line help screens are available to help to guide the user.

The system is very flexible. Standard input and output layouts can be loaded and modified to suit all but the larger and more specialised enterprises. Layouts for these systems can be designed from scratch.

SunAccount itself consists basically of the nominal ledger, sales ledger and purchase ledger applications, offering full multi-currency and multi-company features.

SunAccount's companion module, SunBusiness, offers Invoicing, Inventory Control and Sales Order Processing, and integrates fully with SunAccount.

The SunSystems suite of programs is therefore somewhat less comprehensive than that of most of its rivals. Its ability to link with other packages, however, is one of its strengths, and a number of 30-party packages, such as Bonus! and the Damanpay payroll package, are able to integrate with SunAccount. In addition, the software provides a very easy-to-use transfer facility to enable links to many other popular packages such as Wordstar, Supercalc, Lotus and dBase.

There is also a report generator module SunWriter, available with current releases of the software. However, given that the capability to set up and tailor reports is already built into the software, many users may find this module an unnecessary luxury.

The software's tremendous flexibility becomes apparent when setting up a company on a system. Each company installed is held on a separate database, with a virtually unlimited number of companies possible. Up to 99 accounting periods can be defined, thereby allowing the user to choose any one of the standard options – 4, 12, 13 or 52. All periods can be open for posting at any time, although it is possible to limit postings to only the current period as a means of preventing accidental postings to the wrong period. Account codes can be up to ten characters in length and either numeric or alphanumeric. Grouping of accounts for subtotalling on the trial balance can be based on either the first or the first two digits. The ledgers can set up for departmental and cost centre accounting, using up to five transaction codes. Further codings allow for a considerable amount of analysis within the ledgers.

The input screens can be set up to minimise the amount of keying required. Reversing journals, for period-end accruals, and recurring journals for standing orders are both available.

The budget facilities available are as comprehensive as I have seen from a micro-accounting package. Reports can be set up for this period, this quarter or the year-to-date, comparing actual with budget and with prior periods giving variances, percentage variances and certain ratios. Various forecast figures, based on either actual or budget figures, are also available.

All accounts on the system can be set up as either open item or balance forward. Cash can be posted *on account* as well as to specified invoices, and the ability to part-pay invoices is catered for. Purchase ledger payments can be made based on due dates or by selection of individual invoices. Where selection is based on due dates, it is possible to flag disputed invoices or to suspend individual accounts to prevent payment. The system can cater for two separate sets of payment days and discount percentages for each account. The printing of cheques, remittance advices and statements is supported and a BACS link will be included in version 3 of the software.

Aged debtor and creditor reports are, of course, available and can be significantly tailored to specific users' requirements. Sales invoices, for example, can be aged based on either transaction date or due date. The system holds a credit limit for each debtor and those who go over the limit are flagged as such on the aged debtors report.

Reliability and security
As with most micro accounting packages, audit controls built into the software are not particularly strong, although most of the tools necessary to enable a security conscious user to set up a well controlled environment do exist.

A full transactions audit trail exists through the Journal Listing function and an option at the system set up stage can be set to force the printing of the journal listing immediately after transaction entry. If this is not set it remains up to the user to decide when to print journals. No automatic trail exists, however, of alterations to standing data, though access to standing data files can be password protected.

Reports can be spooled to disk. Once this has been done, the system does not check to ensure that the report has actually been printed so that any spooled report could be deleted within the operating system without being printed. All transaction entries are, however, sequentially numbered so that a simple sequence check could detect any journal not printed.

The multi-user version of the software has a reasonably powerful password facility, using operator identification with up to eleven access levels. The operators can also have personal passwords. The single-user version also now has password facilities as standard.

A back-up and restore function is built into the software. The procedure is well documented in the manual and is very simple to operate. It cannot be used to back-up onto tape cartridges, and users with tape back-up will need to use commands within the operating system to back-up data.

One minor irritation with the software arises at the year end. Although the system successfully clears all profit and loss accounts to zero, it is unable to post the resultant profit or loss to the balance sheet, and a two line journal entry has to be posted in order to do this.

Ease of use and documentation

SunAccount definitely falls into the 'not easy to set up but very powerful' category of software. Once set up, however, it is not difficult to use and contains a number of features designed to make data entry as painless as possible.

The manual is not very well laid out and not particularly easy to follow. A more detailed list of contents at the start of each section would make it easier to follow, although all the necessary information is certainly contained somewhere in the manual. However, it is rather short on useful examples of the various ways in which functions can be set up and the benefits to be derived from the various options.

One laudable feature of the software is that it is being continually updated. This has led to further problems with documentation, however, since notes describing the updates have not been immediately integrated into the manual, but appear as a series of notes in a separate section. However, a new manual incorporating all amendments has now been released.

Support

SunAccount is distributed through a dealer network. There are at present only two Scottish dealers, both based in Edinburgh.

Conclusion

SunAccount is an innovative piece of software which can compete with any other *sophisticated* micro accounting packages in terms of functionality. The difficulty of set up and the lack of local support are likely to deter many potential users in Scotland, and I would say that this is not a suitable package for the first time user who has fairly simple requirements from a computerised accounting system. I would hope, however, that more experienced users who are very clear about their precise requirements would consider using SunAccount. Its flexibility may well mean that it will be able to meet more of their requirements than any other package.

Hardware and costs

The package is available in both single- and multi-user form, with versions available for most of the standard micro operating systems (e.g. MS-DOS, C-DOS, UNIX, XENIX) as well as for a number of minicomputers.

For the single user the minimum memory required under MS-DOS on an IBM compatible PC is 256Kb, although 512Kb is recommended. The SunAccount manual suggests that the system can run on a twin-floppy machine, but that 'this requires some ingenuity, and is not recommended', with which I can only concur.

Finally, costs. The single user, single currency system costs £1,850 and the multicurrency system costs £2,775. The multi-user versions cost £2,950 and £4,425 respectively.

Features Rating Table

Package	OMICRON	SMB PLUS	SUNACCOUNT	TETRAPLAN
	Rating (out of 10)			
Ease of set-up	6	8	5	7
Documentation	6	8	6	7
Performance of accounting functions	9	7	8	8
Ease of use	8	7	7	8
Reporting	8	7	8	7
Security	8	7	7	8
Support (Scotland)	4	5	4	7
Value for money	4	5	8	8
TOTAL (out of 80)	53	54	53	60

Package Information Table

Product Name	OMICRON PowerSystems
Version Number	2.10.
Date of test	January 1988.
Modules Available	Nominal ledger, sales ledger, purchase ledger, foreign currency sales and purchase ledgers, stock control, payroll, purchase order, sales order processing and invoicing, sales analysis, job costing, assets register, financial modelling, report writers, BACS, powerlink.
Cost per Module	Single user – from £900 to £1250, multi-user – from £1500.
Publisher	Omicron Management Software Ltd 51 Holland Street Kensington London W8 7JB Tel: 01-938 2244.
Supplier	As publisher.
What support is available	Direct and dealer based.
Operating system	PC, MS-DOS, UNIX, CDOS, CP/M.
Hardware	Most micros or networks, supporting above operating systems.
Network/multi-user version available	Yes.
Hardware used for tests	Compaq.
Number of UK users	3,000.
First operational	1981.
Report generator available?	Yes.
Links to other packages	Yes, via powerlink.

SMB PLUS	SUNACCOUNT	TETRAPLAN
3.5.	2.4.4.	B4.3.
January 1988.	August 1987.	November 1987.
Sales and purchase ledgers, nominal and reporting, payroll (weekly), payroll (monthly), fixed assets, job/contract costing, invoicing and sales analysis, order entry, stock, purchase order processing, report generator and qPlex IV (for some operating systems only).	SunAccount: Integrated nominal, sales and purchase ledgers. SunBusiness: invoicing, inventory control, sales order processing.	Nominal, sales and purchase ledgers, order entry, invoicing/sales analysis, purchase order processing, stock control, job costing, payroll/SSP, bill of materials, fixed assets, report writer, cash book, BACS and SMP (statutory maternity pay).
Single-user – £850, multi-user from £995 to £2750 for System 36, (subject to finalisation).	System integrated sales, purchases and nominal – £1850 single currency, £2775 multi-currency, (single user).	Single-user – £490, multi-user – from £690 for up to four users to £1790 for 32 licence version.
SMB Business Software Datasolve Ltd Datasolve House 99 Staines Road West Sunbury on Thames Middlesex TW16 7AH. Tel: 0932 785566.	Systems Union Ltd Northampton Lodge Canonbury Square London N1 2AN. Tel: 01-354 3131.	Tetra Business Systems Foundation House Norreys Drive Maidenhead SLX 5BX Tel: 0628 770939.
As publisher. Installation, training, support and bespoke from Datasolve.	As publisher. Telephone hotline, consultancy and courses.	As publisher. Telephone and on site support.
DOS, CPM/86, C-DOS, C-CPM, UNIX, XENIX, SSP, Compact, Regular.	MS-DOS, CP/M, Concurrent DOS, UNIX and VAX.	MS-DOS, XENIX and UNIX.
IBM compatibles and IBM system 36.	All hardware supporting above operating systems.	Hardware supporting above operating systems.
Yes.	Yes.	Yes.
Compaq portable II.	Compaq Deskpro 286 and Epson.	Compaq 286 portable with 640K RAM and 20Mb Hard disk.
1,200	850.	3,000.
1976.	1983.	1979.
Yes.	Yes.	Yes.
Yes, CSV and ASCII output to Lotus, dBase, etc.	Yes.	Yes.

Evaluation Checklists

General Points

		OMICRON	
Performance of Requisite Accounting Functions			
1	Does the software perform the functions which the user wants performed?		
2	Can the software be used by more than one user at the same time?	yes	Normal access rule for networks apply.
3	Can the software support groups of companies/departments/branches?	yes	
	How many such branches or companies can be supported?		999 separate ledgers may be set up. Cost centres may be set up for each branch for income and expenditure analysis. Aggregation possible.
	Can they be consolidated?	no	Aggregation possible via financial modelling system.
4	Is multi-currency processing available?	yes	Special system required.
	What are the maximum number of currencies available?		2 per ledger.
	Is conversion to sterling automatic?	yes	
5	Are sufficient accounting periods provided by the system?		Only 12 or 13 periods nominal ledger allowed. 53 for sales ledger.
	Can these periods be adjusted to suit different user requirements?	yes	Dates of periods may be adjusted by user.
6	Are the ends of accounting periods determined by the user rather than being set by the system?	yes	System sets dates automatically but user may adjust.
7	Can data from all accounting periods be assessed at any given moment?	yes	
	Can previous months be accessed for enquiries or reports?	yes	
8	Does the system prevent posting to more than one accounting period at a time?	no	Historical periods may be re-opened for posting.
	Is it impossible to allocate transactions to future periods or to previous closed months?	no	
9	Does the system permit use of budgets and provide comparisons between budgets and actuals?	yes	Two budget fields available ('original' and revised) for each account but standard reports make little use of these. Reports have to be devised by report generator.
10	Is the maximum value of transactions that can be handled by the system sufficient?		11 integers, 2 decimal places.
11	Is the maximum number of accounts on each ledger (e.g. sales ledger, purchase ledger, nominal ledger) sufficient?	yes	
12	Is the size and format of account numbers adequate and sufficient for analysis purposes?	yes	Format determined by user up to 8 characters for nominal a/c code up to 7. Cost centre up to 7 provided 8 limit not exceeded in aggregate a/c code numeric. Cost centre alpha.
13	Does the associated hardware incorporate enough memory, disk storage and other peripherals for the software to operate satisfactorily?		

	SMB PLUS		SUNACCOUNT		TETRAPLAN
yes		yes		yes	On a network of Xenix system.
yes		yes		yes	
	100 companies. 100 departments per company.		Realistically, limited only by disk space.		Unlimited.
yes		yes		no	But can aggregate using report writer in the nominal ledger.
yes		yes		yes	
	1,296.		Limited only by 5-character code up to 99 currencies within one account.		Unlimited.
yes		yes		yes	
yes	Nominal ledger 12 or 13.		Up to 99.		Up to 13.
no	Unless by bespoke.	yes		yes	User-definable dates.
no	But can decide when to run month ends.	yes	Each period is numbered PP/YY. This is changed manually at the end of each period by entering ledger definition.	yes	
yes		yes		yes	
yes	Up to 99 months history.	yes		yes	
yes		yes	This option is available within ledger definition.	yes	
	Future – no. Previous – yes.	no	Both are available but can be prevented.		To previous – yes. To future – no.
yes	This year, next year budget and forecast.	yes	Password control.	yes	
yes	11 digits then decimal point. 99,999,999,999.99.	yes		yes	
yes		yes		yes	No limits.
yes	Sales ledger and purchase ledger – 12 character alphanumeric. Nominal ledger – 10 digits.	yes	Up to 10 characters.	yes	S/L P/L – 8 characters. N/L – 16 characters.

		OMICRON

14 Does the system offer adequate expansion potential as regards terminals, memory, disk storage capacity and other peripherals?

15 Are the control features provided by the software adequate to support effective user controls?

16 Are complementary clerical procedures to be imposed and effectively monitored by management?

Reliability – Security and Continuity of Processing

1	Does the system facilitate back-up storage?	no	Prompts are issued but DOS back-up has to be used.
	How much time will complete back-up of the system require?		Depends on date and hardware.
2	Does the system facilitate recovery procedures in the event of system failure?	no	DOS restore required.
3	If system failure occurs part way through a batch or transaction, will the operator have to re-input only the batch or transaction being input at the time of the failure?	no	User is required to restore from last back-up.
4	Are there any features provided with the software to help track down processing problems?	no	
5	Are back-up procedures provided within each specific software application or within the operating system?	no	Operating system.
	Are any of these back-up procedures automatic?	no	

Support and Maintenance

1	Will the supplier provide corrections to the program?	yes	Maintenance at 15% of purchase price per year.
2	Will the supplier provide general enhancements to the program?	yes	Maintenance contract required @ 15% of purchase price per year.
	Will these be provided automatically?	yes	
	Will they be given free of charge?	no	
3	Will the software supplier provide 'hot-line' support to assist with immediate problem solving?		
	If so, at what cost?		
4	Is the supplier capable of giving sufficient ongoing education and training and other support?		
5	Can the supplier provide all the hardware, software and maintenance requirements of the user?		
6	Can the supplier provide support in the user's locality?		
7	Is a warranty offered in respect of specification and performance of the system?		
8	Would there be adequate back-up in the event of hardware or software failure?		
9	Will the software supplier make the program source code available to the user, either directly or by deposit with a third party?		
10	If the software is acquired under licence, are there any unduly restrictive conditions in the licence?	no	

The term 'supplier' refers to the supplier of the support and mainteanance, whether or not this is the same as the supplier of the software.

HIGH-PRICE PACKAGES

	SMB PLUS		SUNACCOUNT		TETRAPLAN
	Upgrade costs in line with difference in price. No program or data conversion.				
no		yes	Back-up function on systems menu.	no	Not part of accounting suite.
	Determined by the data size and hardware and system configuration.		Depends on date and hardware.		Dependent on hardware and volume of data.
no		yes		yes	Depends on back-up procedure.
no	If file updating, then requires restore.	yes		no	All transactions since time of input must be re-entered.
no	But see nominal ledger audit options.	yes	Error messages on screen.	yes	System log.
no	Operating system.	yes		no	Operating system.
no		no		no	Can be if running Xenix.
yes	Free of charge corrections.	yes		yes	
yes	To support contract holders.	yes		yes	
yes		no	On request.	no	
no		no	Yes – if maintenance contract.	no	Yes – if customer has a maintenance contract.
yes	Direct from Datasolve.			yes	
yes	Various categories of hot line support at various prices.				Price on application.
	Determined by locality.				
yes	By arrangement.	yes	National computing centre. ESCROW.	yes	
no				no	

OMICRON

Ease of Use
(a) Interactive processing

1. Does the software run under an operating system, which is a commonly accepted standard? — yes — MS-DOS and UNIX.
2. Is the software available concurrently to more than one user? — yes — By network.
3. Can more than one system function be performed concurrenly? — yes
4. Does the software effectively lead the user through the data entry procedures? — yes

    Does the software facilitate immediate error correction? — yes — A/c code and cost centre checked items may not be posted unbalanced.
5. Is the software menu-driven? — yes

    Are such menus restricted by password and application? — yes
6. Are the user screens adequately titled? — yes — But some prompts are poor (e.g. '?' prompts password).
7. Does the system inform the operator which programs or files are being loaded? — no
8. Does the software facilitate file maintenance, back-up and archive copying? — no — Operating system.

(b) User documentation

1. Is the manual clearly laid out and understandable? — yes
2. Is the manual comprehensive and accurate? — yes
3. Is there an index to the manual? — yes — Quality of index is poor.
4. Is it easy to locate specific topics in the manual when required? — yes — For major steps but poor indexing for items of detail.
5. Is it easy to follow through all procedures in the manual? — yes
6. Are completed examples included in the manual? — yes
7. Are help screens available? — no — Some help is provided by prompts at each stage.

    Do they provide detailed on-line instructions on how to use particular features of the software?

    Can they be edited or prepared by the user?
8. Does the documentation clearly specify the actions to be taken by users at each important stage of processing? — yes
9. Will the software supplier provide regular updates of documentation in the event of modifications or revisions? — yes — On payment of maintenance fee.
10. Will the software supplier make the detailed program documentation available to the user, either directly or by deposit with a third party? — yes — Deposit with NCC.

Efficiency

1. Are the various functions of the system menu-driven, or otherwise easy to initiate? — yes

    Is there a good response time in the initiation of functions? — Reasonable.
2. Is data entry easily repeated if similar to previous entry? — yes — Good facilities for repeat a/c no. and text.

HIGH-PRICE PACKAGES

	SMB PLUS		SUNACCOUNT		TETRAPLAN
yes	Several.	yes	MS-DOS, UNIX, XENIX.	yes	DOS, XENIX.
yes		yes		yes	
yes		yes		yes	
yes		yes	Although data entry screens have to be defined initially by the user.	yes	
no	Cumbersome, but necessary to keep portability, considering improvement.	yes	There is an amend option on all relevant screens.	yes	
yes		yes		yes	
yes	By user, and modules.	no		yes	
yes		yes		yes	
yes		yes		yes	
no	Hardware and operating system dependent.	yes		no	
yes		no	Some duplication of information.	yes	
yes		yes	Includes a separate section for update information.	yes	
yes	Re-written in last 18 months.	yes	Several.	no	
yes		no	Particularly with regard to software changes.	yes	
yes		yes		yes	
yes		yes	Sample output report included.	yes	
no	Considering for next version.	yes	Now available as standard.	no	
		yes			
		no			
yes		yes		yes	
yes	Section of updated features.	yes	The manual contains a section of updates.	yes	
yes	By arrangement.	yes		yes	
yes		yes		yes	
yes	Hardware dependent.	yes		yes	
no	e.g. no repeat of narrative on journals.	yes	A repeat key can be used.	no	

	OMICRON	

3 Is there a good response time

    (i) in processing data input? — yes

    (ii) in producing requisite reports? — yes

    (iii) in updating files? — yes

    (iv) in producing back-up files? — N/A

    (v) in deleting redundant information files? — yes

4 Does the system prevent access to a record while it is being updated? — yes

5 Does the system retain a log of file updates until the next occasion on which the relevant information is reported or the relevant file used in a regular control procedure? — no — Available in multi-user system.

6 Can regular reports be esily duplicated if required? — yes

Flexibility
(a) Integration facilities

1 Are the different accounting applications integrated? — yes

    Are they integrated on an item by item basis or are they integrated by weekly or monthly end routines? — Month end or periodic routines at user's choice.

2 Whichever method is used, can the ledger updating process be satisfactorily controlled? — yes

3 Does the software run under an operating system which is a commonly-accepted standard? — yes — MS-DOS or UNIX.

4 Can more than one system function be performed concurrently? — yes

5 Can software be linked to other packages, e.g. word processing, graphics, financial modelling, to provide alternative display and reporting facilities? — yes — By report generator or powerlink utility.

(b) Reporting Flexibility

1 Can the user easily design additional output reports or displays? — yes — Powerful report generator.

2 Is a report generator provided as part of the software or as an option associated with it? — yes — Part of software.

3 Can screen layouts, reports and transaction formats be easily adapted to users' requirements? — yes — Suppression of input not required and order of input determined by user.

4 Does the output of the software facilitate proper control to ensure that decisions are not inadvertently taken on the basis of incorrect information? — yes

(c) Parameter or table facilities

1 If the system uses a lot of standing information which changes frequently or regularly, does the system allow for such changes to be effected through the use of parameters or tables? — yes

2 If so, is the use of such parameters or tables adequately reported? — yes

HIGH-PRICE PACKAGES

SMB PLUS		SUNACCOUNT		TETRAPLAN	
yes		yes	With small data files response times were good. With larger files I would expect production of reports to be more time consuming.	yes	
yes	Hardware dependent.	yes		yes	
yes		yes		yes	
N/A		yes		yes	
yes		yes		yes	
yes		yes		no	
no		no		yes	
yes		yes		yes	
yes	Including payroll to nominal ledger and stock to nominal ledger.	yes	All sales and purchase ledger accounts are included in the nominal ledger.	yes	
	Item by item.		Item by item.		Either – user defined.
yes	But batch 'suspend' facility could have been useful, though on-line update precludes this.	yes		yes	
yes	Several.	yes		yes	
yes		yes		yes	
yes	DOS – Lotus. Xenix – Uniplex. Sys 36 – Query.	yes		yes	
yes	Complex report requires complex learning.	yes			Yes – Reports. No – Displays.
yes		yes	Optional additional module.		A separate report writer module is available.
no	Only by bespoke.	yes	A certain amount of adaption is possible.	no	
yes	Determined by quality of management reports.	yes		yes	
yes	Description files. Tax and NIC tables.	yes		yes	
yes		yes		yes	

	OMICRON
3 Is proper control to be exercised over changes to such parameters to tables?	yes
If so, how? (e.g. through the use of system facilities such as passwords or by inspection of appropriate records)	Passwords.

Software Installation and Training
(a) Financial resources
1 Has account been taken in the budget for system development/acquisition of the full costs of

    initial acquisition?

    initial training?

    future training?

(b) Other resources
2 Is the main equipment to be located in adequate accommodation?

Is this such that staff are not seriously affected by the equipment (e.g. by noise from the printer).

3 Is there sufficient scope for the installation, if required, of communications equipment?

4 Have requisite consumables (e.g. special stationery, filing facilities, fireproof storage) been provided for?

(c) Involvement of software supplier
5 Is the supplier capable of giving sufficient initial education and training and other support?

6 Are potential users permitted to test the software for a trial period before commitment to acquire it?

7 If required, does the supplier have sufficient capable personnel to assist users to convert to the new system?

8 If required, will the supplier provide machine time to enable users to set up files of input data before installation?

(d) Involvement of user personnel
9 Who is to be responsible for running and controlling the system on a regular basis?

Is this person sufficiently competent?

10 Who is to be responsible for the installation and implementation of the system?

Is this person sufficiently competent?

11 Which staff will operate the system?

Do they have sufficient aptitude for computers?

12 Is there adequate cover for staff in the event of illness and holidays?

Package Software Acquisition
Preliminary questions relating to software supplier
1 Does the supplier have a good overall reputation as regards experience and reliability?

2 Does the supplier offer a full range of accounting software?

3 Is the supplier's financial status stable?

Does the supplier demonstrate an adequate capital base, growth and profitability?

SMB PLUS	SUNACCOUNT	TETRAPLAN
yes	yes	yes
Passwords for master file maintenance changes in sales, purchase ledgers, plus payroll.	Passwords.	Controlled by system manager through separate module (t.o.c.)
		Training is supplied with each module, additional training is available on request.
	yes Sale or return.	

	OMICRON

4 Does the supplier have sufficient technical resources to modify or tailor software to suit different users' requirements?

5 Does the supplier have a substantial user base?

Has it shown adequate commitment to existing users and will it provide a list of them?

Has the supplier sold similar systems to that under consideration?

6 Does the supplier offer adequate contractual terms as regards purchase, installation, delivery, support and maintenance?

Are all costs clearly indicated?

Is the date of delivery of all components of the system clearly stated?

7 Is there adequate evidence that the supplier normally meets its contractual obligations?

8 Will the supplier provide in-depth demonstratrions of its software?

Nominal Ledger

General

1 Are the programs menu-driven?	yes	
If 'YES' – can menus be by-passed once the user is familiar with the package?	no	Menus are configurable and do not materially slow down process.
2 Does the system maintain a log of usage?	no	Not on single-user – available on multi-user.
3 Are informative messages produced on-screen whilst running?	yes	Reasonable.
4 Are error messages informative and easy to understand?	yes	
5 Is the system multi-company?	yes	Up to 999.
6 Is the original set-up straightforward?	yes	But long winded due to many options.
7 Is there a copy/restore facility in the package?	no	
8 Does the system cover disciplined taking of back-ups?	no	Prompts for back-ups given.

Documentation
(a) Manual

1 Is the manual clearly laid out and understandable?	yes	
2 Is the manual comprehensive and accurate?	yes	
3 Is there an index?	yes	Quality of index is poor.
4 Is it easy to follow through all procedures?	yes	For major items but poor indexing for items of detail.

HIGH-PRICE PACKAGES

SMB PLUS		SUNACCOUNT		TETRAPLAN	
yes		yes	The system has one main menu listing all the functions of SunAccount. All functions can be accessed from any screen in the system without having to return to the main menu.	yes	
yes	Invoke program by name from any menu.	yes		yes	Menus can be customised.
no		no		yes	
yes		yes		yes	
yes		yes	With more detailed explanation in the manual.	yes	
yes		yes		yes	
yes		no	There is considerable user input necessary in setting up the system.	yes	Dealer experience helpful in the initial stages.
no		yes		no	
no		yes	An option on the system maintenance menu, handled within the system and fully explained in the manual.	no	
yes		no	The same information appears to be duplicated in various parts of the manual.	yes	
yes		yes	Including details of changes caused by all updates to the software – held in a separate section.	yes	
yes		yes	Several.	no	The section pages correspond to display menu options.
yes		no	Particularly with regard to software changes. Updates to manual are not integrated into the original manual.	yes	

		OMICRON
5 Is it easy to locate specific points when required?	yes	
6 Are completed examples included?	yes	

(b) Help screens
7 Are help screens available?	no	

If 'YES' –

Do they provide on-line instructions?
Can they be edited or prepared by the user?

Account Details

1 Is the chart of accounts flexible?	yes	
2 What is the format of the nominal account code?		Must not exceed 8 characters in total. A/c nos. 1–7 characters numeric. Cost centre 1–7 characters alpha.
3 Is cost centre accounting available?	yes	Good hierarchical structure available.
4 What is the maximum number of accounts that can be held?		9,999,999.
5 What is the maximum balance that can be held?		99,999,999,999.99.
6 Can accounts be added/deleted/amended at any time?	no	Added via appropriate menu option.
7 Is file automatically re-sorted when a new account is added?	N/A	Indexed.

If 'NO' – can a re-sort be initiated?

8 Is deletion of an account prevented if it has:–		
a non-zero balance	yes	
a zero balance but postings in the current period	yes	
a zero balance but postings in the year-to-date?	yes	
9 Is a hard copy of changes in account details automatically produced?	no	
10 Are 12 or 13 (or more) accounting periods available?	yes	Only 12 or 13.
11 Can budgets be entered for all revenue accounts?	yes	'Original' and 'revised' budget figures available concurrently.
12 Can separate budgets be entered for each accounting period?	yes	
13 Can this year's results be used to calculate next year's budgets automatically?	yes	

Transactions

1 What is the maximum transaction value that can be entered?		11+2 decimal.
2 Can each journal entry contain an unlimited number of debits and credits?	yes	High enough for all practical puposes.
3 Is each input line numbered?	yes	
4 In a long journal entry is it possible to move between screens to view data already input?	yes	
5 Can previously entered journal lines be edited before accepting the whole journal?	yes	Journals can be held unbalanced but not posted.
6 Does each journal entry have a reference number?	yes	
7 Are accruals and pre-payments routines, which both reverse automatically at the start of the next accounting period available?	yes	

	SMB PLUS		SUNACCOUNT		TETRAPLAN	
yes			yes		yes	
yes			yes	A number of sample output reports are included.	yes	Including sample output.
no			yes		no	On-line instructions available on input screens.
			yes			
			no			
yes			yes	Use of transaction codes enables considerable flexibility of reporting.	yes	
	User defined, up to 4 levels of analysis within up to 10 digits.			Maximum 10 characters, containing alphabetic characters, numeric characters or symbols.		16 characters with up to 5 user definable sections.
yes	Included in above coding scheme.		yes		yes	
no	No theoretical limit – hardware dependent.			Realistically, limited only by disk space.		Unlimited.
	99,999,999,999.99.			17 digits, of which up to 3 can be decimal.		±9,999,999,999.99.
yes			yes		yes	
yes			N/A	Because of the database structure, new accounts always appear in the correct place on reports.	N/A	Not necessary held in sort order.
yes			yes		yes	
yes			yes		no	
yes			yes		no	
no			no	Available but not automatic.	no	
yes	12 or 13. No other option.		yes	UP to 99 accounting periods can be defined.	yes	13 maximum, dates are user definable.
yes			yes	The budget database mirrors the actual database.	yes	
yes			yes		yes	
no			no	A transaction spread option assists the entry of budget figures. In addition, prior year figures are available for all reports in any case.	yes	
	99,999,999,999.99.			15 digits – of which up to 3 can be decimals.		±99,999,999.99.
no	Up to 99.		yes		no	Maximum of 30 journal lines.
yes			yes		no	
yes	But awkward.		yes	By using N = next, B = back, F = first, L = last options at the foot of the screen.	yes	
yes			yes		yes	
yes			yes		yes	
yes			yes		yes	

A GUIDE TO ACCOUNTING SOFTWARE

		OMICRON
8 Can recurring journal entries be provided for automatically?	yes	
9 Is a narrative available for:		
each journal entry	yes	
each line of the journal entry?	yes	
10 Can journal entries be posted to future periods?	yes	
11 Can journal entries be posted to previous periods?	yes	
12 Are all transactions retained on file for at least one period?	yes	
13 Can transactions be retained at the period-end?	yes	
14 Can a ledger date pre-date existing transactions?	yes	

Input Controls

1 Is password control used?	yes	
If 'YES' – give detail		6-digit password. 1 level for user and different password for administrator.
2 Is a hard copy automatically produced for all input?	no	
3 Are journal entries automatically sequentially numbered?	no	
4 If integrated, are automatic postings from other modules included in the numbering sequence?	N/A	
5 If accruals and pre-payments automatically reverse, is the reversal included in the numbering sequence?	N/A	
6 Are the totals, of debit or credit entries, produced for all journal entries?	yes	Totals are produced but agreement can be over-ridden.
If 'YES' – is it necessary that this agrees with a pre-list total?		Totals are produced but agreement can be over-ridden.
7 Is it necessary that all journal entries balance before posting?	yes	Can be stored incomplete unbalanced before posting.
8 Is production of an out-of-balance trial balance prevented?	yes	
9 Do all input screens show clearly:		
type of entry	yes	
the distinction between debits and credits	yes	Dr and Cr used.
10 Can the actual date of posting, or a batch reference, be shown on hard copies of transactions input?	yes	
11 Are the following validated:		
date	yes	
nominal ledger account code	yes	
cost centre code	yes	
If 'NO' – are unidentified/invalid entries posted to a suspense account?	N/A	
– how is suspense account treated?		

HIGH-PRICE PACKAGESS 271

SMB PLUS		SUNACCOUNT		TETRAPLAN	
yes	Diarised.	no	However, journal definitions can be set up for every transaction type, with preset codes, debit/credit, and linking line values.	yes	
no		yes		yes	But field not very large – manual records to back-up journal entry recommended.
yes	But would help if this defaulted to previous line narrative.	yes		yes	
yes		yes		yes	
no		yes		yes	If a parameter flag is set to allow this.
yes		yes		yes	
yes		yes	All accounts can be set as either open item or balance forward.	yes	
yes	i.e. posting date, as user specifies period into which posting.	yes		yes	
yes		yes		yes	
	1. Overall entry password. 2. Specific menu options can be accessed only by authorised users.		3 levels of password available. Multi-user systems up to 10 levels.		Each menu option can be password controlled.
yes	Account transaction only and can be spooled.	no	Can be set up to print all input either immediately or at month end. May be spooled.	no	Period-end processing cannot continue unless audit trails have been printed.
no		yes		yes	Optionally.
N/A		yes		no	Source data numbering follows through.
N/A	Reversals use same journal number at original posting.	yes		no	
	Running total.	yes		yes	
no		no		no	
yes		yes		yes	
yes		yes		yes	
yes		yes		yes	
yes		yes		yes	Separate columns on screen.
yes		yes	Date of posting and journal reference.	yes	
yes		yes		yes	
yes		yes		yes	
yes		yes		yes	Part of account code.
N/A		N/A		N/A	

272   A GUIDE TO ACCOUNTING SOFTWARE

		OMICRON	
12	Is a total produced of all debit/credit transactions processed?	yes	
	If 'YES' – is a report produced at the end of each processing run to reconcile b/f total, transactions processed and c/f total?	yes	Control reports produced at the end of posting run.
13	Is a reconciliation of numbers of accounts produced after amendment of the accounts detail file?	no	
14	Does the system prevent the abnormal termination of programs?	no	But system will lock out when user attempts to return. Back-up will have to be loaded.

Integration

1	Is integration possible with the following:–		
	sales ledger	yes	
	purchase ledger	yes	
	payroll	yes	
2	Can the nominal ledger be updated as often as desired?	yes	
3	Is a hard copy automatically produced at the end of each nominal ledger update?	yes	
4	Is there a sales/purchase ledger printout of the nominal ledger update?	no	
5	Are sales ledger and purchase ledger control accounts agreed to the totals of balances in the individual ledgers?	no	
6	Is there a check that the nominal ledger cannot be updated twice with the same sales/purchase data?	yes	
7	Must the nominal ledger be updated from the sales and purchase ledgers before the period-end is run?	no	Before period-end of sales and purchase ledgers.
8	Must the nominal ledger be in the same period as the sales and purchases ledgers for the update to be carried out?	no	Postings will be matched to period by ledgers.
9	Is there any check that all data processed in the sales/purchase ledgers has been posted to the nominal ledger?	no	
10	Are unidentified/invalid entries held in a nominal ledger suspense account?	yes	
	If 'YES' – how is this treated?		Placed on suspense and have to be manually adjusted.
11	Can the user select whether to update the nominal ledger with individual sales/purchases ledger entries or in total?	no	
	If 'NO' – is the update made in detail or in total?		In total.
12	Is it impossible to post directly to the sales/purchase ledger control accounts?	no	

Output
(a) General

1	Is it necessary to produce an audit trail before the period-end procedure is run?	no	All postings may be retained indefinitely.
2	Does the audit tail enable all transactions to be traced fully through the system?	yes	All postings may be retained indefinitely.

HIGH-PRICE PACKAGES

SMB PLUS		SUNACCOUNT		TETRAPLAN	
yes	Printed during input.	no	Part of journal reconciliation.	yes	
no		N/A		yes	
no		no		no	
yes		yes		yes	
yes	Also links to stock and fixed assets.	yes	All sales ledger and purchase ledger accounts are included in the nominal ledger. There is no separate sales or purchase sub-ledger. There is no payroll module with the package, but there are third-party payroll packages which can be integrated.	yes	
yes		yes		yes	
yes		yes		yes	
yes	Updates are on-line (real time) from sales ledger, purchase ledger.	yes		yes	
yes	During update for sales ledger and purchase ledger.	N/A		no	
yes	During update for sales ledger and purchase ledger.	N/A		yes	
no	No evident check of this.	N/A		no	Not automatically.
yes	One update during input.	N/A		yes	
yes	Updated during sales or purchase ledger input.	N/A		no	
no		N/A		no	
yes	By virtue of immediate update.	N/A		yes	
no	Not required, all validation carried out during input, then posted to nominal ledger. Only adjustments go to suspense o/cs in nominal.	N/A	Yes – if using batch entry procedure.	no	
			Posted to error suspense account and cleared manually.		
no		N/A		yes	
no	Detail.				
no		N/A	No control account in conventional sense since sales ledger is part of nominal ledger.	no	
yes		no	A warning appears on the screen, but printing of the audit trail is not enforced.	yes	
yes		yes		yes	

	OMICRON	
3 Can the actual run date, or batch reference, as well as the current ledger date, be shown on all reports?	yes	
4 Can the following be seen on screen:		
account details	yes	
account transactions	yes	
5 Can a printout of the following be obtained for individual accounts/selected ranges of accounts:		
accounts details	yes	
account transactions	yes	
6 Do all outputs show clearly the distinction between debit and credit entries?	yes	Using Dr and Cr.
7 Are all reports adequately titled?	yes	
8 Do reports provide totals where applicable?	yes	
9 Is the period number shown on reports?	yes	
10 Can the following be produced:		User may design reports as he wishes. These responses apply to standard reports.
trial balance	yes	
ledger account detail report	yes	
profit and loss account	yes	
balance sheet	yes	
11 Does the ledger account detail report show the source of postings and narrative input?	yes	
12 Does the ledger account detail report show either the full account history or balance b/f together with the current period's transactions?	yes	
13 Are all report pages numbered sequentially, with the end of report identified?	yes	
14 Can reports be temporarily retained on file for subsequent printing?	no	Can be done but not easily.
If 'YES' – are such files protected from deletion?	no	
15 Is a report generator available for use with the nominal ledger module?	yes	
16 Can transaction files for all previous periods be retained in the system to permit enquiries and reports?	yes	
(b) Trial Balance; P&L and Balance Sheet		
1 Does the package provide for flexible formatting of profit and loss account and balance sheet?	yes	

HIGH-PRICE PACKAGES 275

	SMB PLUS		SUNACCOUNT		TETRAPLAN
yes		yes	All reports show run date and ledger date or period where appropriate.	yes	
yes		yes		yes	
yes		yes		yes	
yes		yes		yes	
yes		yes		yes	
yes		yes	Either in separate headed columns, or, if only one column, C or D beside amount.	yes	
yes		yes		yes	
yes		yes		yes	
yes		yes		yes	
yes		yes		yes	
yes		yes		yes	
yes	Generated using the nominal report generator.	yes		yes	Using report writer.
yes	Generated using the nominal report generator.	yes		yes	Using report writer.
yes		yes		yes	
yes		yes	Every account can be set up as either open item or balance forward.	yes	Year-to-date transactions or current period transactions may be displayed.
yes	But, no specific 'end of report' message.	yes	'End of report' appears at the foot of all reports.	yes	
yes		yes		yes	
no	But difficult to delete other than deliberately within operating system.	no		no	
yes		yes		yes	Part of nominal ledger module.
yes		yes	Period cleardown is not essential at the month end or year end.	yes	
yes		yes		yes	

A GUIDE TO ACCOUNTING SOFTWARE

		OMICRON	
2	Can the following be produced for both the current period and the year-to-date:		
	trial balance	yes	
	profit and loss account	yes	
	balance sheet	yes	
	If 'YES' – is it clearly shown whether a report is for the current period or year-to-date?	yes	
3	Can the following show budgets:		
	trial balance	yes	Report generator must be used.
	profit and loss account	yes	
	If 'YES' – can budgets be omitted if wished?	yes	
4	Can the following reports show comparative figures:		
	trial balance	yes	
	profit and loss account	yes	
	balance sheet	yes	
	If 'YES' – can comparatives be omitted?	yes	
	– can two years' comparatives be shown?	no	
5	Are budgets worked out from the period number as calculated by the number of period-end procedures run?	yes	If required.
6	Are budget variances calculated?		
	If 'YES' are they shown as:		
	value	yes	Report generator must be used.
	percentages	yes	
	both	yes	
7	Do budget reports provide for exception reporting?		Not easily.
8	Does the package provide for a trial balance to be produced for each cost centre?	no	Cost centre cannot be used in balance sheet.
9	Does the package provide for a profit and loss account and balance sheet for each cost centre?	yes	
10	Does the package provide for totalling of like items across cost centres?	yes	
11	Can trial balance production be varied by:		
	printing a range of accounts	yes	
	subtotalling on any chosen digit of account code?	N/A	
12	Can vertical percentages be calculated in the profit and loss account?	yes	Using report generator.
13	Can a report be produced to show the breakdown of profit and loss account and balance sheet figures?	yes	Account contact can be printed.

Year End

1	Can balance sheet items be carried forward and profit and loss account items be cleared automatically at the year-end?	yes	

HIGH-PRICE PACKAGES 277

	SMB PLUS	SUNACCOUNT		TETRAPLAN	
yes	Both on same report.	yes		yes	
yes	User generated.	yes		yes	
yes	User generated.	yes		yes	
yes		yes	Own headings can also be specified.	yes	
yes		yes		no	
yes	Report generator.	yes		yes	
	No – Trial Balance. Yes – Others.	yes		yes	
no		yes		yes	
yes	Report generator.	yes		yes	
yes	Report generator.	yes		yes	
yes	Report generator.	yes		no	
no		no		no	
yes		yes		yes	By period indicator.
		yes		yes	
yes	Report generator.	yes		yes	
yes	Report generator.	yes		yes	
yes	Report generator.	yes		yes	
no	no	yes			Can be done using report writer.
yes		yes		yes	User can determine order used when requesting prints.
yes	Report generator.	yes		yes	
yes	Report generator.	yes		yes	
no	But similar reports can be produced via report generator.	yes		yes	
no		no	Only on first or first two or first three digits.	no	
yes	Report generator.	yes		yes	Using inbuilt report generator.
yes	Could create detailed and summary versions of each.	yes		yes	
yes	Balance sheet a/cs balance become opening balance for next year.	yes		yes	

		OMICRON
2 Can the destination of individual account balances be specified or are all balances cleared at the year-end transferred into one account only?	no	One account only.

Sales Ledger

General

1 Are the programs menu-driven?	yes	
If 'YES' – can menus be by-passed once the user is familiar with the package?	no	
2 Does the system maintain a log of usage?	no	Yes for multi-user.
3 Are informative messages produced on-screen whilst running?	yes	
4 Are error messages informative and easy to understand?	yes	Reasonable.
5 Is the system multi-company?	yes	999 companies.
6 Is the original set-up straightforward?	yes	Essential to read manual.
7 Is there a copy/restore facility in the package?	no	
8 Does the system cover disciplined taking of back-ups?	yes	Prompts back-up before major updates.

Documentation
(c) Manual

1 Is the manual clearly laid out and understandable?	yes	
2 Is the manual comprehensive and accurate?	yes	
3 Is there an index?	yes	Quality of index poor.
4 Is it easy to follow through all procedures?	yes	
5 Is it easy to locate specific points when required?	yes	For major items but poor indexing for items of detail.
6 Are completed examples included?	yes	

(b) Help screens

7 Are help screens available?	no	
If 'YES':		
Do they provide on-line instructions?		
Can they be edited or prepared by the user?		

Customer Details

1 What is the format of the customer account code?		4 digit numeric.
2 What other customer details are held?		Name/Address/Postcode/Phone/ Discount terms. (No contact name). New version – 12 user options.
Do these seem to be sufficient in general?	yes	
3 What is the maximum number of accounts that can be held?		9999.
4 Can customer details be added/deleted/amended at any time?	no	Via appropriate menu only.
5 Is file re-sorted automatically when a new customer is added?	N/A	Indexed files.
If 'NO' – can a re-sort be initiated?		

HIGH-PRICE PACKAGES

	SMB PLUS		SUNACCOUNT		TETRAPLAN
	Net profit and loss total transferred to profit and loss account.		A manual entry has to be made to post profit to retained earnings.		A journal must be raised to distribute the profit manually.
yes		yes		yes	
yes	Invoke progam by name from any menu.	yes		yes	
no		no		yes	
yes		yes		yes	
yes		yes		yes	
yes		yes		yes	
yes		no		yes	Dealer experience helpful.
no		yes		no	
no		yes		no	
yes		no		yes	
yes		yes		yes	
yes		yes		no	The section pages correspond to display menu options.
yes		no		yes	
yes		no		yes	
yes		yes		yes	Including sample output.
no		yes			Instructions included in input screens.
		yes			
		no			
	4–8 digits, alphanumeric.		Maximum 10 characters, containing alphabetic characters, numeric characters or symbols.		8 characters (alphanumeric) must be unique entry.
	Usual details plus: Credit stop, settlement discount, 6 ageing periods, last invoice, last receipt, sales – year-to-date, costs – last year, this year		Up to 5 user defined analysis categories, look-up code, credit limit, due date days, address, telephone number, contact name.		Name, address, alpha sort code, 6 analysis codes, an 8 character alternate code to access an account – non-unique entry.
yes		yes		yes	The alternative code could be longer. Its use could be improved.
	No practical limit, data storage dependent.		Realistically, limited only by disk space.		Unlimited.
yes		yes		yes	Unless open balance is on the account (deletion).
yes		N/A	Indexed files (database).	N/A	Not necessary held in sort order.

280 A GUIDE TO ACCOUNTING SOFTWARE

	OMICRON	
6 Is deletion of a customer prevented if the account has:		
an outstanding balance	yes	
a zero balance but a b/f turnover	yes	Deleted at year end if flagged.
7 Is a hard copy of changes in customer details automatically produced?	no	
If 'NO' – can a hard copy be taken?	yes	

Transactions

1 Can the system be open item?	yes	
2 Are the following inputs possible:		
invoices	yes	
credit notes	yes	
cash received	yes	
cash refunded	yes	Can be individually defined.
discounts	yes	
journal entries	yes	
write-offs	yes	
3 Can an invoice be analysed to several different sales categories?	yes	
4 Are different VAT codes possible for different items within one invoice?	yes	
5 Are all transactions retained on file for at least one period?	yes	
6 Can a ledger date pre-date existing transactions?	yes	

Matching/Allocations
(a) Balance forward

1 Is the balance b/f aged?	no	
2 Can cash be allocated automatically?	N/A	
If 'YES' – how is the allocation made?		
– can this be over-ridden?		
3 Can cash be allocated manually?	N/A	
If 'YES' – does the package check that cash allocated = amount received?		
How is any such difference treated?		
4 Can credit notes/journal entries be allocated to previous periods?	N/A	
5 Can cash in advance be held and later allocated to subsequent periods?	N/A	
6 Can cash be held unallocated?	N/A	

(b) Open item

7 Are outstanding transactions displayed for allocation?	yes	

HIGH-PRICE PACKAGES

SMB PLUS		SUNACCOUNT		TETRAPLAN	
yes		yes		yes	
yes		yes		no	
no		no		no	
yes		yes		yes	
yes		yes		yes	Or balance forward – all accounts must be open item or balance forward.
yes		yes		yes	
yes		yes		yes	
yes		yes		yes	
yes	As received but sign changed.	yes		yes	
yes		yes	Using user defined entry screens.	yes	
yes	Between accounts.	yes		yes	
yes	But only as 'adjust', and must process appropriate journal in nominal ledger out of suspense.	yes		yes	Using journal entries.
yes		yes		yes	Up to 10 including VAT.
yes	Separate invoice posting routine for these.	yes		yes	
yes		yes		yes	Until a clear closed items command is issued.
yes		yes		yes	
yes	By period.	yes		yes	
no		yes		yes	But manual intervention required.
			Oldest first.		Oldest first.
yes		yes		yes	
yes		yes		yes	
yes		yes		yes	
	Process as unallocated cash.	yes	Difference not permitted.		Routine cannot be completed.
yes		yes		yes	
yes		yes		yes	
yes		yes		yes	
yes		yes		yes	

282 A GUIDE TO ACCOUNTING SOFTWARE

		OMICRON
8 Can cash be allocated automatically?	yes	
If 'YES' – how is the allocation made?		Using range option within an account to allocate over a range of transactions – end of day routine allocates automatically if transaction net zero.
– can this be over-ridden?	yes	
9 Can cash be allocated manually?	yes	
If 'YES' – does the package check that cash allocated = cash received?	yes	
How is any difference treated?		Unallocated or written off as discount.
10 Can an over/underpayment of an invoice be recorded?	yes	
11 How often are settled items deleted from file?		Monthly if required.
12 Can credit notes be set against the invoices to which they refer?	yes	
13 Can journal entries be set against the invoices/credit notes to which they refer?	yes	
14 Can cash in advance be held and later allocated to invoice?	yes	
15 Can cash be held unallocated?	yes	
– how is this treated		Unallocated cash.

Input Controls

1 Is password control used?	yes	
If 'YES' – give details		6 characters, 2 levels. 1 for user, 1 for administration.
2 Is a hard copy automatically produced for all input?	no	
3 Are batch totals automatically produced for all transactions input?	yes	
If 'YES' – what is the procedure if this does not agree with a pre-list total?		Reports differences, warning but may be over-ridden.
4 Is it necessary that invoices, cash and adjustments are input in separate batches?	yes	
5 Are batches automatically sequentially numbered?	no	
If 'NO' – can they be so numbered?	yes	Not automatically.
6 Is a report produced at the end of each processing run to reconcile b/f total, transactions processed and c/f total?	yes	
If 'NO' – is a control balance produced at the end of each posting run?		

HIGH-PRICE PACKAGES

	SMB PLUS		SUNACCOUNT		TETRAPLAN
yes		yes		yes	
	Oldest first.		On a range of transaction dates, accounting periods or transaction references.		Oldest first.
yes		yes		yes	
yes		yes		yes	
yes		yes		yes	
	Process as unallocated.		Not permitted.		Routine cannot be completed.
yes		yes		yes	Under-payment leaves balance due. Over-payment left as unallocated.
	Monthly – cleared to 'history' file.		Whenever a period cleardown is performed.		When required.
yes		yes		yes	
yes		yes		yes	
yes		yes	Cash is posted first against a debtor account, and allocated to invoices using a separate entry screen.	yes	
yes		yes		yes	
	Routine available for subsequent allocation. Aged by date of entry. Reports specific to unallocated cash are available.		Unallocated credit.		Current-period unallocated debit.
yes		yes		yes	
	1. Overall log-on. 2. Specific users only permitted to use protected routines.		3 levels single-user, up to 10 levels muti-user.		Each menu option can be password protected.
yes	All transactions only – can be spooled.	no	Can be set up to print immediately after input.	no	Period-end processing cannot continue unless the audit trail has been printed.
yes		yes		yes	
	Warning given. User must investigate, out posting to file will proceed.		Amendments can be made prior to posting.		Batch cannot be accepted.
yes		yes	Would generally be entered via different entry screens.	yes	
no		yes	Batches being simply journals which are sequentially numbered.	yes	Optionally.
yes	User could allocate from a sequential series.				
no		no		no	
yes	Appears on audit trail and screen.	no		no	

	OMICRON	

7 Are the following validated:

date	yes	
customer account number	yes	
VAT code	yes	
goods value	yes	
sales analysis code	no	
8 Is VAT calculated to check the figure input?	no	
9 Is the gross figure agreed to goods+ VAT?	yes	
10 Is discount calculated to check the figure input?	no	
11 Can the actual date of posting, or batch reference, be shown on hard copies of transactions input?	yes	
12 Does the screen always indicate that the sales ledger, as opposed to the purchase ledger, is running?	yes	
13 Do all input screens show clearly:		
type of entry	yes	
the distinction between debits and credits	yes	
14 Is there any check that the same entry is not input twice?	no	
15 Is there a warning if a customer exceeds the credit limit? If 'YES' – what action is required?	no	Report available.
16 Is it impossible for new accounts to be created during processing?	yes	
17 Is a reconciliation of numbers of accounts produced after amendment of the customer detail file?	no	
18 Does the system prevent the abnormal termination of programs?	no	But system will not restart – back-up is required.

Integration

1 Can the sales ledger be integrated with an invoicing module?	yes	
2 Can the sales ledger be integrated with a nominal ledger module?	yes	
3 Can the nominal ledger be updated as often as desired?	yes	
4 Is a hard copy automatically produced at the end of each nominal ledger update?	yes	
5 Is there a sales ledger print-out (as well as a nominal ledger print-out) of the nominal ledger update?	no	
6 Are the following automatically posted to the appropriate nominal ledger accounts:		
discount	yes	
discount written back	yes	
bad debts written off	yes	
contras with purchase ledger	no	But could be set up in parameters.

HIGH-PRICE PACKAGES   285

SMB PLUS		SUNACCOUNT		TETRAPLAN	
yes		yes		yes	
yes		yes		yes	
yes		N/A	The VAT percentage is manually entered into the applicable journal definition.	yes	
yes		yes		yes	
yes		yes		yes	
no		yes	Set up by user in journal definition.	no	
yes		yes	Set up by user in journal definition.	yes	
yes		yes	Set up by user in journal definition.	no	
yes		yes		yes	
yes		N/A	Allocation screen shows account type (i.e. debtor or creditor).	yes	
yes		yes	Set up by user.	yes	
yes		yes		yes	
yes	Invoice reference duplicates are flagged during input.	no	Can be visual check by account display.	yes	Cannot duplicate references.
no	Only in order entry routine.	yes		no	Yes if order entry is used.
			Operator override decision.		There is a controlled over-ride facility.
yes		yes		no	
no		no		no	
yes		yes		yes	
yes		yes		yes	
yes		yes	Debtor accounts are included in the nominal ledger.	yes	
no	Updated on line in real time mode. No choice of frequency.	N/A	Real time update.	yes	
yes		N/A		no	
yes		N/A		no	
yes		yes		yes	
yes	If via credit note, otherwise 'no'.	yes		no	
no	To suspense.	yes	Specific journals could be defined for each case.	no	Nominal ledger journal entry required.
no	To suspense.	yes		no	

286. A GUIDE TO ACCOUNTING SOFTWARE

		OMICRON
7 Are any invalid/unidentified entries posted to a suspense account?	yes	Could be set up in params.
If 'NO' – how are they treated?		Left for manual correction.
If 'YES' – how is the suspense account treated?		
8 Is the sales ledger control balance agreed to the total of the balances in the sales ledger?	no	
9 Can current and future periods be maintained simultaneously?	yes	
10 Is there a check that transactions cannot be posted twice to the nominal ledger?	yes	
11 Must the nominal ledger be updated from the sales ledger before the period-end is run?	no	
12 Must the nominal ledger and the sales ledger be in the same period for the update to be carried out?	no	Postings matched to period by ledgers.
13 Is there any report/warning that transactions posted to the sales ledger have not yet been posted to the nominal ledger?	yes	

Output

1 Is it necessary to produce an audit trail before the period-end procedure is run?	no	
2 Does the audit trail enable all transactions to be traced fully through the system?	yes	
3 Can the actual run date, or batch reference, as well as current ledger date, be shown on reports?	yes	
4 Can the following be produced:		
list of master file information	yes	
aged debtors report	yes	
VAT report	yes	
ledger detail report	yes	
customer statements	yes	
customer name and address labels	yes	
debt collection letters	yes	
5 Does the customer statement show:		
all o/s transactions together with all items settled in the current period	yes	If open item.
or all o/s transactions only	yes	Can be done.
or the balance b/f and the current period's transactions	yes	If balance forward.
or just the current balance	no	
6 Does the customer statement:		
show discount separately	yes	
show ageing	yes	
allow special messages	no	Yes if using report writer.
allow for suppression of erroneous postings and their corrections	no	

HIGH-PRICE PACKAGES

SMB PLUS		SUNACCOUNT		TETRAPLAN	
N/A	Should be none as validated and updated to nominal immediately.	N/A – for standard processing; Yes – if using batch entry procedure.		no	
					Badly! Batch entries can be lost. Errors displayed on display and system log.
			Error suspense cleared manually.		
no		N/A	Part of nominal ledger.	no	Not automatically.
yes	Not within sales ledger, but sales can be ahead of nominal.	yes		no	
N/A		N/A		yes	
N/A	Updated simultaneously.	N/A		no	
N/A	Updated simultaneously.	N/A		no	A futures file is used, nominal should always equal or lag sales ledger.
N/A	Updated simultaneously.	N/A		yes	
yes		no		yes	
yes		yes		yes	
yes		yes	All reports show run date and ledger date or period where appropriate.	yes	Automatic.
yes		yes		yes	
yes		yes		yes	
yes		yes		yes	
yes		yes		yes	
yes		yes		yes	
yes		no	Although data can be easily transferred to other word processing or database packages.	yes	
yes		no		yes	4 levels of severity.
yes		yes	Options.	yes	
no		yes	Options.		
no		yes	Options.	yes	
no		yes	Options.	yes	
yes		yes		no	
yes		yes		yes	
yes		yes		yes	
yes		yes		no	

288 A GUIDE TO ACCOUNTING SOFTWARE

	OMICRON
7 Can the following screens be seen:	
customer details	yes
customer transactions	yes
8 Can hard copies of the following be obtained for individual accounts/selected ranges of accounts:	
customer details	yes
customer transactions	yes
9 Does the ledger account detail report/copy statements show:	
the source of all postings	yes
how part payments and allocations have been treated	yes
either the full account history or balance b/f together with the current period's transactions?	yes
10 Does the aged analysis show for each customer:	
total balance o/s	yes
credit limit	yes
11 Is ageing strictly by transaction date?	yes
If 'NO' – how is ageing done?	
12 Does the aged analysis show unallocated cash separately?	no
If 'NO' – how is it aged?	Netted off against period of payment recorded.
13 Do all outputs show clearly the distinction between debits and credits?	yes
14 Are all reports adequately titled?	yes
15 Do reports provide totals where applciable?	yes
16 Can report production be varied by:	
printing a range of accounts	yes
printing, by e.g., area/rep?	no Can be produced via report generator.
17 Is the period number shown on reports?	yes
18 Are all report pages sequentially numbered with the end of report identified?	yes Totals signify end.
19 Is a sales analysis possible?	yes Via report generator.
20 Can reports be temporarily retained on file for subsequent printing?	yes
If 'YES' – are such files protected from deletion?	no
21 Is a report generator available for use with the sales ledger module?	yes
22 Can transaction files for previous periods be retained in the system to permit enquiries and reports?	yes

Purchase Ledger

General

1 Are programs menu-driven?	yes
If 'YES' – can menus be by-passed once the user is familiar with the package?	no

HIGH-PRICE PACKAGES

SMB PLUS		SUNACCOUNT		TETRAPLAN	
yes		yes		yes	
yes		yes		yes	
yes		yes		yes	
yes		yes		yes	
yes		yes		yes	
no	Other than by user applying appropriate reference.	yes		yes	
yes		yes		yes	
yes		yes		yes	
no	But, variety of credit control reports available.	yes		yes	
yes		no	Can be by due date or transaction date.	no	Can be by due date on aged debtor printout.
yes		yes		yes	
yes		yes		yes	
yes		yes		yes	
yes		yes		yes	
yes		yes		yes	
yes		yes		yes	
yes	As at date, and date printed.	yes		yes	
yes	No special 'end of report' message.	yes		yes	
yes		yes	By use of up to 5 transaction analysis codes.	yes	
yes		yes		yes	
no	No special protection, user could deliberately delete.	no		no	
yes		yes		yes	A separate report writer module is available.
yes	Up to 99 periods in 'history' file.	yes	Period cleardown not essential.	yes	But are cleared on running closed item program.

| yes | | yes | System has one main menu listing all the key functions of SunAccount. | yes | |
| yes | Invoke progam by name from any menu. | yes | All functions can be accessed from any screen in the system. | yes | Menus can be customised. |

		OMICRON	
2	Does the system maintain a log of usage?	no	
3	Are informative messages produced on-screen whilst running?	yes	
4	Are error messages informative and easy to understand?	yes	Reasonable.
5	Is the system multi-company?	yes	
6	Is the original set-up straightforward?	yes	
7	Is there a copy/restore facility in the package?	no	
8	Does the system cover disciplined taking of back-ups?	yes	Reminds before major updates.

Documentation
(a) Manual

1	Is the manual clearly laid out and understandable?	yes	
2	Is the manual comprehensive and accurate?	yes	
3	Is there an index?	yes	Quality of index poor.
4	Is it easy to follow through all procedures?	yes	
5	Is it easy to locate specific points when required?	yes	For major items but poor indexing for items of detail.
6	Are completed examples included?	yes	

(b) Help screens

7	Are help screens available?	no	
	If 'YES':		
	Do they provide on-line instructions?		
	Can they be edited or prepared by the user?		

Supplier Details

1	What is the format of the supplier account code?		4-digit numeric.
2	What other supplier details are held?		Name/address/postcode/phone/discount terms. No contact name.
	Do these seem to be sufficient in general?	yes	But poor.
3	What is the maximum number of accounts that can be held?		9999.
4	Can supplier details be added/deleted/amended at any time?	no	Via appropriate menu option only.
5	Is file re-sorted automatically when a new supplier is added?	yes	
	If 'NO' – can a re-sort be initiated?		
6	Is deletion of a supplier prevented if the account has:		
	an outstanding balance	yes	
	a zero balance but a b/f turnover?	yes	
7	Is a hard copy of changes in supplier details automatically produced?	no	
	If 'NO' – can a hard copy be taken?	yes	

HIGH-PRICE PACKAGES

SMB PLUS		SUNACCOUNT		TETRAPLAN	
no		no		yes	
yes		yes		yes	
yes		yes	With more detailed explanation in the manual.	yes	
yes		yes		yes	
yes		no	Considerable user input necessary in setting up the system.	yes	
no		yes		no	
no		yes	An option on the system maintenance menu, handled within the system and fully explained in the manual.	no	
yes		no	Same information duplicated in various parts of the manual.	yes	
yes		yes		no	The section pages correspond to display menu options.
yes		yes		yes	
yes		no	Particularly with regard to software updates where the information is not integrated into the original manual.	yes	
yes		yes		yes	
yes		yes	See nominal ledger.	yes	Including sample output.
no		yes		no	
		yes			On-line instructions available on input screens.
		no			
	4–8 digits alphanumeric.		Maximum 10 characters, containing alphabetic characters, numeric characters or symbols.		8 characters (alphanumeric).
	User plus – credit stop, bank details, payment terms, purchases – year to date, purchases – last year, 6 periods ageing.		Up to 5 user-defined analysis categories, look-up code, credit limit, payment days (2), discount days and % (2), address, telephone no., contact name.		Name, address, banking details, settlement terms, 3 analysis codes, alpha sort code, an 8 character alternative code to access an account – non unique entry.
yes		yes		yes	
	No practical limit, determined by disk space.		Realistically limited only by disk space.		Unlimited.
yes		yes		yes	Unless an open balance is on the account.
yes		N/A	Indexed sequential.	N/A	Not necessary.
yes		yes		yes	
yes		yes		no	
no		no		no	
yes		yes		yes	

A GUIDE TO ACCOUNTING SOFTWARE

		OMICRON	
Transactions			
1 Can the system be open item?	yes	No option must be open.	
2 Are the following inputs possible:			
invoices	yes		
credit notes	yes		
manual payments	yes		
cash refunded	yes		
discounts	yes		
3 Can an invoice be analysed to several different expense categories?	yes		
4 Are different VAT codes possible for different items within one invoice?	yes		
5 Are all transactions retained on file for at least one period?	yes		
6 Can a ledger pre-date existing transactions?	yes		
7 Can 2 references be input for an invoice (own and supplier's reference)?	yes		
Matching/Allocations			
(a) Balance forward			
1 Is the balance b/f aged?	N/A		
2 Can cash be allocated automatically?	N/A		
If 'YES' – how is the allocation made?	N/A		
– can this be overridden?	N/A		
3 Can cash be allocated automatically?	N/A		
If 'YES' – does the package check that cash allocated = amount paid?	N/A		
How is any such difference treated?	N/A		
4 Can credit notes/journal entries be allocated to previous periods?	N/A		
5 Can cash in advance be held and later allocated to subsequent periods?	N/A		
(b) Open item			
6 Are outstanding transactions displayed for allocation?	yes		
7 Can cash be allocated automatically?	yes	During automatic payments routine.	
If 'YES' – how is the allocation made?		Using automatic payments run plus if balance on a/c is zero, system automatically allocates all transactions on the account during end of day.	
– can this be over-ridden?	yes	Amend suggested payment.	
8 Can cash be allocated manually?	yes		
If 'YES' – does the package check that cash allocated = cash paid?	yes		
How is any difference treated?		Balance o/s accept with diffs.	
9 Can an over/underpayment of an invoice be recorded?	no	Yes if allocation routine used.	
10 How often are settled items deleted from file?		Monthly if required.	

HIGH-PRICE PACKAGES

SMB PLUS		SUNACCOUNT		TETRAPLAN	
yes		yes		yes	Or balance forward.
yes		yes		yes	All accounts must be open item or balance forward. No mixing allowed.
yes		yes		yes	
yes		yes	Using user-defined entry screens.	yes	
yes		yes		yes	
yes		yes		yes	Through journal entries.
yes		yes		yes	Up to 10 including VAT.
yes	Separate posting routine.	yes		yes	
yes		yes		yes	Until a clear closed items command is issued.
yes		yes		yes	Purchase ledger entries must have a date in the current period.
yes		yes	By using description field.	yes	
yes	By period.	yes		yes	
yes		no		yes	
	Auto payments routine.				Oldest first.
yes				yes	
yes		yes		yes	
yes		yes		yes	
	Unallocated cash transaction.		Over/underpayment not permitted.		Routine cannot be completed.
yes		yes		yes	
yes		yes		yes	
yes		yes		yes	
yes	Via auto-payments routine.	yes		yes	
			On a range of transaction dates, accounting periods or transaction references.		Oldest first.
yes	Review of proposed payments.	yes		yes	
yes				yes	
yes		yes		yes	
	Unallocated cash transaction.		Not permitted.		Routine cannot be completed.
yes		yes		yes	Underpayment leaves balance due, overpayment is left unallocated.
	Monthly – cleared to 'history' file.		Users choice – whenever period cleardown is performed.		When required.

		OMICRON	
11	Can credit notes be set against the invoices to which they refer?	yes	
12	Can journal entries be set against the invoices/credit notes to which they refer?	yes	
13	Can cash in advance be held and later allocated to invoice?	yes	
14	Can cash be held unallocated?	yes	
	– how is this treated?		Unallocated item.

Input Controls

		OMICRON	
1	Is password control used?	yes	
	If 'YES' – give details		6-character.
2	Is a hard copy automatically produced for all input?	no	
3	Are batch totals automatically produced for all transactions input?	yes	Reports difference but may be over-ridden.
	If 'YES' – what is the procedure if this does not agree with a pre-list total?		Difference recorded on audit reports.
4	Is it necessary that invoices, cash and adjustments are input in separate batches?	yes	
5	Are batches automatically sequentially numbered?	no	
	If 'NO' – can they be so numbered?	yes	Not automatically.
6	Is a report produced at the end of each processing run to reconcile b/f total, transactions processed and c/f total?	yes	This report is produced at end of day procedure.
	If 'NO' – is a control balance produced at the end of each posting run?		
7	Are the following validated:		
	date	yes	
	supplier account number	yes	
	VAT code	yes	
	goods value	yes	
	analysis code	no	
8	Is VAT calculated to check figure input?	no	
9	Is the gross figure agreed to goods+VAT?	yes	
10	Is discount calculated to check the figure input?	no	
11	Can the actual date of posting, or batch reference, be shown on hard copies of transactions input?	yes	
12	Does the screen always indicate that the purchase ledger, as opposed to the sales ledger, is running?	yes	
13	Do all input screens show clearly:–		
	type of entry	yes	
	the distinction between debits and credits?	yes	
14	Is there any check that the same entry is not input twice?	no	
15	Is there a warning if a supplier is overpaid?	no	But flagged on report.

HIGH-PRICE PACKAGES

	SMB PLUS		SUNACCOUNT		TETRAPLAN
yes		yes		yes	
yes		yes		yes	
yes		yes	Cash is posted first against a supplier account and allocated to invoices using a separate entry screen.	yes	
yes		yes	Unallocated cash.	yes	Current period unallocated credit.
	Allocated according to date of entry and reported in aged format.				
yes		yes		yes	
	1. Overall log-in. 2. Specific users only permitted to use protected routines.		3 levels single user, up to 10 levels multi-user.		Each menu option can be password protected.
yes	All transactions only – can be spooled.	no	Can be set up to print immediately after input.	no	Period-end processing cannot continue unless the audit trail has been printed.
yes		yes		yes	
	Warning given and user must investigate. Posting to file will proceed.		Uncorrected entries rejected.		Batch cannot be accepted.
yes		yes	Would generally be input via different entry screens.	yes	
no		yes	Batches being simply journals which are sequentially numbered.	yes	Optionally.
yes	User could allocate from a sequential series.				
no		no		yes	
yes	On screen and audit trail.	no			
yes		yes		yes	
yes		yes		yes	
yes		N/A	The VAT % is manually entered into the applicable journal definition.	yes	
yes		yes		yes	
yes		yes		yes	
no		yes	Set up by user in journal definition.	no	
yes		yes	Set up by user in journal definition.	yes	
yes		yes	Set up by user in journal definition.	no	
yes		yes		yes	
yes		yes	In effect.	yes	
yes		yes	Set up by user.	yes	
yes		yes		yes	
yes	Invoice reference duplicates are flagged during input.	no		yes	Cannot duplicate reference.
no	But obvious.	no		no	

		OMICRON	
16	Is it impossible for new accounts to be created during processing?	yes	Can exit processing temporarily to create new a/c and return to batch.
17	Is a reconciliation of numbers of accounts produced after amendment of the customer detail file?	yes	
18	Does the system prevent the abnormal termination of programs?	no	Will not allow restart. Back-up copies must be used.

Integration

		OMICRON	
1	Can the purchase ledger be integrated with a job-costing module?	yes	
2	Can the purchase ledger be integrated with a nominal ledger module?	yes	
3	Can the nominal ledger be updated as often as desired?	yes	
4	Is a hard copy automatically produced at the end of each nominal ledger update?	yes	
5	Is there a purchase ledger print-out (as well as a nominal ledger print-out) of the nominal ledger update?	no	
6	Are the following automatically posted to the appropriate nominal ledger accounts:		
	discount	yes	
	discount written back	yes	
	contras with sales ledger?	no	Can be set up in parameters.
7	Are any invalid/unidentified entries posted to a suspense account?	yes	
	If 'NO' – how are they treated?		
	If 'YES' – how is the suspense account treated?		Left for manual correction.
8	Is the purchase ledger control balance agreed to the total of the balances in the purchase ledger?	no	
9	Can current and future periods be maintained simultaneously?	yes	Warning if posting to other than current.
10	Is there a check that transactions cannot be posted twice to the nominal ledger?	yes	
11	Must the nominal ledger be updated from the purchase ledger before the period-end is run?	yes	Before period end of purchase ledger but warning given.
12	Must the nominal ledger and the purchase ledger be in the same period for the update to be carried out?	no	Batches can be posted to other than current period.
13	Is there any report/warning that transactions posted to the purchase ledger have not yet been posted to the nominal ledger?	yes	

Output

		OMICRON	
1	Is it necessary to produce an audit trail before the period end procedure is run?	no	
2	Does the audit trail enable all transactions to be traced fully through the system?	yes	
3	Can the actual run date, or batch reference, as well as current ledger date, be shown on reports?	yes	

HIGH-PRICE PACKAGES

SMB PLUS		SUNACCOUNT		TETRAPLAN	
yes		yes		no	
no		no		no	
yes		yes		yes	
yes		yes	The conversion module can be used for costing together with the transaction analysis codes.	yes	
yes		yes	Supplier accounts are included in the nominal ledger.	yes	
no	Update on line in real time mode, no choice of frequency.	N/A	Real time update.	yes	
yes		N/A		no	
yes		N/A		yes	
yes		yes	Specific journals could be defined for each case.	yes	
yes	If via credit, otherwise 'no'.	yes		yes	
no	To suspense.	yes		no	
N/A	Should be none, as validated and updated to nominal immediately.	no		no	
no		N/A	Not possible unless using batch processing. Part of TB to be corrected by journal. Part of nominal ledger.	no	Not automatically.
yes		yes		yes	
N/A		N/A		yes	
N/A	Updated simultaneously.	N/A		no	
N/A	Updated simultaneously.	N/A		no	
N/A	Updated simultaneously.	N/A		yes	
yes		no		yes	
yes		yes		yes	
yes		yes	All reports show run date and ledger date or period date where appropriate.	yes	

		OMICRON
4 Can the following be produced:		
list of master file information	yes	
aged creditors report	yes	
VAT report	yes	
ledger detail report	yes	
remittance advices	yes	
supplier name and address labels	yes	
suggested payments	yes	
cheques	yes	
5 Can remittance advices show:		
individual invoices	yes	
discount	yes	
supplier's references	yes	
6 Can the following screens be seen:		
supplier details	yes	
supplier transactions	yes	
7 Can hard copies of the following be obtained for individual accounts/selected ranges of accounts:–		
supplier details	yes	
supplier transactions	yes	
8 Does the ledger account detail report show:		
the source of all postings	yes	
how part payments and allocations have been treated	yes	
either the full account history or balance b/f together with the current period's transactions?	yes	
9 Is ageing strictly by transactions date?	no	
If 'NO' – how is ageing done?		Can be any no. of days from: doc dates, period start date, period-end date.
10 Does the aged analysis show unallocated cash separately?	no	
If 'NO' – how is it aged?		Netted off against period payment recorded.
11 Do all outputs show clearly the distinction between debits and credits?	yes	
12 Are all reports adequately titled?	yes	
13 Do reports provide totals where applicable?	yes	
14 Can report production be varied by:		
printing a range of accounts	yes	
printing by, e.g., area	no	Can be done via report generator only.
15 Is the period number shown on reports?	yes	
16 Are all report pages sequentially numbered with the end of report identified?	yes	End identified by totals.

HIGH-PRICE PACKAGES 299

	SMB PLUS		SUNACCOUNT		TETRAPLAN
yes		yes		yes	
yes		yes		yes	
yes		yes		yes	
yes		yes		yes	
yes		yes		yes	
yes		no	Although date can be easily transferred to word processing packages.	yes	
yes		yes	By setting appropriate dates on the aged creditors report.	yes	
yes		yes		yes	
yes		yes		yes	
yes		yes		yes	
yes		yes		yes	
yes		yes		yes	
yes		yes		yes	
yes		yes		yes	
yes		yes		yes	
yes		yes		yes	
no	User would have to input a matching reference no.	yes		no	
yes		yes		yes	
yes		no	Due date or transaction date.	no	Also by due date.
yes		yes		yes	
yes		yes		yes	
yes		yes		yes	
yes		yes		yes	
yes		yes		yes	
yes		yes		yes	
yes	Date produced, and 'as at' date.	yes		yes	
yes	No specific 'end of report' message.	yes		yes	

A GUIDE TO ACCOUNTING SOFTWARE

		OMICRON
17 Is a purchase analysis possible?	yes	
18 Can reports be temporarily retained on file for subsequent printing?	no	
If 'YES' – are such files protected from deletion?		
19 Is a report generator available for use with the purchase ledger module?	yes	
20 Can transaction files for previous periods be retained in the system to permit enquiries and reports?	yes	
Payments/Cheque Writing		
1 Can the system write cheques?	yes	
If 'YES' – is the payment posted automatically to the purchase ledger?	yes	
2 Is there an automatic cheque writing facility? If 'YES':		
is a list of suggested payments printed in advance of the cheques?	yes	
is the total cash requirement printed in advance of the cheques?	yes	
can the automatic payment routine be aborted if either of the above is not satisfactory?	yes	
3 Can the following payment/report options be selected:		
individual invoice selection	yes	
supplier selection	yes	
pay all invoices of a certain age	yes	
pay according to due date	yes	
pay all invoices except those marked not to be paid	yes	
other (specify)		Items with discount available.
4 Is discount automatically calculated by the payment routine?	yes	
5 Can invoices be held as disputed?	yes	
If 'YES' – can a report of disputed invoices be produced?	yes	By various categories of dispute.

	SMB PLUS	SUNACCOUNT		TETRAPLAN	
yes		yes	By the use of up to 5 transaction analysis codes.	yes	
yes		yes		yes	
	No special protection. User could deliberately delete.	no		no	
yes		yes		yes	A separate report writer module is available.
yes	Up to 99 periods in 'history' file.	yes	Period cleardown not essential.	yes	Until closed items are cleared.
yes		yes		yes	
yes		yes		yes	
		yes		yes	
yes		yes	Aged creditors using appropriate date.	yes	
yes		yes	As above after entering 'Withhold Payment' where appropriate.	yes	
yes		yes		yes	
yes		yes		no	
yes	Range of supplier nos., or individually from through ledger.	yes		no	
yes		yes		no	
yes		yes		yes	
yes		yes		yes	
yes		yes		yes	
yes	By moving due date to future, 'but' list is produced for such invoices.	yes		yes	
yes		no		yes	

Other Packages

Summaries	**304**
Package Information Table	**306**
Evaluation Checklists:	
General Points	**308**
Performance of Requisite Accounting Functions	308
Reliability – Security and Continuity of Processing	310
Support and Maintenance	310
Ease of Use	312
(a) Interactive Processing	312
(b) User Documentation	312
Efficiency	312
Flexibility	314
(a) Integration Facilities	314
(b) Reporting Flexibility	314
(c) Parameter or Table Facilities	314
Software Installation and Training	316
(a) Financial Resources	316
(b) Other Resources	316
(c) Involvement of Software Supplier	316
(d) Involvement of User Personnel	316
Package Software Acquisition	316
Preliminary Questions Relating to Software Supplier	316
Nominal Ledger	**318**
General	318
Documentation	318
(a) Manual	318
(b) Help Screens	320
Account Details	320

Transactions	320
Input Controls	322
Integration	324
Output	324
(a) General	324
(b) Trial Balance; P&L and Balance Sheet	326
Year End	328

Sales Ledger 328

General	328
Documentation	330
(a) Manual	330
(b) Help screens	330
Customer Details	330
Transactions	330
Matching/Allocations	332
(a) Balance Forward	332
(b) Open Item	332
Input Controls	334
Integration	336
Output	336

Purchase Ledger 340

General	340
Documentation	340
(a) Manual	340
(b) Help screens	342
Supplier Details	342
Transactions	342
Matching/Allocations	344
(a) Balance Forward	344
(b) Open Item	344
Input Controls	344
Integration	346
Output	348
Payments/Cheque Writing	350

The details of these packages may be of interest to the reader but it should be remembered that the summaries and evaluations were completed wholly by the manufacturers.

Summary of BOS

BOS Software Ltd produces an integrated range of application software. The software runs on some mini- and most micro-computers and is available for single-user, multi-user and networked systems using the BOS operating system. The user price for most modules is single-user – £400 and multi-user £950.

The following business software modules are available:
- Nominal ledger
- Purchase ledger
- Sales ledger
- Payroll
- Purchase order processing
- Job costing
- BACS
- Invoicing
- Sales order processing
- Stock control
- Fixed assets
- Cash book
- Manufacturer

BOS software is sold through a network of 200 local dealers throughout the UK. For an annual service charge users can receive whole-time support and new versions of the software.

Summary of Business Desk

The Business Desk suite of accounting packages is suitable for a very wide range of business types and requirements. The base package comprises fully integrated sales, purchase and nominal ledgers. The other packages in the suite incorporate sales invoicing, stock control, sales order processing and purchase order processing. There is a simple upgrade path between packages.

Both single- and multi-user options are available.

Features include comprehensive audit trails and automatic VAT processing. A number of reports and documents, such as sales invoices, may be designed by the user.

The package is available for a wide range of operating systems (such as MS-DOS, C-DOS and UNIX), and a number of networking systems.

Summary of FACT

FACT is a fully integrated accounting system for micro computers consisting of five modules: sales, purchase and nominal ledgers, management reporting and fixed assets.

Other systems, including CMG's ORDERFACT order processing package, can be linked to FACT through the powerful batch input routines. There is also a two-way link between FACT and the Lotus 1-2-3 and Symphony spreadsheet packages.

FACT is written, marketed and supported exclusively by CMG who aim to provide a complete service including training and a helpline.

Multi-user facilities allow access from up to sixteen screens simultaneously with full record locking. Up to 99 companies can be held, each with its own accounting currency and every company can hold invoice details in foreign currencies.

FACT can be fully password protected. Entry of a security number and matching password can give access to a single option from one menu, every option from every menu or any other combination.

Up to thirteen accounting periods can be set up. Postings are allowed to both the current and future accounting periods, which allows closing of the various ledgers at different times. Double entry disciplines are maintained throughout and a full audit trail is provided, by means of daybooks, for all types of transaction.

Summary of Shortlands Gold

Shortlands software offers users the advanced features, flexibility and powerful reporting needed in today's business environment. Developed originally on UNIX, the software is available across the UNIX, XENIX, DOS and Novell Network environments, and is therefore suitable for the medium to large company that is running departmental accounts or has subsidiary company interests.

Large value transaction fields and a floating decimal point allow even the largest companies to be catered for in any currency.

The requirement in today's business environment for fast and effective reporting is catered for with Shortlands management report writer. This allows reports such as profit and loss, balance sheet and department reports to be produced in the users own format with variance reporting against budgets and last years figures.

For many businesses the tracking of money is vital and Shortlands multi-currency cash book and reconciliation facilities as well as comprehensive payments interrogation programs allow users to see how much they are paying, what discounts they can take advantage of and how much is in the bank.

The software is also muti-company, with no limit to the number of companies held on the system. With the provision of both consolidation and inter-company posting routines, it can provide accurate group company figures.

Package Information Table

Product Name	BOS
Version Number	6.0
Modules Available	Nominal, sales and purchase ledgers, payroll, purchase order processing, sales order processing, invoicing, BACS, stock control, fixed assets, cash book and manufacturer.
Cost per Module	Single-user – £400 multi-user – from £690.
Publisher	BOS Software Ltd, 87–9 Saffron Hill, London EC1N 8QU. Tel: 031831 8811.
Supplier	As publisher.
What support is available	Training centres, from dealers, hotline and software updating.
Operating system	BOS.
Hardware	Most minis and micros e.g., IBMPC, XT, AT, PS/2 and VAX.
Network/multi-user version available	Yes.
Number of UK users	12,000.
First operational	1979.
Report generator available?	Yes.
Links to other packages	Yes.

BUSINESS DESK	FACT	SHORTLANDS GOLD
5. Nominal, sales and purchase ledgers, invoicing, stock, sales order processing, and purchase order processing.	5. Nominal, sales and purchase ledgers, fixed assets, management reporting.	3.1. Nominal, sales, cost and purchase ledgers, management report, writer, cash book, time sheet recording, customer order processing, stock control, fixed assets, payroll and sales report writer.
£300 to £1000.	Single-user – £700, multi-user – £1050.	Single-user – £1000 except report writer at £250 and fixed assets and time sheets at £700, multi-user – £1500 except report writer at £500 and fixed assets and time sheets at £1000.
Paxton Computers Ltd, 28 New Street, St Neots, Cambridge PE19 1AJ. Tel: 0480 217777.	Computer Management Group (UK) Ltd, Sunley House, Bedford Park, Croydon CR0 2AP Tel: 01-680 7027 041-221 8193.	Shortlands Computing Services Ltd, Clyde House, Reform Road, Maidenhead SL6 8BU Tel: 0628 75227.
As publisher. Contract with Paxton or dealer.	As publisher. Hotline, software maintenance, training, installation assistance and consultancy.	As publisher. Telephone hotline, software updating, installation and training courses and user group.
PC-DOS, MS-DOS, C-CP/M, C-DOS, XENIX, UNIX-V and networks. IBM compatibles, ICL and NCR Tower.	DOS. IBM-PC, XT/AT and compatibles.	UNIX, XENIX, DOS and Novell network. Altos, AT & T 3b2, IBM, 6150 (AIX), IBM-PC, XT, AT, PS/2 and compatibles, Apricot, Compaq, NCR Tower and Prime.
Yes. 2,500 Version 1 – 1981. Version 5 – 1987.	Yes. 250. 1984.	Yes. 500+. 1982.
No.	Yes, for nominal ledger	Yes.
Yes.	Yes, Lotus/Symphony.	Yes, input and output links.

Evaluation Checklists

General Points

Performance of Requisite Accounting Functions		BOS
1 Does the software perform the functions which the user wants performed?	yes	
2 Can the software be used by more than one user at the same time?	yes	Multi-user and/or local area network.
3 Can the software support groups of companies/departments/branches?	yes	
How many such branches or companies can be supported.		100 companies. 100 departments.
Can they be consolidated?	yes	Report generator available.
4 Is multi-currency processing available?	yes	
What are the maximum number of currencies available?		99.
Is conversion to sterling automatic?	yes	
5 Are sufficient accounting periods provided by the system?	yes	13 per year.
Can these periods be adjusted to suit different user requirements?	yes	Flexible.
6 Are the ends of accounting periods determined by the user rather than being set by the system?	yes	
7 Can data from all accounting periods be assessed at any given moment?	yes	
Can previous months be accessed for enquiries or reports?	yes	Once a month is closed it cannot be modified.
8 Does the system prevent posting to more than one accounting period at a time?	no	2 possible open periods current and future or prior and current.
Is it impossible to allocate transactions to future periods or to previous closed months?	no	Once a month is closed, it cannot be modified.
9 Does the system permit use of budgets and provide comparisons between budgets and actuals?	yes	
10 Is the maximum value of transactions that can be handled by the system sufficient?	yes	No limit except by size of disk.
11 Is the maximum number of accounts on each ledger (e.g. sales ledger, purchase ledger, nominal ledger) sufficient?	yes	No limit except by size of disk.
12 Is the size and format of account numbers adequate and sufficient for analysis purposes?		10 characters in NL. 7 in SL/PL.
13 Does the associated hardware incorporate enough memory, disk storage and other peripherals for the software to operate satisfactorily?		
14 Does the system offer adequate expansion potential as regards terminals, memory, disk storage capacity and other peripherals?		
15 Are the control features provided by the software adequate to support effective user controls?	yes	

BUSINESS DESK		FACT		SHORTLANDS GOLD	
yes		yes		yes	
yes		yes		yes	
yes		yes		yes	
	99.		99.		Unlimited.
no		yes		yes	
no		yes		yes	
			10.		Unlimited.
		yes		yes	
yes	Any number.	yes	13.	yes	Up to 13 periods.
yes		yes		yes	User-definable.
yes		yes		yes	
no		yes		yes	
no		yes		yes	
yes		no	Warning if outside current period.	no	
no		no	Password protected.	no	Future period posting allowed. Previous periods can only be accessed in nominal ledger through specific program.
no		yes		yes	
yes		yes		yes	11 figures before decimal point (transaction level). 13 figures before decimal point (totals).
yes	No maximum set by the package.	yes		yes	
	6-character alphanumeric for sales and purchases. 4+2 for nominal ledger.		8-character in nominal ledger, sales ledger and purchase ledger.		12 characters in nominal ledger, 10 in sales ledger and purchase ledger.
		yes		yes	
yes		yes		yes	

	BOS

16 Are complementary clerical procedures to be imposed and effectively monitored by management?

Reliability – Security and Continuity of Processing

1 Does the system facilitate back-up storage?	yes	Warnings if forgotten.
How much time will complete back-up of the system require?		About 1 minute per day for small/medium system.
2 Does the system facilitate recovery procedures in the event of system failure?	yes	Recovery procedures available.
3 If system failure occurs part way through a batch or transaction, will the operator have to re-input only the batch or transaction being input at the time of the failure?	yes	
4 Are there any features provided with the software to help track down processing problems?	yes	Debug reports.
5 Are back-up procedures provided within each specific software application or within the operating system?		Both.
Are any of these back-up procedures automatic?	no	Warning if not done.

Support and Maintenance

1 Will the supplier provide corrections to the program?	yes	Annual maintenance charge.
2 Will the supplier provide general enhancements to the programs?	yes	
Will these be provided automatically?	no	
Will they be given free of charge?	no	Small maintenance/service charge.
3 Will the software supplier provide 'hotline' support to assist with immediate problem solving?	yes	
If so, at what cost?		Included in annual maintenance charge.
4 Is the supplier capable of giving sufficient ongoing education and training and other support?	yes	Two training centres and tutorials sent through post.
5 Can the supplier provide all the hardware, software and maintenance requirements of the user?		
6 Can the supplier provide support in the user's locality?		200 dealers.
7 Is a warranty offered in respect of specification and performance of the system?	yes	Covered by support licence.
8 Would there be adequate back-up in the event of hardware or software failure?		
9 Will the software supplier make the program source code available to the user, either directly or by deposit with a third party?	yes	To third party (dealer).
10 If the software is acquired under licence, are there any unduly restrictive conditions in the licence?	no	

The term 'supplier' refers to the supplier of the support and maintenance, whether or not this is the same as the supplier of the software.

OTHER PACKAGES 311

BUSINESS DESK		FACT		SHORTLANDS GOLD	
yes		yes		no	Within operating system.
			Depends on size of files. Uses efficient data compression techniques.		Variable – depending on data. Could take 20–30 minutes.
yes		yes		yes	From previous back-ups.
		yes	Usually can just input the current document.	yes	
yes		yes		yes	
	With each application.		Within software application.		Operating system only.
yes		yes			Can be set up to be on XENIX and UNIX systems.
yes		yes		yes	
yes		yes		yes	Free to clients with support contracts.
no		yes		yes	
	Possibly – dependent upon the nature of the changes.	no	£85 per month for hotline service and enhancements.	yes	
yes		yes		yes	
	10% of package price annually.		£85 per month for hotline service and enhancements.		Free to clients with support contracts.
		yes		yes	
		yes		yes	Hardware maintenance handled by MBS engineering.
					Supported from Maidenhead.
		yes		yes	
		no		yes	
no		no		no	

Ease of Use
(a) Interactive processing

		BOS	
1	Does the software run under an operating system, which is a commonly accepted standard?	yes	BOS.
2	Is the software available concurrently to more than one user?	yes	Multi-tasking, multi-user.
3	Can more than one system function be performed concurrently?	yes	
4	Does the software effectively lead the user through the data entry procedures?	yes	
	Does the software facilitate immediate error correction?	yes	
5	Is the software menu-driven?	yes	
	Are such menus restricted by password and application?	yes	Password and operator i.d.
6	Are the user screens adequately titled?	yes	
7	Does the system inform the operator which programs or files are being loaded?	no	
8	Does the software facilitate file maintenance, back-up and archive copying?	yes	

(b) User documentation

1	Is the manual clearly laid out and understandable?	yes	
2	Is the manual comprehensive and accurate?	yes	
3	Is there an index to the manual?	yes	
4	Is it easy to locate specific topics in the manual when required?	yes	
5	Is it easy to follow through all procedures in the manual?	yes	Tutorial section.
6	Are completed examples included in the manual?	yes	
7	Are help screens available?	no	Can be set up by user.
	Do they provide detailed on-line instructions on how to use particular features of the software?		
	Can they be edited or prepared by the user?		
8	Does the documentation clearly specify the actions to be taken by users at each important stage of processing?	yes	
9	Will the software supplier provide regular updates of documentation in the event of modifications or revisions?	yes	Included in maintenance charge.
10	Will the software supplier make the detailed program documentation available to the user, either directly or by deposit with a third party?	yes	To dealer.

Efficiency

1	Are the various functions of the system menu-driven, or otherwise easy to initiate?	yes	
	Is there a good response time in the initiation of functions?	yes	

OTHER PACKAGES

BUSINESS DESK	FACT	SHORTLANDS GOLD	
yes	yes	yes	DOS, XENIX and UNIX.
yes	yes	yes	
yes	yes	yes	
yes	yes	yes	
yes	yes	yes	On-line validation.
yes	yes	yes	
yes	yes	yes	
yes	yes	yes	
yes	yes	no	
yes	yes	yes no	File maintenance. Back-up is through the operating system.
yes	yes	yes	
yes	yes	yes	
no	yes	yes	
yes	yes	yes	
yes	yes	yes	
no	yes	yes	
no	yes	no	
	yes		
	no		
yes	yes	yes	
	yes	yes	
no	no		Can be negotiated.
yes	yes	yes	
yes	yes	yes	

		BOS	
2	Is data entry easily repeated if similar to previous entry?	yes	Default response.
3	Is there a good response time:		
	(i) in processing data input?	yes	
	(ii) in producing requisite reports?	yes	
	(iii) in updating files?	yes	
	(iv) in producing back-up files?	yes	
	(v) in deleting redundant information files?	yes	
4	Does the system prevent access to a record while it is being updated?	yes	Full record locking.
5	Does the system retain a log of file updates until the next occasion on which the relevant information is reported or the relevant file used in a regular control procedure?	yes	Event logging for main menu.
6	Can regular reports be easily duplicated if required?	yes	

Flexibility

(a) Integration facilities

		BOS	
1	Are the different accounting applications integrated?	yes	
	Are they integrated on an item by item basis or are they integrated by weekly or monthly end routines?		It varies.
2	Whichever method is used, can the ledger updating process be satisfactorily controlled?	yes	
3	Does the software run under an operating system which is a commonly accepted standard?		BOS.
4	Can more than one system function be performed concurrently?	yes	Multi-user.
5	Can software be linked to other packages, e.g. word processing, graphics, financial modelling, to provide alternative display and reporting facilities?	yes	WP, graphics, spreadsheet.

(b) Reporting flexibility

		BOS	
1	Can the user easily design additional output reports or displays?		
2	Is a report generator provided as part of the software or as an option associated with it?		Yes for some modules.
3	Can screen layouts, reports and transaction formats be easily adapted to user requirements?		
4	Does the output of the software facilitate proper control to ensure that decisions are not inadvertently taken on the basis of incorrect information?	yes	

(c) Parameter or table facilities

		BOS	
1	If the system uses a lot of standing information which changes frequently or regularly, does the system allow for such changes to be effected through the use of parameters or tables?	yes	
2	If so, is the use of such parameters or tables adequately reported?	yes	

OTHER PACKAGES 315

BUSINESS DESK		FACT		SHORTLANDS GOLD	
no	But standard comments and default analysis codes.	yes	Where applicable.	yes	
yes		yes		yes	
yes		yes		yes	
yes		yes		yes	
yes		yes		yes	
yes		yes		yes	
yes		yes		yes	
no		no		yes	
yes		yes		yes	
yes		yes		yes	
	Item by item.		Item by item.		In some instances item by item – in others by running specific update programs.
yes		yes		yes	
yes		yes		yes	
yes		yes		yes	
yes		yes		yes	Via q Plex IV report generator.
no		yes		yes	Via q Plex IV report generator.
no		yes		yes	As an option.
	Some reports.	yes	But not policy to do so.		Screen layouts – no. Transaction formats – no. Reports – yes.
		yes		yes	
		yes		yes	
		yes		yes	

	BOS

3 Is proper control to be exercised over changes to such parameters or tables? — yes

If so, how? (e.g. through the use of system facilities such a password or by inspection of appropriate records). — Passwords.

Software Installation and Training
(a) Financial resources
1 Has account been taken in the budget for system development/acquisition of the full costs of:

   initial acquisition?

   initial training?

   future training?

(b) Other resources
2 Is the main equipment to be located in adequate accommodation?

   Is this such that staff are not seriously affected by the equipment (e.g. by noise from the printer).

3 Is there sufficient scope for the installation, if required, of communications equipment?

4 Have requisite consumables (e.g. special stationery, filing facilities, fireproof storage) been provided for?

(c) Involvement of software supplier
5 Is the supplier capable of giving sufficient initial education and training and other support? — yes

6 Are the potential users permitted to test the software for a trial period before commitment to acquire it? — no — Can visit other sites.

7 If required, does the supplier have sufficient capable personnel to assist users to convert to the new system? — yes

8 If required, will the supplier provide machine time to enable users to set up files of input data before installation? — yes

(d) Involvement of user personnel
9 Who is to be responsible for running and controlling the system on a regular basis? Is this person sufficiently competent?

10 Who is to be responsible for the installation and implementation of the system?

   Is this person sufficiently competent?

11 Which staff will operate the system?

   Do they have sufficient aptitude for computers?

12 Is there adequate cover for staff in the event of illness and holidays?

Package Software Acquisition
Preliminary questions relating to software supplier
1 Does the supplier have a good overall reputation as regards experience and reliability?

2 Does the supplier offer a full range of accounting software?

3 Is the supplier's financial status stable?

   Does the supplier demonstrate an adequate capital base, growth and profitability?

OTHER PACKAGES 317

BUSINESS DESK		FACT		SHORTLANDS GOLD	
		yes		yes	
			By password.		Password protection.
		yes	Marketed and supported by CMG.	yes	Marketed and supplied by Shortlands.
		yes		yes	
		yes		yes	
		yes		yes	

		BOS
4 Does the supplier have sufficient technical resources to modify or tailor software to suit different users' requirements?		
5 Does the supplier have a substantial user base?		
Has it shown adequate commitment to existing users and will it provide a list of them?		
Has the supplier sold similar systems to that under consideration?		
6 Does the supplier offer adequate contractual terms as regards purchase, installation, delivery, support and maintenance?		
Are all costs clearly indicated?		
Is the data of delivery of all components of the system clearly stated?		
7 Is there adequate evidence that the supplier normally meets its contractual obligations?		
8 Will the supplier provide in-depth demonstrations of its software?		

Nominal Ledger

General

1 Are the programs menu driven?	yes	
If 'YES' – can menus be by-passed once the user is familiar with the package?	yes	Menus are not displayed if reply typed ahead.
2 Does the system maintain a log of usage?	yes	Event logging from main menu.
3 Are informative messages produced on-screen whilst running?	yes	
4 Are errors messages informative and easy to understand?	yes	
5 Is the system multi-company?	yes	Up to 99 companies.
6 Is the original set-up straightforward?	yes	'Skeleton' company accounts and statement format set up.
7 Is there a copy/restore facility in the package?	yes	
8 Does the system cover disciplined taking of back-ups?	yes	

Documentation

(a) Manual

1 Is the manual clearly laid out and understandable?	yes	
2 Is the manual comprehensive and accurate?	yes	
3 Is there an index?	yes	
4 Is it easy to follow through all procedures?	yes	Tutorial.
5 Is it easy to locate specific points when required?	yes	Reference section based on a menu-by-menu basis.
6 Are completed examples included?	yes	

OTHER PACKAGES 319

BUSINESS DESK		FACT		SHORTLANDS GOLD	
yes		yes		yes	
yes		yes		no	
no		yes		yes	
yes		yes		yes	
yes		yes	Messages are also listed in manual.	yes	
yes		yes		yes	If required.
yes		yes		yes	
yes	Utility.	yes		no	Via operating system.
yes		yes		no	Explained in manuals.
yes		yes		yes	
yes		yes		yes	
no		yes	Numerical and alphabetical.	yes	
yes		yes		yes	
yes		yes		yes	
no		yes		yes	

320 A GUIDE TO ACCOUNTING SOFTWARE

		BOS

(b) Help screens

7 Are help screens available?	no	Can be set up by user.
If 'YES' –		
Do they provide on-line instructions?		
Can they be edited or prepared by the user?		

Account Details

1 Is the chart of accounts flexible?	yes	
2 What is the format of the nominal account code?		Flexible. 10 alphanumeric+2-digit department+2-digit company codes.
3 Is cost centre accounting available?	yes	Departmental accounting.
4 What is the maximum number of accounts that can be held?		Limited only by disk size.
5 What is the maximum balance that can be held?		£999,999,999.99.
6 Can accounts be added/deleted/amended at any time?	yes	Cannot be deleted if non-zero balance.
7 Is file automatically re-sorted when a new account is added?	N/A	Indexed sequential file.
If 'NO' – can a resort be initiated?		
8 Is deletion of an account prevented if it has:		
a non-zero balance	yes	
a zero balance but postings in the current period	yes	
a zero balance but postings in the year-to-date?	yes	
9 Is a hard copy of changes in account details automatically produced?	no	Optional.
10 Are 12 or 13 (or more) accounting periods available?		13
11 Can budgets be entered for all revenue accounts?	yes	
12 Can separate budgets be entered for each accounting period?	yes	
13 Can this year's results be used to calculate next year's budgets automatically?	yes	

Transactions

1 What is the maximum transaction value that can be entered?		£999,999,999.99.
2 Can each journal entry contain an unlimited number of debits and credits?		Up to 9,999.
3 Is each input line numbered?	yes	
4 In a long journal entry is it possible to move between screens to view data already input?	yes	
5 Can previously entered journal lines be edited before accepting the whole journal?	yes	
6 Does each journal entry have a reference number?	yes	
7 Are accruals and pre-payments routines, which both reverse automatically at the start of the next accounting period, available?	yes	
8 Can recurring journal entries be provided for automatically?	yes	

OTHER PACKAGES 321

BUSINESS DESK		FACT		SHORTLANDS GOLD	
no		yes		no	
		yes			
		no			
yes		yes	Main accounts and sub accounts available.	yes	Very flexible.
	4-alphanumeric + 2-digit cost centre.		8 numeric.		Up to 12 alphanumeric available.
yes		yes		yes	Up to 6 levels of subtotalling.
	No maximum.		No maximum.		No maximum.
	£999,999,999.99.		£999,999,999.99.		13 figures before decimal place.
yes		yes		yes	Not deleted if balance on account.
N/A	Indexed, ensures correct sequence.	N/A	Index ensures correct sequence.	yes	
yes		yes		yes	
yes		no		yes	
yes	If required.	no		yes	
no		no		yes	
	Any number.	yes	13.	yes	
no		yes		yes	
no		yes		yes	
no		yes	Via two way links to Lotus.	no	
	£99,999,999.99.		£999,999,999.99.		11 figures before the decimal place.
no	15 in total.	no	Maximum 53 lines.	no	Limit of 100 entries.
yes		yes		yes	
N/A		yes		yes	
yes		yes		yes	
yes		yes		yes	
no		yes		yes	
no		yes		yes	

		BOS
9 Is a narrative available for:		
each journal entry	yes	
each line of the journal entry	yes	
10 Can journal entries be posted to future periods?	yes	Standing journals available.
11 Can journal entries be posted to previous periods?	yes	One previous open period.
12 Are all transactions retained on file for at least one period?	yes	Selective purge available.
13 Can transactions be retained at the period-end?	yes	
14 Can a ledger date pre-date existing transactions?	no	

Input Controls

1 Is password control used?	yes	
If 'YES' – give detail		3 levels of password.
2 Is a hard copy automatically produced for all input?	yes	
3 Are journal entries automatically sequentially numbered?	yes	
4 If integrated, are automatic postings from other modules included in the numbering sequence?	yes	
5 If accruals and pre-payments automatically reverse, is the reversal included in the numbering sequence?	yes	
6 Are totals, of debit or credit entries, produced for all journal entries?	yes	
If 'YES' – is it necessary that this agrees with a pre-list total?	yes	Control total for batch can be amended.
7 Is it necessary that all journal entries balance before posting?	yes	
8 Is production of an out-of-balance trial balance prevented?	yes	
9 Do all input screens show clearly:		
type of entry	yes	
the distinction between debits and credits	yes	
10 Can the actual date of posting, or a batch reference, be shown on hard copies of transactions input?	yes	
11 Are the following validated:		
date	yes	
nominal ledger account code	yes	
cost centre code	yes	Department code.
If 'NO' – are unidentified/invalid entries posted to a suspense account?		
– how is suspense account treated?		
12 Is a total produced of all debit/credit transactions processed?	yes	
If 'YES' – is a report produced at the end of each processing run to reconcile b/f total, transactions processed and c/f total?	yes	

OTHER PACKAGES 323

BUSINESS DESK		FACT		SHORTLANDS GOLD	
yes		yes		yes	
yes		yes		yes	
no		yes		yes	Up to 4 future periods.
yes		yes	Password protected.	no	But prior period adjustments can be posted through a special program.
yes		yes		yes	
yes		yes		yes	Up to 13 prior periods can be kept.
yes		yes		yes	
yes		yes		yes	
	Program level.		Each menu option can either be free or blocked for a particular password.		Password protected at (a) company level (b) module level (c) program level
yes		yes		yes	
yes		no		no	
yes		no		no	
		no		no	
yes		yes		yes	
no		no		no	
yes		yes		yes	
yes		yes		yes	
yes		yes		yes	
yes		yes		yes	
yes		yes		yes	
yes		yes		yes	
yes		yes		yes	
yes		yes		yes	As part of nominal ledger account code.
yes		yes		yes	
yes		no		yes	

	BOS
13 Is a reconciliation of numbers of accounts produced after amendment of the accounts detail file?	no
14 Does the system prevent the abnormal termination of programs?	yes

Integration

	BOS
1 Is integration possible with the following:	
sales ledger	yes
purchase ledger	yes
payroll	yes
2 Can the nominal ledger be updated as often as desired?	yes
3 Is a hard copy automatically produced at the end of each nominal ledger update?	yes
4 Is there a sales/purchase ledger print-out of the nominal ledger update?	yes
5 Are sales ledger and purchase ledger control accounts agreed to the totals of balances in the individual ledgers?	yes
6 Is there a check that the nominal ledger cannot be updated twice with the same sales/purchases data?	yes
7 Must the nominal ledger be updated from the sales and purchases ledgers before the period-end is run?	no
8 Must the nominal ledger be in the same period as the sales and purchases ledgers for the update to be carried out?	no
9 Is there any check that all data processed in the sales/purchase ledgers has been posted to the nominal ledger?	yes
10 Are unidentified/invalid entries held in a nominal ledger suspense account?	yes
If 'YES' – how is this treated?	The user should journal items out of this account.
11 Can the user select whether to update the nominal ledger with individual sales/purchase ledger entries or in total?	yes
If 'NO' – is the update made in detail or in total?	
12 Is it impossible to post directly to the sales/purchase ledger control accounts?	no

Output

(a) General

	BOS
1 Is it necessary to produce an audit trail before the period-end procedure is run?	yes
2 Does the audit trail enable all transactions to be traced fully through the system?	yes
3 Can the actual run date, or batch reference, as well as the current ledger date, be shown on all reports?	yes
4 Can the following be seen on screen:	
account details	yes
account transactions	yes
5 Can a print-out of the following be obtained for individual accounts/selected ranges of accounts:	
account details	yes
account transactions	yes

OTHER PACKAGES

BUSINESS DESK		FACT		SHORTLANDS GOLD	
no		no		no	
yes		yes	A special recovery procedure must be followed by the user to re-enter the system.	yes	
yes		yes		yes	
yes		yes		yes	
no		yes		yes	
yes		yes		yes	
no		yes		yes	
yes		yes	Combined Report.	yes	
yes	Via validate program.		By user verification.	yes	
yes		yes	Transactions posted to sales ledger and purchase ledger will only update nominal ledger once.	yes	
yes		yes		yes	
	Yes – purchase ledger. No – sales ledger.	yes		no	
yes	Automatic update.	yes		yes	
N/A		yes		yes	
			As part of the nominal ledger.		User must investigate and correct.
no		no		yes	
	Detail except to debtors, creditors and VAT control.		Action dependent on setting for each nominal account.		
yes		no		yes	
yes		no	Automatically produced.	no	Produced automatically on data input.
yes		yes		yes	
yes		no		yes	
yes		yes		yes	
yes		yes		yes	
yes		yes		yes	
yes		yes		yes	

		BOS
6 Do all outputs show clearly the distinction between debit and credit entries?	yes	
7 Are all reports adequately titled?	yes	
8 Do reports provide totals where applicable?	yes	
9 Is the period number shown on reports?	no	Period start and end dates shown.
10 Can the following be produced:		
trial balance	yes	
ledger account detail report	yes	
profit and loss account	yes	Up to 45 user definable reports.
balance sheet	yes	Up to 45 user definable reports.
11 Does the ledger account detail report show the source of postings and narrative input?	yes	
12 Does the ledger account detail report show either the full account history or balance b/f together with the current period's transactions?	yes	
13 Are all report pages numbered sequentially, with the end of report identified?	yes	Date and time shown.
14 Can reports be temporarily retained on file for subsequent printing?	yes	Optional spooler.
If 'YES' – are such files protected from deletion?	yes	
15 Is a report generator available for use with the nominal ledger module?	yes	
16 Can transaction files for all previous periods be retained in the system to permit enquiries and reports?	yes	
(b) Trial balance; P&L and balance sheet		
1 Does the package provide for flexible formatting of profit and loss account and balance sheet?	yes	
2 Can the following be produced for both the current period and the year-to-date:		
trial balance	yes	
profit and loss account	yes	
balance sheet	yes	
If 'YES' – is it clearly shown whether a report is for the current period or year-to-date?	yes	
3 Can the following show budgets:		
trial balance	yes	Period performance options on trial balance menu.
profit and loss account	yes	
If 'YES' – can budgets be omitted if wished?	yes	

OTHER PACKAGES 327

BUSINESS DESK		FACT		SHORTLANDS GOLD	
yes		yes		yes	
yes		yes	Either system standard description or user's own.	yes	
yes		yes		yes	
yes	Where applicable.	yes		yes	
yes		yes		yes	
yes		yes		yes	
yes		yes	Via extended trial balance or management reports module.	yes	Through management report writer.
yes		yes		yes	
yes		yes		yes	
yes	As required.	yes	Either is available.	yes	
yes		yes		yes	
yes		yes		yes	
no		no		no	
no		yes		yes	
no		no		yes	
yes		yes	Via management reports module.	yes	Via management report wirter.
yes		yes		yes	
yes		yes	Via management reports module.	yes	
yes		yes	Via management reports module.	yes	
yes		yes	Via management reports module.	yes	
no		no		yes	
no		yes	Via management reports module.	yes	
		yes	Via management reports module.		No – from trial balance. Yes – from profit and loss.

		BOS
4 Can the following reports show comparative figures:		
trial balance	yes	Period performance options on trial balance.
profit and loss account	yes	
balance sheet	yes	
If 'YES' – can comparatives be omitted?	yes	
– can two years' comparatives be shown	no	
5 Are budgets worked out from the period number as calculated by the number of period-end procedures run?	yes	
6 Are budget variances calculated?	yes	
If 'YES' are they shown as:		
value	yes	
percentages	no	
both	no	
7 Do budget reports provide for exception reporting?	no	
8 Does the package provide for a trial balance to be produced for each cost centre?	yes	Departmental reporting.
9 Does the package provide for a profit and loss account and balance sheet for each cost centre?	yes	Departmental reporting.
10 Does the package provide for totalling of like items across cost centres?	yes	Departmental reporting.
11 Can trial balance production be varied by:		
printing a range of accounts	yes	
subtotalling on any chosen digit of account code	no	
12 Can vertical percentages be calculated in the profit and loss account?	yes	
13 Can a report be produced to show the breakdown of profit and loss account and balance sheet figures?	yes	
Year End		
1 Can balance sheet items be carried forward and profit and loss account items be cleared automatically at the year-end?	yes	
2 Can the destination of individual account balances be specified or are all balances cleared at the year-end transferred into one account only?		One account.

Sales Ledger

General		
1 Are the programs menu-driven?	yes	
If 'YES' – can menus be by-passed once the user is familiar with the package?	yes	Menus are not displayed if reply typed ahead.
2 Does the system maintain a log of usage?	yes	Event logging from main menu.
3 Are informative messages produced on-screen whilst running?	yes	
4 Are errors messages informative and easy to understand?	yes	
5 Is the system multi-company?	yes	

OTHER PACKAGES

BUSINESS DESK		FACT		SHORTLANDS GOLD	
no		no		yes	
no		yes	Via management reports module.	yes	
no		yes	Via management reports module.	yes	
		yes		yes	
		no		no	
N/A		no		no	
N/A		yes	Via management reports module.	yes	
		yes	Via management reports module.	yes	
		yes	Via management reports module.	yes	
		yes	Via management reports module.	yes	
N/A		no		yes	
no		yes		yes	
yes		yes	Via management reports module.	yes	
yes		yes	Via management reports module.	yes	
yes		yes		yes	
no		yes		yes	
no		yes	Via management reports module.	yes	
yes		yes		yes	
yes		yes		yes	
	All cleared profit and loss accounts to one account in balance sheet for profit retained.		One account only for each company.		Profit and loss items transferred to one account only.
yes		yes		yes	
yes		yes		no	
no		yes		yes	
yes		yes		yes	
yes		yes	Messages are also listed in manual.	yes	
yes		yes		yes	If required.

	BOS

6 Is the original set-up straightforward? — yes
7 Is there a copy/restore facility in the package? — yes
8 Does the system cover disciplined taking of back-ups? — yes

Documentation
(a) Manual

1 Is the manual clearly laid out and understandable? — yes
2 Is the manual comprehensive and accurate? — yes
3 Is there an index? — yes
4 Is it easy to follow through all procedures? — yes | Tutorial.
5 Is it easy to locate specific points when required? — yes | Reference section based on a menu-by-menu basis.
6 Are completed examples included? — yes

(b) Help screens

7 Are help screens available? — no | Can be set up by user.

If 'YES' –

Do they provide on-line instructions?

Can they be edited or prepared by the user?

Customer Details

1 What is the format of the customer account code? | Flexible. Up to 7 alphanumeric.
2 What other customer details are held? | Currency, up to 242 address, credit limit, terms and discount details, nearest warehouse etc....

Do these seem to be sufficient in general? — yes

3 What is the maximum number of accounts that can be held? | Limited only by computer disk size.
4 Can customer details be added/deleted/amended at any time? — yes | Cannot delete if outstanding transactions.
5 Is file re-sorted automatically when a new customer is added? — N/A | Indexed sequential.

If 'NO' – can a re-sort be initiated?

6 Is deletion of a customer prevented if the account has:

   an outstanding balance — yes

   a zero balance but a b/f turnover — yes

7 Is a hard copy of changes in customer details automatically produced? — yes | Option in system parameter.

If 'NO' – can a hard copy be taken?

Transactions

1 Can the system be open item? — yes

OTHER PACKAGES

BUSINESS DESK		FACT		SHORTLANDS GOLD	
yes		yes		yes	
yes	Utility.	yes		no	In operating system.
yes		yes		no	But the manuals clearly explain how and when to take back-ups.
yes		yes		yes	
yes		yes		yes	
no		yes	Numerical and alphabetical.	yes	
yes		yes		yes	
yes		yes		yes	
no		yes		yes	
no		yes		no	
		yes			
		no			
	6 alphanumeric.		8 numeric.	yes	Up to 10 alphanumeric.
	Name, address, notes, credit details, settlement discount details, turnover.		Name, address, telephone no., debtor group, credit limit, bank a/c no. Due term in days, turnover.		Name, address, credit limit, payment terms, discount % allowed, 5 user-defined extra fields for additional information.
yes		yes		yes	
	No maximum.		No maximum.		Unlimited.
yes		yes		yes	No deletions if balance on account.
N/A	Indexed files.	N/A	Index ensures correct sequence.	yes	
yes		yes		yes	
no		no	The existence of settled invoices will preclude deletion.	yes	
no		no		yes	
yes		yes			
yes		yes	Mandatory.	yes	

	BOS	
2 Are the following inputs possible:		
invoices	yes	
credit notes	yes	
cash received	yes	
cash refunded	yes	Journals.
discounts	yes	
journal entries	yes	
write-offs	yes	Journals.
3 Can an invoice be analysed to several different sales categories?	yes	
4 Are different VAT codes possible for different items within one invoice?	yes	
5 Are all transactions retained on file for at least one period?	yes	
6 Can a ledger date pre-date existing transactions?	no	

Matching/Allocations

(a) Balance forward

	BOS	
1 Is the balance b/f aged?	yes	
2 Can cash be allocated automatically?	yes	
If 'YES' – how is the allocation made?		Oldest first or any later %'s balance-selected.
– can this be overriden	yes	
3 Can cash be allocated manually?	yes	
If 'YES' – does the package check that cash allocated = amount received?	yes	
How is any such difference treated?		Available for subsequent allocation or can be left unallocated.
4 Can credit notes/journal entries be allocated to previous periods?	no	
5 Can cash in advance be held and later allocated to subsequent periods?	yes	
6 Can cash be held unallocated?	yes	

(b) Open item

	BOS	
7 Are outstanding transactions displayed for allocation?	yes	
8 Can cash be allocated automatically?	yes	
If 'YES' – how is the allocation made?		Oldest first or any later selection.
– can this be over-ridden?	yes	
9 Can cash be allocated manually?	yes	
If 'YES' does the package check that cash allocated = cash received?	yes	
How is any difference treated?		Available for subsequent allocation or can be left unallocated.
10 Can an over/under-payment of an invoice be recorded?	yes	

OTHER PACKAGES 333

BUSINESS DESK		FACT		SHORTLANDS GOLD	
yes		yes		yes	Ranges of invoices can be paid.
yes		yes		yes	
yes		yes		yes	
yes		yes		yes	
yes		yes		yes	
yes		yes		yes	
yes		yes		yes	
yes		yes	By using different revenue a/c's.	yes	Up to 50 on each.
yes		N/A	VAT is input by amount. VAT codes not used.	yes	
yes		yes	User controls retention period.	yes	
yes		yes		yes	
yes		N/A	System is open-item.	no	
yes	Oldest first.				Ranges of invoices can be paid.
yes				yes	
yes				yes	
yes				yes	
	Not allowed.				Not allowed.
yes				no	
yes				yes	
no				yes	
yes		yes		yes	
yes		yes			
	Oldest first.		By date of invoice.		Ranges of invoices can be paid.
yes		yes		yes	
yes		yes		yes	
yes		yes	Error message if not equal.	yes	
			System can be 'forced' to accept either amount allocated or amount received.		Not allowed.
yes		yes		yes	

	BOS
11 How often are settled items deleted from file?	Optional purge.
12 Can credit notes be set against the invoices to which they refer?	yes
13 Can journal entries be set against the invoices/credit notes to which they refer?	yes
14 Can cash in advance be held and later allocated to invoice?	yes
15 Can cash be held unallocated?	yes
– how is this treated	Shown as unallocated cash on statement.

Input Controls

	BOS
1 Is password control used?	yes
If 'YES' – give detail	3 levels of password.
2 Is a hard copy automatically produced for all input?	yes
3 Are the batch totals automatically produced for all transactions input?	yes
If 'YES' – what is the procedure if this does not agree with a pre-list total?	Can amend the details so control total matches.
4 Is it necessary that invoices, cash and adjustments are input in separate batches?	yes
5 Are batches automatically sequentially numbered?	yes
If 'NO' – can they be so numbered?	
6 Is a report produced at the end of each processing run to reconcile b/f total, transactions processed and c/f total?	yes Optional.
If 'NO' – is a control balance produced at the end of each posting run?	
7 Are the following validated:	
date	yes
customer account number	yes
VAT code	yes
goods value	yes If invoicing or sales order processing.
sales analysis code	yes
8 Is VAT calculated to check figure input?	yes
9 Is the gross figure agreed to goods+VAT?	yes
10 Is discount calculated to check the figure input?	yes
11 Can the actual date of posting, or batch reference, be shown on hard copies of transactions input?	yes
12 Does the screen always indicate that the sales ledger, as opposed to the purchase ledger, is running?	no Not always necessary.
13 Do all input screens show clearly:	
type of entry	yes
the distinction between debits and credits	yes
14 Is there any check that the same entry is not input twice?	Batch numbering.

BUSINESS DESK		FACT		SHORTLANDS GOLD	
	Every period.		When user operates option.		If 'open-item' – after month end update. If 'never-cleared' – never.
yes		yes	Separate entry to match.	yes	
yes		yes		yes	
yes		yes		yes	
yes		yes		yes	
	Transactions held until period end allocated.		Cash must be allocated to a dummy invoice number.		Flagged as COA (cash on account) – can be allocated at later date.
no		yes		yes	
			Each menu option can either be free or blocked for a particular password.	yes	Password protection at:- (a) company level (b) module level (c) program level
no		yes		yes	
	On audit trails.	yes		yes	If batching opted for.
		yes	User must make correction if necessary in subsequent batch.		User not prevented from accepting batch but difference is shown on audit trail.
yes		no		yes	
yes		yes		no	
				yes	
	If required – must be run before period end.	no		yes	
		no			
yes		yes		yes	
yes		yes		yes	
yes		no	Not used.	yes	
yes		yes	Document must balance.	yes	
yes		yes		yes	
yes		no		no	But validation is being included in next release (3.2).
yes		yes		yes	
yes		no		yes	
yes		yes		yes	
yes		yes		yes	
yes		yes		yes	
yes		yes		yes	
no		yes	Duplicate invoice numbers are not permitted.	yes	

	BOS	
15 Is there a warning if a customer exceeds the credit limit?	yes	
If 'YES' – what action is required?		None.
16 Is it impossible for new accounts to be created during processing?	no	
17 Is a reconciliation of numbers of accounts produced after amendment of the customer detail file?	no	
18 Does the system prevent the abnormal termination of programs?	yes	

Integration

1 Can the sales ledger be integrated with an invoicing module?	yes	
2 Can the sales ledger be integrated with a nominal ledger module?	yes	
3 Can the nominal ledger be updated as often as desired?	yes	
4 Is a hard copy automatically produced at the end of each nominal ledger update?	yes	
5 Is there a sales ledger print-out (as well as a nominal ledger print-out) of the nominal ledger update?	yes	Optional.
6 Are the following automatically posted to the appropriate nominal ledger accounts:		
discount	yes	
discount written back	no	Journal adjustment.
bad debts written off	no	Journal adjustment.
contras with purchase ledger	no	Journal adjustment.
7 Are any invalid/unidentified entries posted to a suspense account?	yes	
If 'NO' – how are they treated?		
If 'YES' – how is the suspense account treated?		Can be journalled in nominal ledger.
8 Is the sales ledger control balance agreed to the total of the balances in the sales ledger?	yes	
9 Can current and future periods be maintained simultaneously?	yes	2 periods.
10 Is there a check that transactions cannot be posted twice to the nominal ledger?	yes	
11 Must the nominal ledger be updated from the sales ledger before the period-end is run?	no	
12 Must the nominal ledger and the sales ledger be in the same period for the update to be carried out?	no	
13 Is there any report/warning that transactions posted to the sales ledger have not yet been posted to the nominal ledger?	no	

Output

1 Is it necessary to produce an audit trail before the period-end procedure is run?	yes	
2 Does the audit trail enable all transactions to be traced fully through the system?	yes	
3 Can the actual run date, or batch reference, as well as current ledger date, be shown on reports?	yes	

OTHER PACKAGES 337

BUSINESS DESK		FACT		SHORTLANDS GOLD	
yes		yes	Printed on sales ledger.	yes	Only if customer order processing.
	Operator key depression.		None.		
yes		no		yes	
no		no		no	
yes		no	A special recovery procedure must be followed by the user to re-enter the system.	yes	
yes		yes		yes	
yes		yes		yes	
yes		yes		yes	
no		yes		yes	
yes		yes	Combined report.	yes	
yes		yes		yes	
yes		yes		yes	
yes		yes		yes	
yes		yes		yes	
no	Not allowed – validated on input.	yes		no	Not allowed at all – validated on input.
			Part of nominal ledger.		
yes			Only by user verification.	yes	
no		yes	Next period only.	yes	1 future period only.
yes		yes	Transactions posted to sales ledger will only update nominal ledger once.	yes	
yes	Automatic update.	yes		yes	
no		yes		no	
N/A		yes	A period end cannot be run if transactions are outstanding.	yes	
yes		no	Automatically produced.	yes	Automatically produced when period end run, as well as on data input.
yes		yes		yes	
yes		no		yes	

	BOS	
4 Can the following be produced:		
list of master file information	yes	
aged debtors report	yes	
VAT report	yes	
ledger detail report	yes	
customer statements	yes	
customer name and address labels	no	Report generator.
debt collection letters	yes	Word processing interface.
5 Does the customer statement show:		
all o/s transactions together with all items settled in the current period	yes	Open item.
or all o/s transactions only		
or the balance b/f and the current period's transactions	yes	Balance forward.
or just the current balance		
6 Does the customer statement:		
show discount separately	no	
show ageing	yes	
allow special messages	yes	
allow for suppression of erroneous postings and their corrections	no	
7 Can the following screens be seen:		
customer details	yes	
customer transactions	yes	
8 Can hard copies of the following be obtained for individual accounts/selected ranges of accounts:		
customer details	yes	
customer transactions	yes	
9 Does the ledger account detail report/copy statements show:		
the source of all postings	yes	
how part payments and allocations have been treated	yes	
either the full account history or balance b/f together with the current period's transactions	yes	
10 Does the aged analysis show for each customer:		
total balance o/s	yes	
credit limit	yes	
11 Is ageing strictly by transaction date?	no	
If 'NO' – how is ageing done.		Choice of ageing periods.

BUSINESS DESK	FACT		SHORTLANDS GOLD	
yes	yes		yes	
yes	yes	By invoice date or by due date.	yes	
yes	no		yes	
yes	yes		yes	
yes	yes		yes	
yes	yes		yes	
no	no			Through qPlex IV report generator.
yes	yes	If option selected.	yes	
yes { All options available.	yes	If option selected.	no	
yes	no	Open item.	yes	If 'balance brought' forward, type of account.
yes	no		no	
yes	no		yes	
yes	no		no	
yes	yes		no	
no	no		no	
yes	yes		yes	
yes	yes		yes	
yes	yes		yes	
yes	yes		yes	
yes	yes		yes	
yes	yes		yes	
yes	yes	Full a/c history.	yes	
yes	yes		yes	
yes	no		yes	
yes	no		no	
		Either by invoice date or by due date.		Can be aged by invoice date or due date.

		BOS	
12	Does the aged analysis show unallocated cash separately?	yes	
	If 'NO' – how is it aged?		
13	Do all outputs show clearly the distinction between debits and credits?	yes	
14	Are all reports adequately titled?	yes	
15	Do reports provide totals where applicable?	yes	
16	Can report production be varied by:		
	printing a range of accounts	yes	
	printing by, e.g., area/rep.	yes	Sales analysis.
17	Is the period number shown on reports?	no	Period start and end date.
18	Are all report pages sequentially numbered with the end of report identified?	yes	Date and time shown.
19	Is a sales analysis possible?	yes	
20	Can reports be temporarily retained on file for subsequent printing?	yes	Optional spooler.
	If 'YES' – are such files protected from deletion?	yes	
21	Is a report generator available for use with the sales ledger module?	yes	
22	Can transaction files for previous periods be retained in the system to permit enquiries and reports?	yes	

Purchase Ledger

General

1	Are the programs menu-driven?	yes	
	If 'YES' – can menus be by-passed once the user is familiar with the package?	yes	Menus are not displayed if reply typed ahead.
2	Does the system maintain a log of usage?	yes	Event logging from main menu.
3	Are informative messages produced on-screen whilst running?	yes	
4	Are error messages informative and easy to understand?	yes	
5	Is the system multi-company?	yes	
6	Is the original set-up straightforward?	yes	
7	Is there a copy/restore facility in the package?	yes	
8	Does the system cover disciplined taking of back-ups?	yes	

Documentation
(a) Manual

1	Is the manual clearly laid out and understandable?	yes	
2	Is the manual comprehensive and accurate?	yes	
3	Is there an index?	yes	
4	Is it easy to follow through all procedures?	yes	Tutorial.
5	Is it easy to locate specific points when required?	yes	Reference section based on a menu-by-menu basis.
6	Are completed examples included?	yes	

OTHER PACKAGES 341

BUSINESS DESK		FACT		SHORTLANDS GOLD	
yes		no		no	
			By posting date.		Aged from date of input.
yes		yes		yes	
yes		yes	Either system standard descriptions or user's own.	yes	
yes		yes		yes	
yes		yes		yes	
yes		yes	Debtor group range.	yes	
	Where appropriate.	yes		yes	
yes		yes		yes	
no		yes	By revenue account number or by extracting transactions to Lotus (in nominal ledger).	no	Only if customer order processing and stock installed.
yes		yes		yes	
no		no		no	
no		no		yes	qPlex IV report generator.
no		no		yes	
yes		yes		yes	
yes		yes		no	
no		yes		yes	
yes		yes		yes	
yes		yes	Also listed in manual.	yes	
yes		yes		yes	If required.
yes		yes		yes	
yes	Utility.	yes		no	Via operating system.
yes		yes		no	Explained in manuals.
yes		yes		yes	
yes		yes		yes	
no		yes	Numerical and alphabetical.	yes	
yes		yes		yes	
yes		yes		yes	
no		yes		yes	

(b) Help screens

		BOS
7 Are help screens available?	no	Can be set up by user.

If 'YES'

    Do they provide on-line instructions?

    Can they be edited or prepared by the user?

Supplier Details

1 What is the format of the supplier account code?		Flexible. Up to 7 alphanumeric.
2 What other supplier details are held?		Discount and terms details, factor details, address, etc.
Do these seem to be sufficient in general?	yes	
3 What is the maximum number of accounts that can be held?		Limited only by disk size.
4 Can supplier details be added/deleted/amended at any time?	yes	Cannot be deleted if outstanding transactions.
5 Is file re-sorted automatically when a new supplier is added?	N/A	Indexed sequential.
If 'NO' – can a re-sort be initiated?		
6 Is deletion of a supplier prevented if the account has:		
an outstanding balance	yes	
a zero balance but a b/f turnover	yes	
7 Is a hard copy of changes in supplier details automatically produced?	yes	Option in system parameters.
If 'NO' – can a hard copy be taken?	yes	

Transactions

1 Can the system be open item?	yes	
2 Are the following inputs possible:		
invoices	yes	
credit notes	yes	
manual payments	yes	
cash refunded	yes	Using journals.
discounts	yes	
3 Can an invoice be analysed to several different expense categories?	yes	
4 Are different VAT codes possible for different items within one invoice?	yes	
5 Are all transactions retained on file for at least one period?	yes	
6 Can a ledger date pre-date existing transactions?	yes	
7 Can 2 references be input for an invoice (own and supplier's reference)?	yes	

	BUSINESS DESK		FACT		SHORTLANDS GOLD	
no		yes		no	
		yes			
		no			
	6 alphanumeric.		8 numeric.		Up to 10 characters alphanumeric.
	Name, address, notes, aged balances and turnover.		Name, address, telephone no., creditor group, bank a/c no., due terms in days, turnover.		Name, address, payment terms. % discount received, 5 user-defined extra fields, e.g. for contact, telephone, telex area etc.
yes		yes		yes	
	No maximum.		No maximum.		No limit.
yes		yes		yes	No deletion if balance on account.
N/A	Indexed.	N/A	Index ensures correct sequence.	N/A	
				yes	
yes		yes		yes	
no		no	The existence of settled invoices will preclude deletion.	yes	
no		no		yes	
yes		yes			
yes		yes	Mandatory.	yes	
yes		yes		yes	
yes		yes		yes	
yes		yes		yes	
yes		yes		yes	
yes		yes		yes	
yes		yes	By using different nominal ledger expense a/c's.	yes	Up to 50 on each.
yes		N/A	VAT codes not used. VAT is input by amount.	yes	
yes		yes	User controls retention periods.	yes	
yes		yes		yes	
yes		yes		yes	

Matching/Allocations
(a) Balance forward

		BOS
1 Is the balance b/f aged?	yes	
2 Can cash be allocated automatically?	yes	
If 'YES' – how is the allocation made?		
– can this be over-ridden?	yes	
3 Can cash be allocated manually?	yes	
If 'YES' – does the package check that cash allocated = amount paid?	yes	Available for subsequent allocation.
How is any such difference treated?		
4 Can credit notes/journal entries be allocated to previous periods?	no	
5 Can cash in advance be held and later allocated to subsequent periods?	yes	

(b) Open item

6 Are outstanding transactions displayed for allocation?	yes	
7 Can cash be allocated automatically?	yes	
If 'YES' – how is the allocation made?		Oldest first or any later selection.
– can this be over-ridden?	yes	
8 Can cash be allocated manually?	yes	
If 'YES' does the package check that cash allocated = cash paid?		
How is any difference treated?		Available for subsequent allocation, or can be left unallocated.
9 Can an over/underpayment of an invoice be recorded?	yes	
10 How often are settled items deleted from file?		Optional purge.
11 Can credit notes be set against the invoices to which they refer?	yes	
12 Can journal entries be set against the invoices/credit notes to which they refer?	yes	
13 Can each in advance be held and later allocated to invoice.	yes	
14 Can cash be held unallocated?	yes	
– how is this treated?		Shown as unallocated code on remittance advice.

Input Controls

1 Is password control used?	yes	
If 'YES' – give detail		3 levels of password.
2 Is a hard copy automatically produced for all input?	yes	
3 Are batch totals automatically produced for all transactions input?	yes	
If 'YES' – what is the procedure if this does not agree with a pre-list total?		Can amend the details so control total matches.
4 Is it necessary that invoices, cash and adjustments are input in separate batches?	yes	

OTHER PACKAGES

BUSINESS DESK		FACT		SHORTLANDS GOLD	
yes		N/A	System is open item.	no	
yes				yes	
	Oldest first or any later balance selected.				By various ranges, i.e. by currency, due date, discount ranges of customers etc.
yes				yes	
yes				yes	
yes				yes	
	Not allowed.				Not allowed.
yes				no	
yes				yes	
yes		yes		yes	
yes		yes		yes	
	Oldest first.		By date *or* due date of invoice		By various ranges, i.e. by currency, due date, discount, ranges of customers, etc.
yes		yes		yes	
yes		yes		yes	
yes		yes	Error message if not equal.	yes	
			System can be 'forced' to accept either amount allocated or amount received.		Not allowed.
yes		yes		yes	
	Period end.		When user operates option.		If 'open item' after month end, if 'never cleared' – never.
yes		yes	Separate entry to match.	yes	
yes		yes		yes	
yes		yes		yes	
yes		yes		yes	
	Payment transactions held till allocated.		Cash must be allocated to a dummy invoice number.		Flagged as cash on account.
no		yes		yes	
			Each menu option can either be free or blocked for a particular password.		(a) company level (b) module level (c) program level (d) system wide level
no		yes		yes	
	On audit trails.	yes		yes	Optional.
			User must make correction if necessary in subsequent batch.		Difference shown on audit trail if posted.
yes		no		yes	

A GUIDE TO ACCOUNTING SOFTWARE

		BOS	
5	Are batches automatically sequentially numbered?	yes	
	If 'NO' – can they be so numbered?		
6	Is a report produced at the end of each processing run to reconcile b/f total, transactions processed and c/f total?	yes	
	If 'NO' – is a control balance produced at the end of each posting run?		
7	Are the following validated:		
	date	yes	
	supplier account number	yes	
	VAT code	yes	
	goods value	yes	If purchase order processing used.
	analysis code	yes	
8	Is VAT calculated to check figure input?	yes	
9	Is the gross figure agreed to goods+VAT?	yes	
10	Is discount calculated to check the figure input?	yes	
11	Can the actual date of posting, or batch reference, be shown on hard copies of transactions input?	yes	
12	Does the screen always indicate that the purchase ledger, as opposed to the sales ledger, is running?		Not always – only when necessary.
13	Do all input screens show clearly:		
	type of entry	yes	
	the distinction between debits and credits	yes	
14	Is there any check that the same entry is not input twice?	no	
15	Is there a warning if a supplier is overpaid?	no	
16	Is it impossible for new accounts to be created during processing?	no	
17	Is a reconciliation of numbers of accounts produced after amendment of the customer detail file?	no	
18	Does the system prevent the abnormal termination of progams?	yes	

Integration

1	Can the purchase ledger be integrated with a job costing module?	yes	
2	Can the purchase ledger be integrated with a nominal ledger module?	yes	
3	Can the nominal ledger be updated as often as desired?	yes	
4	Is a hard copy automatically produced at the end of each nominal ledger update?	yes	
5	Is there a purchase ledger print out (as well as a nominal ledger print out) of the nominal ledger update?	yes	Optional.
6	Are the following automatically posted to the appropriate nominal ledger accounts:		
	discount	yes	
	discount written back	no	Journal adjustment.
	contras with sales ledger	no	Journal adjustment.

OTHER PACKAGES 347

BUSINESS DESK		FACT		SHORTLANDS GOLD	
yes		yes		no	
				yes	
	As required, must be run by period end.	no		yes	
		no			
yes		yes		yes	
yes		yes		yes	
yes		no	Not used.	yes	
yes		yes	Document must balance.	yes	
yes		yes		yes	
yes		no		no	To be included in next release.
yes		yes		yes	
yes		no		yes	
yes		yes		yes	
yes		yes		yes	
yes		yes		yes	
yes		yes		yes	
no		yes	Duplicate invoice numbers are not permitted.	yes	
yes		no		no	
yes		no		yes	
no		no		no	
yes		no	A special recovery procedure must be followed by the user to re-enter the system.	yes	
no		no		yes	
yes		yes		yes	
yes		yes		yes	
no		yes		yes	
yes		yes	Combined report.	yes	
yes		yes		yes	
yes		yes		yes	
yes		yes		yes	

		BOS
7	Are any invalid/unidentified entries posted to a suspense account?	yes
	If 'NO' – how are they treated?	
	If 'YES' – how is the suspense account treated?	Can be journalled in nominal ledger.
8	Is the purchase ledger control balance agreed to the total of the balances in the purchase ledger?	yes
9	Can current and future periods be maintained simultaneously?	yes — 2 periods.
10	Is there a check that transactions cannot be posted twice to the nominal ledger?	yes
11	Must the nominal ledger be updated from the purchase ledger before the period-end is run?	no
12	Must the nominal ledger and the purchase ledger be in the same period for the update to be carried out?	no
13	Is there any report/warning that transactions posted to the purchase ledger have not yet been posted to the nominal ledger?	no

Output

		BOS
1	Is it necessary to produce an audit trail before the period-end procedure is run?	yes
2	Does the audit trail enable all transactions to be traced fully through the system?	yes
3	Can the actual run date, or batch reference, as well a current ledger date, be shown on reports?	yes
4	Can the following be produced:	
	list of master file information	yes
	aged creditors reports	yes
	VAT report	yes
	ledger detail report	yes
	remittance advices	yes
	supplier name and address labels	yes
	suggested payments	yes
	cheques	yes
5	Can remittance advices show:	
	individual invoices	yes
	discount	no
	supplier's reference	yes
6	Can the following screens be seen:	
	supplier details	yes
	supplier transactions	yes
7	Can hard copies of the following be obtained for individual accounts/selected ranges of accounts:	
	supplier details	yes
	supplier transactions	yes

OTHER PACKAGES 349

BUSINESS DESK		FACT		SHORTLANDS GOLD	
no	Validated on input.	yes		no	
	Not allowed.				Not allowed.
			Part of nominal ledger.		
yes		no	Only by user verification.	yes	
no		yes	Next period only.	yes	
yes		yes		yes	
yes		yes		yes	
yes		yes		no	
N/A		yes	A period end cannot be run if transactions are outstanding.	yes	
yes		no	Automatically produced.		Automatically produced when period end run.
yes		yes		yes	
yes		no		yes	
yes		yes		yes	
yes		yes		yes	
yes		no		yes	
yes		yes		yes	
yes		yes		yes	
yes		yes		yes	
no		yes		yes	
yes		yes		yes	+ Giros.
yes		yes		yes	
yes		no		yes	
no		yes		yes	
yes		yes		yes	} Same program.
yes		yes		yes	
yes		yes		yes	
yes		yes		yes	

350 A GUIDE TO ACCOUNTING SOFTWARE

		BOS	
8	Does the ledger account detail report show:		
	the source of all postings	yes	
	how part-payments and allocations have been treated	yes	
	either the full account history or balance b/f together with the current period's transactions?	yes	
9	Is ageing strictly by transaction date?	no	
	If 'NO' – how is ageing done?		Choice of ageing.
10	Does the aged analysis show unallocated cash separately?	yes	
	If 'NO' – how is it aged?		
11	Do all outputs show clearly the distinction between debits and credits?	yes	
12	Are all reports adequately titled?	yes	
13	Do reports provide totals where applicable?	yes	
14	Can report production be varied by:		
	printing a range of accounts?	yes	
	printing by, e.g. area?	yes	Account type.
15	Is the period number shown on reports?	no	Start and end date of period.
16	Are all report pages sequentially numbered with the end of report identified?	yes	Date and time.
17	Is a purchase analysis possible?	yes	
18	Can reports be temporarily retained on file for subsequent printing?	yes	Optional spooler.
	If 'YES' – are such files protected from deletion?	yes	
19	Is a report generator available for use with the purchase ledger module?	yes	
20	Can transaction files for previous periods be retained in the system to permit enquiries and reports?	yes	

Payments/Cheque Writing

		BOS	
1	Can the system write cheques?	yes	
	If 'YES' – is the payment posted automatically to the purchase ledger?	yes	
2	Is there an automatic cheque writing facility? If 'YES':	yes	
	is a list of suggested payments printed in advance of the cheques?	yes	
	is the total cash requirement printed in advance of the cheques?	yes	
	can the automatic payment routine be aborted if either of the above is not satisfactory?	yes	
3	Can the following payment/report options be selected:		
	individual invoice selection	yes	
	supplier selection	yes	
	pay all invoices of a certain age	yes	
	pay according to due date	yes	
	pay all invoices except these marked not to be paid	yes	
	other (specify)		Payment priority number allocated to each application.

OTHER PACKAGES 351

BUSINESS DESK		FACT		SHORTLANDS GOLD	
yes		yes		yes	
yes		yes		yes	
yes		yes	Full a/c history.	yes	
yes		no		no	
			Either by invoice date or by due date.		Invoice or due date.
yes		no		yes	On each account.
			By posting date.		
yes		yes		yes	
yes		yes	Either system standard descriptions or user's own.	yes	
yes		yes		yes	
yes		yes		yes	
yes		yes	Credit or group range.	yes	
yes	Where applicable.	yes		yes	
yes		yes		yes	
no		yes	Via nominal ledger.	yes	
yes		yes		yes	
no		no		yes	
no		no		yes	qPlex IV.
no		no		yes	
yes		yes		yes	
yes		yes		yes	
no		yes		yes	
N/A		yes		yes	
N/A		yes		yes	
N/A		yes		yes	
		yes		yes	
		yes		yes	
		yes		yes	
		yes		yes	
		yes		yes	
		yes	By credit or account group.		By currency.

	BOS
4 Is discount automatically counted by the payment routine?	yes
5 Can invoices be held as disputed?	yes
If 'YES' – can a report of disputed invoices be produced?	no

OTHER PACKAGES 353

BUSINESS DESK	FACT	SHORTLANDS GOLD
no	no	yes
no	yes	yes
	no	yes

Part 4
Appendices

Appendix 1
Information Technology Statement – Good Accounting Software

Introduction

The Institute of Chartered Accountants of Scotland recognises the need to give clear guidance to a wide audience on the qualities which contribute to well-designed accounting software. This Statement is therefore directed to those involved in the development, marketing, selection or implementation of accounting software.

The Statement deals with the essential criteria of good accounting software. It will be supplemented from time to time by separately published material intended to give guidance at a more detailed level on other aspects of software selection.

Except where specifically stated otherwise, the contents of the Statement are intended to be equally applicable to all accounting software, whether developed in house or externally.

The Statement is divided into two parts. Part I is a summary of the matters addressed by the Statement. Part II is a commentary on these matters.

Part I

Summary

1. The suitability of accounting software for each particular user will always be dependent upon that user's individual requirements. These requirements should therefore always be fully considered before software is acquired. The quality of the software developers or suppliers should also be considered at the outset (paragraphs 6–10).
2. Subject to these considerations, this Statement sets out the criteria and other factors which determine the quality of accounting software itself (paragraphs 11–14).
3. Fundamentally, good accounting software should:
– be capable of supporting the accounting functions for which it was designed (paragraphs 15–16).

- provide facilities to ensure the completeness, accuracy and continuing integrity of these accounting functions (paragraphs 17–30).
- be effectively supported and maintained (paragraphs 31–35).

4. It is also desirable that good accounting software should:
- be easy to learn, understand and operate (paragraphs 36–44).
- make the best practical use of available resources (paragraph 45).
- accommodate limited changes to reflect specific user requirements (paragraphs 46–60).

5. It is also essential, when software is implemented, for appropriate support and training to be available (paragraphs 61–67).

Part II

Commentary
Judgmental Factors in Software Assessment

6. This Statement deals with the essential criteria of good accounting software and with aspects of its installation which need particular attention if the full potential benefits of the system are to be achieved.

7. However, it should be recognised at the outset that accounting software cannot be assessed solely by reference to its intrinsic features in a mechanistic way. Significant elements of judgment, unrelated to the characteristics of the sofware itself, must always be applied when deciding or advising on the acquisition of accounting software for a particular user.

8. The following matters are particularly important and should always be considered before software is developed or acquired:
- the requirements of the potential user for financial and management information, which should be determined explicitly before any software is developed or acquired:
- the status, reputation and expertise of the software developers or suppliers.

9. In the case of packaged software, it is prudent to determine the number of current users of the package, whether they find it satisfactory for their purposes and whether the supplier is apparently following a course of steady improvement and development. However, these need not be the only factors in deciding whether to acquire a particular package. For example, a new entrant to the software market may be able to provide compensating advantages, such as proximity and individual attention, despite the lack of a track record.

10. In considering these matters, some users may feel obliged to trade off the quality of software against its cost. In doing so, however, they may sacrifice the benefits of better financial or management information which in the long term would have been more valuable.

Criteria of Good Accounting Software
Introduction
11. Subject to the matters mentioned in paragraphs 6–10 above, the criteria of good accounting software are applicable whatever the circumstances of its use. Any software which does not meet these criteria is unlikely to be generally acceptable as good software, even if some of its users find it satisfactory for their particular purposes and even though many users find acceptable ways of overcoming its deficiencies.

12. Certain criteria of good accounting software are fundamental and need to be satisfied before consideration of any others. They relate to the need for the software to perform the requisite accounting functions, to be reliable and to be properly supported and maintained. These criteria are discussed more fully in paragraphs 15–35 below.

13. Other criteria are less fundamental but nevertheless desirable. They relate to the need for the software to be easy to use, to be efficient and to offer flexibility in operation. These criteria are discussed more fully in paragraphs 36–60 below.

14. The procedures surrounding the installation of accounting software and the provision of initial training in its use, though not criteria of the software itself, are factors which directly determine its subsequent effectiveness. These matters are therefore considered in paragraphs 61–67 below.

Performance of requisite accounting functions
15. Accounting software, if it is to be considered sastisfactory, will be capable of properly performing the accounting functions for which it was designed. Two of the main reasons for dissatisfaction with accounting software are that it does not meet the specifications or reasonable expectations of its potential users and that it does not conform to the claims of its developer or supplier.

16. Accounting software should therefore perform the functions which:
– are claimed for it;
– it purports to perform;
– are required by statute;
– constitute good accounting practice;
– provide sufficient information to enable users to comply with the disclosure requirements of relevant regulatory authorities.

Reliability
17. Good accounting software, like all other good software, will perform its designated functions consistently, accurately and predictably.

18. It will therefore provide features to help ensure the completeness, accuracy and continuing integrity of the accounting process. These features must help users to maintain:

- full accounting records (paragraphs 19–23);
- accounting controls (paragraphs 24–27);
- security and continuity of processing (paragraphs 28–30).

Full accounting records

19. It should always be possible for users, by reference to the records maintained by the computer system, to trace any transaction item between its entry into the computer system and its incorporation into the final accounts or other relevant records.

20. Such a transaction trail is sometimes referred to as an audit trail. However, this suggests that such records are mainly of interest to auditors, whereas in fact they are of primary relevance to the users of the system and to those responsible for its management.

21. The retention of a full record of all accounting transactions is essential because:
- it enables users to verify the results of processing;
- in the event of processing interruption it can be used to ensure that processing is restarted at the correct point;
- it helps to ensure that the requirements of the Companies Act 1985 and other statutory requirements are fulfilled and that the requisite VAT accounting records are maintained.

22. Such a transaction trail, particularly in a small computer system, will often consist of reports or other legible output (e.g. copy customer statements), but may also take the form of records maintained on computer-accessible media, provided that such records are readily retrievable in legible form if required. In any event, such reports or records should include, or readily permit the retrieval of, all relevant control totals and value totals.

23. Such records should fully reflect the processing of items input either manually or directly from other computer systems. They should also fully incorporate all data generated by the system itself. Reports which constitute such records should be presented logically. Such records, whether printed or held on computer files, need to be retained in an orderly manner for as long as reference may need to be made to them.

Accounting controls

24. Acounting software can only be satisfactory if proper accounting controls can be exercised in connection with its use. Accounting controls should be designed to ensure or maximise:
- the completeness, accuracy and authorisation of input;
- the completeness and accuracy of processing;
- the security of data stored on computer files.

25. Such accounting controls may be exercised by means of either:
- manual control procedures involving the use of reports produced by the software;
- programmed control procedures incorporated in the software, designed to impose direct control over aspects of its operation or the continuing integrity of data processed by it (e.g. programmed checks that accounting ledgers remain in balance).

In most instances there will be a mixture of both types of control procedure.

26. Reports produced by the system should facilitate manual control procedures both over the operation of the software and over the integrity of the accounting records. Details of all amendments to standing data maintained on computer files should always be reported so that the correctness of the amendments can be checked.

27. Programmed control procedures are part of the processing carried out by the system. However, the results of such programmed control procedures should always be reported, even if they reveal nothing which requires any action, so that the user can confirm that the procedures have been carried out. Any discrepancies, unusual conditions or errors should also be reported so that the necessary action can be taken in relation to them.

Security and continuity of processing

28. Good accounting software will provide facilities to assist in maintaining the security and continuity of processing.

29. Program and data files can be lost or corrupted by a variety of different causes. When this happens, and the data or programs need to be recreated, considerable inconvenience may result. The software should therefore provide facilities for the user to take copies of programs and data at appropriate points during processing. At critical points, for example immediately before the end of an accounting period, the software should force the user to take data copies. Most of these copies need be retained only for a short period until the next copy is taken. Users should set the times of taking copies so as to minimise the need to re-enter data.

30. When a loss or corruption occurs the copy files may be used to restore the position as it was before the problem arose. In most cases this involves some re-processing of data and sometimes data needs to be re-input before the re-processing can take place. In any case, the software should be able to demonstrate, after such a recovery, that the resulting files are all fully restored.

Support and maintenance

31. Accounting software is likely to be used for a considerable time, during which there may be changes in the user's detailed requirements. These may be caused either by changes in the user's own circumstances (e.g. business

expansion) or by external factors (e.g. changes in methods of indirect taxation). In addition the software itself may need to be updated to enable it to be used with more advanced hardware, or to be corrected in relation to obscure errors which come to light during continued use. The user must therefore be sure that the system will be properly supported during its useful life.

32. If software is developed in-house, sufficient resources should be available from the outset to ensure that it can be properly maintained.

33. Purchasers of packaged software should seek a warranty with regard to specification, performance and support in the event of software failure. Such a support agreement should preferably be arranged with the company which wrote the software, and may be linked with an arrangement for the user to receive such updates to the software as may from time to time become appropriate.

34. The organisation which is to provide continuing support for the software should be sound and stable. In this connection, the following matters are particularly important:
– turnover and profitability (if the organisation is small, whether it is part of a large group of companies committed to providing continued financial support to its subsidiaries);
– number and expertise of key staff;
– availability of support in the user's locality;
– availability of an updating service at a reasonable cost;
– whether names of existing customers are made available;
– whether the software is written in a commonly-used programming language;
– whether master versions of the software and related documentation are kept with a third party so that customers can have continued support even if, for whatever reason, the original support organisation is no longer able or willing to provide it.

35. Sometimes, accounting software can only be used with one particular type of hardware. In such cases, equivalent consideration needs to be given, before the software is acquired, to the availability, quality and cost of support for the hardware.

Ease of use

36. Good accounting software will be easy to learn, understand and operate. This will be achieved by features such as:
– interactive processing (paragraphs 37–39);
– user documentation (paragraphs 40–44).

Interactive processing

37. The distinguishing characteristic of interactive processing is that, via a terminal, the user has immediate access to the functions of the system. While

the user is executing these functions the system responds with clear and helpful prompts and messages.
38. The system presents the user with visual prompts and messages which:
- request input from the user;
- identify input validation errors;
- show what processing is being performed;
- identify processing errors and malfunctions.
39. With interactive software the user is able without delay:
- to input, review and amend transaction data and reference data;
- to execute file maintenance, back-up, archive copying and other housekeeping functions.

User documentation
40. User documentation includes all the written material provided to assist the user to operate the software quickly and efficiently.
41. Documentation should include manuals, which should be properly indexed and cross-referenced. They should be easy to read, interpret and understand, and should not assumed prior knowledge or availability of immediate support.
42. Many systems supplement the manuals by permitting the user to invoke on-screen help facilities, which explain the operation of the software at particular points during processing.
43. Documentation for the benefit of users should explain fully and clearly:
- the contents of all output screens and reports;
- all system commands and functions;
- all error messages and appropriate remedial actions;
and additionally should explain clearly how the software:
- should be implemented;
- should be operated on a regular basis;
- should be controlled;
- should be safeguarded against misuse or corruption.
44. Documentation should also give examples of how to use the facilities of the software to the best advantage (e.g. in setting up an effective system of nominal ledger codes).

Efficiency
45. Good accounting software will, like other good software, make the best use of available resources within the constraints imposed by other criteria. For example, the software should operate as quickly as is consistent with adequate programmed control routines and the need to produce the necessary routine accounting reports.

Flexibility
46. Good accounting software will accommodate limited changes to reflect user requirements and will be easy to expand and upgrade. This will often involve the use of features such as:
– integration facilities (paragraphs 47–53);
– reporting flexibility (paragraphs 54–57);
– parameter (or table) facilities (paragraphs 58–60).

Integration facilities
47. Integration of accounting software is the process whereby the data entered into one application or sub-system is used to update files in other applications or sub-systems without the need to re-enter the data manually, thereby reducing data entry time, increasing efficiency and minimising the risk of error.
48. Most accounting software is modular. This means that each application (i.e. sales ledger, purchase ledger, etc.) operates separately from the others. Where such modules can be linked together they are often described as integrated.
49. The method of integration differs from case to case. Some software provides for immediate integration (i.e. as soon as a transaction is input). Other software provides for subsequent integration (e.g. it is carried out at the end of each batch or each day). Some applications may work on a combination of both methods.
50. If more than one application is to be installed by a computer user it is advisable to select software which provides for controlled integration (i.e. it is immediately apparent what information is being transferred across from one application to another and there is clear evidence of how each application is affected).
51. Where the data used in an accounting system also needs to be used in other processes (e.g. forecasting; narrative reporting), the ability to communicate with other types of system (e.g. spreadsheet; word processing) may also be desirable.
52. With fully integated software, no operator intervention is required, after prime data input, in order to ensure that the effect of a transaction is fully recorded within the accounting system. A fully integrated accounting system will update all the relevant files automatically, thereby saving the time which would otherwise have been needed to carry out these updates individually. In these circumstances, users should still exercise controls over the completeness of the integration process.
53. The integration of modular software can often be equally effective, provided that there is satisfactory control over the timing and effect of updating all the relevant files.

Reporting flexibility

54. All accounting software provides for the output of standard reports. However, these reports may not always be adequate to meet the user's requirements. For example, the user may from time to time need information which was not foreseen when the reporting requirements of the system were first specified.

55. Accounting software therefore often provides flexible reporting facilities so that users can design additional output to suit their particular requirements.

56. It should be recognised that flexibility is not a substitute for the proper planning and control of essential reports, and that over-reliance on flexible reporting facilities can give rise to weak controls over the production and use of accounting information. Nevertheless reporting flexibility brings significant advantages, because it allows for the speedy production of special management reports at minimal cost to the user.

57. Reporting flexibility can be provided either within the accounting software itself, or in some cases by means of a separate report generator with which it can be integrated.

Parameter (or table) facilities

58. A parameter is a pre-determined item of standing information that is likely to require frequent or regular amendment. Such items, rather than being incorporated directly into the software itself, may be held in tables to which the software makes reference when required.

59. Parameters allow users to tailor processing to their changing needs. If a parameter table is used, the software makes reference to an item in the table each time processing involves the use of, for example, the basic VAT rate. Thus, when a change to the rate occurs, it is only necessary to alter one figure in the table without altering the software at all. This saves time and also avoids the possibility of introducing errors into the software itself.

60. However, it is important that changes to tables are correct. Good accounting software should therefore:
- print out table updates, or the full table after any updating, for specific checking;
- provide evidence, on the relevant output, of the contents of tables used during processing.

Software Installation and Training

61. In order that good accounting software may be fully effective in practice, there is a need for good installation procedures and training in its use.

Installation procedures

62. A careful study of the particular requirements of the user should be made, taking into account the level of computer literacy among the staff, the number of staff who may use the system and the proposed level of involvement of management. The amount of time needed to learn and understand the full potential of a piece of software varies considerably, depending on the experience of the user, and is often underestimated.

63. The installation of a computerised accounting system can be fraught with problems if it is not planned properly. The basis installation procedures include setting the relevant timetable, testing the systems and converting the data. Attention should also be given to providing the requisite space, furniture, ancillary equipment, and consumables. The supplier or other adviser should be in a position to provide guidance for users on details connected with all these matters. Installation assistance is particularly important in organisations which do not employ qualified accountants or data processing specialists. It is also important in organisations which cannot allocate experienced staff to manage the installation because resources are already fully stretched.

Training

64. Training assists the user to understand the facilities of the software. It may be supplied in the form of personal or class tuition, or through video, audio or written self-tuition materials.

65. Users and potential users may have little experience of business computer systems or of training others. In such cases it is essential, before the software is acquired, for users to be satsified that adequate training facilities are available (often from the supplier of the software by means of formal training or follow up visits after installation).

66. Further training and assistance from the software supplier, or from a satisfactory alternative source, may also be required if there is a high staff turnover or if an improved version of the software is subsequently developed or acquired.

67. A complete training programme will include:
- introduction to and familiarisation with the different hardware components of the system;
- a broad over-view of the software and specific instruction in the use of its functions and commands;
- experience of actually using the system by entering test data and learning how to extract reports.

Conclusion

68. Users are often dependent on the continued correct operation of accounting software for many of their business functions. This Statement

therefore sets out the fundamental factors which potential users should take into account when acquiring or evaluating accounting software, and the criteria and associated features which determine its quality.

Appendix 2
Evaluation Checklist

This appendix gives a blank questionnaire to allow readers to perform their own evaluations of packages in which they are interested. The questionnaire was produced by the Institute of Chartered Accountants of Scotland's Information Technology Committee and is divided into four sections:

General Points: (pages 372–378)
Nominal Ledger (pages 378–384)
Sales Ledger (pages 384–390)
Purchase Ledger (pages 391–397)

Notes on questionnaire

1. As noted in the Institute's Information Technology Statement No. 2 the quality of any piece of accounting software depends on its appropriateness to a particular user's needs. This questionnaire offers suggestions of the sort of factors which are always likely to be relevant to the evaluation of accounting software. However, it will still be necessary, before it is used in any particular context, for it to be adapted to the precise circumstances and needs of the individual user.

2. This questionnaire is designed to be used in conjunction with the detailed checklists, published separately, relating to the specific features of different accounting software modules.

3. Depending on the particular context in which the questionnaire is used, some of the answers to questions will inevitably be more important than others. Users should identify the specific functions of software which they consider essential, as opposed to those which they regard as useful but less vital. Users should review the results of the completed questions with this in mind.

4. It is nevertheless highly unlikely, and is not in practice necessary, that the answer to every question will be entirely satisfactory. Users of the

questionnaire must always make a considered judgement whether any major shortcoming, or combination of minor shortcomings, renders the software unacceptable to them.

5. Subject to these considerations, and as far as possible, the questionnaire is designed so that the answer 'yes' to any question is likely to be more satisfactory than the answer 'no'.

6. The same question is occasionally asked under more than one heading within the questionnaire. In such cases, the question is particularly important for more than one reason.

Package Information Sheet

PRODUCT NAME

VERSION NUMBER

DATE OF TESTS

MODULES AVAILABLE

COST PER MODULE

PUBLISHER

SUPPLIER

WHAT SUPPORT IS AVAILABLE?

OPERATING SYSTEM

HARDWARE

NETWORK/MULTI-USER VERSION AVAILABLE?

HARDWARE USED FOR TESTS

NUMBER OF UK USERS

FIRST OPERATIONAL

REPORT GENERATOR AVAILABLE?

LINKS TO OTHER PACKAGES

SPECIAL FEATURES

Questionnaire

General Points

Performance of Requisite Accounting Functions

	Y/N	COMMENTS
1 Does the software perform the functions which the user wants performed?		
2 Can the software be used by more than one user at the same time?		
3 Can the software support groups of companies/departments/branches?		
How many such branches or companies can be supported.		
Can they be consolidated?		
4 Is multi-currency processing available?		
What is the maximum number of currencies available?		
Is conversion to Sterling automatic?		
5 Are sufficient accounting periods provided by the system?		
Can these periods be adjusted to suit different user requirements?		
6 Are the ends of accounting periods determined by the user rather than being set by the system?		
7 Can data from all accounting periods be assessed at any given moment?		
Can previous months be accessed for enquiries or reports?		
8 Does the system prevent posting to more than one accounting period at a time?		
Is it impossible to allocate transactions to future periods or to previous closed months?		
9 Does the system permit use of budgets and provide comparisons between budgets and actuals?		
10 Is the maximum value of transactions that can be handled by the system sufficient?		
11 Is the maximum number of accounts on each ledger (e.g. sales ledger, purchase ledger, nominal ledger) sufficient?		
12 Is the size and format of account numbers adequate and sufficient for analysis purposes?		
13 Does the associated hardware incorporate enough memory, disk storage and other peripherals for the software to operate satisfactorily?		

	Y/N	COMMENTS

14 Does the system offer adequate expansion potential as regards terminals, memory, disk storage capacity and other peripherals?

15 Are the control features provided by the software adequate to support effective user controls?

16 Are complementary clerical procedures to be imposed and effectively monitored by management?

Reliability – Security and Continuity of Processing
1 Does the system facilitate back-up storage?

How much time will complete back up of the system require?

2 Does the system facilitate recovery procedures in the event of system failure?

3 If system failure occurs part way through a batch or transaction, will the operator have to re-input only the batch or transaction being input at the time of the failure?

4 Are there any features provided with the software to help track down processing problems?

5 Are back-up procedures provided within each specific software application or within the operating system?

Are any of these back-up procedures automatic?

Support and Maintenance
1 Will the supplier provide corrections to the program?

2 Will the supplier provide general enhancements to the programs?

Will these be provided automatically?

Will they be given free of charge?

3 Will the software supplier provide 'hot-line' support to assist with immediate problem solving?

If so, at what cost?

4 Is the supplier capable of giving sufficient ongoing education and training and other support?

5 Can the supplier provide all the hardware, software and maintenance requirements of the user?

	Y/N	COMMENTS
6 Can the supplier provide support in the user's locality?		
7 Is a warranty offered in respect of specification and performance of the system?		
8 Would there be adequate back-up in the event of hardware or software failure?		
9 Will the software supplier make the program source code available to the user, either directly or by deposit with a third party?		
10 If the software is acquired under licence, are there any unduly restrictive conditions in the licence?		

The term 'supplier' refers to the supplier of the support and maintenance, whether or not this is the same as the supplier of the software.

Ease of Use
(a) Interactive processing

	Y/N	COMMENTS
1 Does the software run under an operating system, which is a commonly-accepted standard?		
2 Is the software available concurrently to more than one user?		
3 Can more than one system function be performed concurrently?		
4 Does the software effectively lead the user through the data entry procedures?		
Does the software facilitate immediate error correction?		
5 Is the software menu-driven?		
Are such menus restricted by password and application?		
6 Are the user screens adequately titled?		
7 Does the system inform the operator which programs or files are being loaded?		
8 Does the software facilitate file maintenance, back-up and archive copying?		

(b) User documentation

	Y/N	COMMENTS
1 Is the manual clearly laid out and understandable?		
2 Is the manual comprehensive and accurate?		
3 Is there an index to the manual?		
4 Is it easy to locate specific topics in the manual when required?		
5 Is it easy to follow through all procedures in the manual?		

	Y/N	COMMENTS

6 Are completed examples included in the manual?

7 Are help screens available?

Do they provide detailed on-line instruction on how to use particular features of the software?

Can they be edited or prepared by the user?

8 Does the documentation clearly specify the actions to be taken by users at each important stage of processing?

9 Will the software supplier provide regular updates of documentation in the event of modifications or revisions?

10 Will the software supplier make the detailed program documentation available to the user, either directly or by deposit with a third party?

Efficiency
1 Are the various functions of the system menu-driven, or otherwise easy to initiate?

Is there a good response time in the initiation of functions?

2 Is data entry easily repeated if similar to previous entry?

3 Is there a good response time

   (i) in processing data input?

   (ii) in producing requisite reports?

   (iii) in updating files?

   (iv) in producing back-up files?

   (v) in deleting redundant information files?

4 Does the system prevent access to a record while it is being updated?

5 Does the system retain a log of file updates until the next occasion on which the relevant information is reported or the relevant file used in a regular control procedure?

6 Can regular reports be easily duplicated if required?

Flexibility
(a) Integration facilities
1 Are the different accounting applications integrated?

Are they integrated on an item by item basis or are they integrated by weekly or monthly end routines?

	Y/N	COMMENTS

2 Whichever method is used, can the ledger updating process be satisfactorily controlled?

3 Does the software run under an operating system which is a commonly-accepted standard?

4 Can more than one system function be performed concurrently?

5 Can software be linked to other packages, e.g. word processing, graphics, financial modelling, to provide alternative display and reporting facilities?

(b) Reporting flexibility
1 Can the user easily design additional output reports or displays?

2 Is a report generator provided as part of the software or as an option associated with it?

3 Can screen layouts, reports and transaction formats be easily adapted to users' requirements?

4 Does the output of the software facilitate proper control to ensure that decisions are not inadvertently taken on the basis of incorrect information?

(c) Parameter or table facilities
1 If the system uses a lot of standing information which changes frequently or regularly, does the system allow for such changes to be effected through the use of parameters or tables?

2 If so, is the use of such parameters or tables adequately reported?

3 Is proper control to be exercised over changes to such parameters or tables?

If so, how? (e.g. through the use of system facilities such as passwords or by inspection of appropriate records)

Software Installation and Training
(a) Financial resources
1 Has account been taken in the budget for system development/acquisition of the full costs of

    initial acquisition?

    initial training?

    future training?

(b) Other resources
2 Is the main equipment to be located in adequate accommodation?

Is this such that staff are not seriously affected by the equipment (e.g. by noise from the printer).

	Y/N	COMMENTS

3   Is there sufficient scope for the installation, if required, of communications equipment?

4   Have requisite consumables (e.g. special stationery, filing facilities, fireproof storage) been provided for?

(c) Involvement of software supplier
5   Is the supplier capable of giving sufficient initial education and training and other support?

6   Are potential users permitted to test the software for a trial period before commitment to acquire it?

7   If required, does the supplier have sufficient capable personnel to assist users to convert to the new system?

8   If required, will the supplier provide machine time to enable users to set up files of input data before installation?

(d) Involvement of user personnel
9   Who is to be responsible for running and controlling the system on a regular basis?

Is this person sufficiently competent?

10   Who is to be responsible for the installation and implementation of the system?

Is this person sufficiently competent?

11   Which staff will operate the system?

Do they have sufficient aptitude for computers?

12   Is there adequate cover for staff in the event of illness and holidays?

Package Software Acquisition
Preliminary questions relating to software supplier
1   Does the supplier have a good overall reputation as regards experience and reliability?

2   Does the supplier offer a full range of accounting software?

3   Is the supplier's financial status stable?

Does the supplier demonstrate an adequate capital base, growth and profitability?

4   Does the supplier have sufficient technical resources to modify or tailor software to suit different users' requirements?

	Y/N	COMMENTS

5 Does the supplier have a substantial user base?

Has it shown adequate commitment to existing users and will it provide a list of them?

Has the supplier sold similar systems to that under consideration?

6 Does the supplier offer adequate contractual terms as regards purchase, installation, delivery, support and maintenance?

Are all costs clearly indicated?

Is the date of delivery of all components of the system clearly stated?

7 Is there adequate evidence that the supplier normally meets its contractual obligations?

8 Will the supplier provide indepth demonstrations of it software?

Nominal Ledger

General
1 Are programs menu driven?

    If 'YES' – can menus be bypassed once the user is familiar with the package?

2 Does the system maintain a log of usage?

3 Are informative messages produced on-screen whilst running?

4 Are error messages informative and easy to understand?

5 Is the system multi-company?

6 Is the original set-up straightforward?

7 Is there a copy/restore facility in the package?

8 Does the system cover disciplined taking of back-ups?

Documentation
(a) Manual
1 Is the manual clearly laid out and understandable?

2 Is the manual comprehensive and accurate?

3 Is there an index?

4 Is it easy to follow through all procedures?

5 Is it easy to locate specific points when required?

6 Are completed examples included?

APPENDIX 2 379

Y/N	COMMENTS

(b) Help screens
7 Are help screens available?
   If 'YES' –

   Do they provide on-line instructions?

   Can they be edited or prepared by the user?

Account Details
1 Is the chart of accounts flexible?

2 What is the format of the nominal account code?

3 Is cost centre accounting available?

4 What is the maximum number of accounts that can be held?

5 What is the maximum balance that can be held?

6 Can accounts be added/deleted/amended at any time?

7 Is file automatically re-sorted when a new account is added?

   If 'NO' – can a re-sort be initiated?

8 Is deletion of an account prevented if it has:

   a non-zero balance

   a zero balance but postings in the current period

   a zero balance but postings in the year-to-date

9 Is a hard copy of changes in account details automatically produced?

10 Are 12 or 13 (or more) accounting periods available?

11 Can budgets be entered for all revenue accounts?

12 Can separate budgets be entered for each accounting period?

13. Can this year's results be used to calculate next year's budgets automatically?

Transactions
1 What is the maximum transaction value that can be entered?

2 Can each journal entry contain an unlimited number of debits and credits?

3 Is each input line numbered?

4 In a long journal entry is it possible to move between screens to view data already input?

	Y/N	COMMENTS

5 Can previously entered journal lines be edited before accepting the whole journal?

6 Does each journal entry have a reference number?

7 Are accruals and prepayments routines, which both reverse automatically at the start of the next accounting period, available?

8 Can recurring journal entries be provided for automatically?

9 Is a narrative available for:

    each journal entry

    each line of the journal entry

10 Can journal entries be posted to future periods?

11 Can journal entries be posted to previous periods?

12 Are all transactions retained on file for at least one period?

13 Can transactions be retained at the period-end?

14 Can a ledger date pre-date existing transactions?

Input Controls

1 Is password control used?

    If 'YES' – give details

2 Is a hard copy automatically produced for all input?

3 Are journal entries automatically sequentially numbered?

4 If integrated, are automatic postings from other modules included in the numbering sequence?

5 If accruals and prepayments automatically reverse, is the reversal included in the numbering sequence?

6 Are totals, of debit or credit entries, produced for all journal entries?

    If 'YES' – is it necessary that this agrees with a pre-list total?

7 Is it necessary that all journal entries balance before posting?

8 Is production of an out-of-balance trial balance prevented?

	Y/N	COMMENTS

9 Do all input screens show clearly:

   type of entry

   the distinction between debits and credits

10 Can the actual date of posting, or a batch reference, be shown on hard copies of transactions input?

11 Are the following validated:

   date

   Nominal Ledger account code

   Cost Centre code

   If 'NO' – are unidentified/invalid entries posted to a suspense account?

   – how is the suspense account treated?

12 Is a total produced of all debit/credit transactions processed?

   If 'YES' – is a report produced at the end of each processing run to reconcile b/f total, transactions processed and c/f total?

13. Is a reconciliation of numbers of accounts produced after amendment of the accounts detail file?

14 Does the system prevent the abnormal termination of programs?

Integration

1 Is integration possible with the following:

   Sales Ledger

   Purchase Ledger

   Payroll

2 Can the Nominal Ledger be updated as often as desired?

3 Is a hard copy automatically produced at the end of each Nominal Ledger update?

4 Is there a Sales/Purchase Ledger print-out of the Nominal Ledger update?

5 Are Sales Ledger and Purchase Ledger control accounts agreed to the totals of balances in the individual ledgers?

6 Is there a check that the Nominal Ledger cannot be updated twice with the same Sales/Purchase data?

7 Must the Nominal Ledger be updated from the Sales and Purchase Ledgers before the period-end is run?

	Y/N	COMMENTS

8 Must the Nominal Ledger be in the same period as the Sales and Purchases Ledgers for the update to be carried out?

9 Is there any check that all data processed in the Sales/Purchase Ledgers has been posted to the Nominal Ledger?

10 Are unidentified/invalid entries held in a Nominal Ledger suspense account?

    If 'YES' – how is this treated?

11 Can the user select whether to update the Nominal Ledger with individual Sales/Purchases Ledger entries or in total?

    If 'NO' – is the update made in detail or in total?

12. Is it impossible to post directly to the sales/purchase ledger control accounts?

Output
(a) General

1 Is it necessary to produce an audit trail before the period end procedure is run?

2 Does the audit trail enable all transactions to be traced fully through the system?

3 Can the actual run date, or batch reference, as well as the current ledger date, be shown on all reports?

4 Can the following be seen on screen:

    account details

    account transactions

5 Can a print-out of the following be obtained for individual accounts/selected ranges of accounts:

    account details

    account transactions

6 Do all outputs show clearly the distinction between debit and credit entries?

7 Are all reports adequately titled?

8 Do reports provide totals where applicable?

9 Is the period number shown on reports?

10 Can the following be produced:

    Trial Balance

    Ledger Account Detail Report

    Profit and Loss Account

    Balance Sheet

APPENDIX 2   383

	Y/N	COMMENTS

11 Does the ledger account detail report show the source of postings and narrative input?

12 Does the ledger account detail report show either the full account history or balance b/f together with the current period's transactions?

13 Are all report pages numbered sequentially, with the end of report identified?

14 Can reports be temporarily retained on file for subsequent printing?

    If 'YES' – are such files protected from deletion?

15 Is a report generator available for use with the Nominal Ledger module?

16 Can transaction files for all previous periods be retained in the system to permit enquiries and reports?

(b) Trial Balance; P&L and Balance Sheet

1 Does the package provide for flexible formatting of Profit and Loss Account and Balance Sheet?

2 Can the following be produced for both the current period and the year-to-date:

    Trial Balance

    Profit and Loss Account

    Balance Sheet

    If 'YES' – is it clearly shown whether a report is for the current period or year-to-date?

3 Can the following show budgets:

    Trial Balance

    Profit and Loss Account

    If 'YES' – can budgets be omitted if wished?

4 Can the following reports show comparative figures:

    Trial Balance

    Profit and Loss Account

    Balance Sheet

    If 'YES' – can comparatives be omitted?
          – can two years' comparatives be shown?

5 Are budgets worked out from the period number as calculated by the number of period-end procedures run?

	Y/N	COMMENTS

6 Are budget variances calculated?
 If 'YES' are they shown as:
   value
   percentages
   both		

7 Do budget reports provide for exception reporting?		
8 Does the package provide for a Trial Balance to be produced for each Cost Centre?		
9 Does the package provide for a Profit and Loss Account and Balance Sheet for each Cost Centre?		
10 Does the package provide for totalling of like items across Cost Centres?		

11 Can trial balance production be varied by:
   printing a range of accounts
   subtotalling on any chosen digit of account code		

12 Can vertical percentages be calculated in the Profit and Loss Account?		
13 Can a report be produced to show the breakdown of Profit and Loss Account and Balance Sheet figures?		

Year End

	Y/N	COMMENTS
1 Can Balance Sheet items be carried forward and Profit and Loss Account items be cleared automatically at the year-end?		
2 Can the destination of individual account balances be specified or are all balances cleared at the year-end transferred into one account only?		

Sales Ledger

General

	Y/N	COMMENTS
1 Are programs menu driven? If 'YES' – can menus be bypassed once the user is familiar with the package?		
2 Does the system maintain a log of usage?		
3 Are informative messages produced on-screen whilst running?		
4 Are error messages informative and easy to understand?		
5 Is the system multi-company?		
6 Is the original set-up straightforward?		

	Y/N	COMMENTS

7 Is there a copy/restore facility in the package?

8 Does the system cover disciplined taking of back-ups?

Documentation
(a) Manual
1 Is the manual clearly laid out and understandable?

2 Is the manual comprehensive and accurate?

3 Is there an index?

4 Is it easy to follow through all procedures?

5 Is it easy to locate specific points when required?

6 Are completed examples included?

(b) Help screens
7 Are help screens available?

   If 'YES' –

      Do they provide on-line instructions?

      Can they be edited or prepared by the user?

Customer Details
1 What is the format of the customer account code?

2 What other customer details are held?

   Do these seem to be sufficient in general?

3 What is the maximum number of accounts that can be held?

4 Can customer details be added/deleted/amended at any time?

5 Is file re-sorted automatically when a new customer is added?

   If 'NO' – can a re-sort be initiated?

6 Is deletion of a customer prevented if the account has:–

   an outstanding balance

   a zero balance but a b/f turnover

7 Is a hard copy of changes in customer details automatically produced?

   If 'NO' – can a hard copy be taken?

Transactions
1 Can the system be open item?

	Y/N	COMMENTS

2 Are the following inputs possible:
   invoices
   credit notes
   cash received
   cash refunded
   discounts
   journal entries
   write-offs

3 Can an invoice be analysed to several different sales categories?

4 Are different VAT codes possible for different items within one invoice?

5 Are all transactions retained on file for at least one period?

6 Can a ledger date pre-date existing transactions?

Matching/Allocations
(a) Balance forward
1 Is the balance b/f aged?

2 Can cash be allocated automatically?
   If 'YES' – how is the allocation made?
       – can this be over-ridden?

3 Can cash be allocated manually?
   If 'YES' – does the package check that cash allocated = amount received?
       How is any such difference treated?

4 Can credit notes/journal entries be allocated to previous periods?

5 Can cash in advance be held and later allocated to subsequent periods?

6 Can cash be held unallocated?

(b) Open item
7 Are outstanding transactions displayed for allocation?

8 Can cash be allocated automatically?
   If 'YES' – how is the allocation made?
       – can this be over-ridden?

9 Can cash be allocated manually?
   If 'YES' – does the package check that cash allocated = cash received?
       How is any difference treated?

10 Can an over/underpayment of an invoice be recorded?

11 How often are settled items deleted from file?

	Y/N	COMMENTS

12 Can credit notes be set against the invoices to which they refer?

13. Can journal entries be set against the invoices/credit notes to which they refer?

14 Can cash in advance be held and later allocated to invoice?

15 Can cash be held unallocated?

– how is this treated?

Input Controls
1 Is password control used?
If 'YES' – give details

2 Is a hard copy automatically produced for all input?

3 Are batch totals automatically produced for all transactions input?

If 'YES' – what is the procedure if this does not agree with a pre-list total?

4 Is it necessary that invoices, cash and adjustments are input in separate batches?

5 Are batches automatically sequentially numbered?

If 'NO' – can they be so numbered?

6 Is a report produced at the end of each processing run to reconcile b/f total, transactions processed and c/f total?

If 'NO' – is a control balance produced at the end of each posting run?

7 Are the following validated:

date

customer account number

VAT code

goods value

sales analysis code

8 Is VAT calculated to check figure input?

9 Is the gross figure agreed to goods+VAT?

10 Is discount calculated to check the figure input?

11 Can the actual date of posting, or batch reference, be shown on hard copies of transactions input?

12 Does the screen always indicate that the Sales Ledger, as opposed to the Purchase Ledger, is running?

	Y/N	COMMENTS

13 Do all input screens show clearly:

    type of entry

    the distinction between debits and credits

14 Is there any check that the same entry is not input twice?

15 Is there a warning if a customer exceeds the credit limit?

    If 'YES' – what action is required?

16 Is it impossible for new accounts to be created during processing?

17 Is a reconciliation of numbers of accounts produced after amendment of the customer detail file?

18 Does the system prevent the abnormal termination of programs?

Integration

1 Can the sales ledger be integrated with an invoicing module?

2 Can the sales ledger be integrated with a nominal ledger module?

3 Can the nominal ledger be updated as often as desired?

4 Is a hard copy automatically produced at the end of each nominal ledger update?

5 Is there a Sales Ledger print-out (as well as a Nominal Ledger print-out) of the Nominal Ledger update?

6 Are the following automatically posted to the appropriate nominal ledger accounts:

    Discount

    Discount written back

    Bad Debts written off

    Contras with purchase ledger

7 Are any invalid/unidentified entries posted to a suspense account?

    If 'NO' – how are they treated?

    If 'YES' – how is the suspense account treated?

8 Is the sales ledger control balance agreed to the total of the balances in the sales ledger?

9 Can current and future periods be maintained simultaneously?

10 Is there a check that transactions cannot be posted twice to the Nominal Ledger?

	Y/N	COMMENTS

11 Must the Nominal Ledger be updated from the Sales Ledger before the period-end is run?

12 Must the Nominal Ledger and the Sales Ledger be in the same period for the update to be carried out?

13 Is there any report/warning that transactions posted to the Sales Ledger have not yet been posted to the Nominal Ledger?

Output

1 Is it necessary to produce an audit trail before the period end procedure is run?

2 Does the audit trail enable all transactions to be traced fully through the system?

3 Can the actual run date, or batch reference, as well as current ledger date, be shown on reports?

4 Can the following be produced:

    List of Master File information

    Aged Debtors Report

    VAT Report

    Ledger Detail Report

    Customer Statements

    Customer Name and Address labels

    Debt Collection letters?

5 Does the customer statement show:

    all o/s transactions together with all items settled in the current period

    or all o/s transactions only

    or the balance b/f and the current period's transactions

    or just the current balance

6 Does the customer statement:

    show discount separately

    show ageing

    allow special messages

    allow for suppression of erroneous postings and their corrections

7 Can the following screens be seen:

    customer details

    customer transactions

	Y/N	COMMENTS

8 Can hard copies of the following be obtained for individual accounts/selected ranges of accounts:

   customer details

   customer transactions

9 Does the Ledger Account Detail Report/ copy statements show:

   the source of all postings

   how part payments and allocations have been treated

   either the full account history or balance b/f together with the current period's transactions

10 Does the Aged Analysis show for each customer:

   total balance o/s

   credit limit

11 Is ageing strictly by transaction date?

   If 'NO' – how is ageing done?

12 Does the Aged Analysis show unallocated cash separately?

   If 'NO' – how is it aged?

13 Do all outputs show clearly the distinction between debits and credits?

14 Are all reports adequately titled?

15 Do reports provide totals where applicable?

16 Can report production be varied by:

   printing a range of accounts

   printing by e.g. area/rep

17 Is the period number shown on reports?

18 Are all report pages sequentially numbered with the end of report identified?

19 Is a sales analysis possible?

20 Can reports be temporarily retained on file for subsequent printing?

   If 'YES' – are such files protected from deletion?

21 Is a report generator available for use with the Sales Ledger module?

22 Can transaction files for previous periods be retained in the system to permit enquiries and reports?

	Y/N	COMMENTS

Purchase Ledger

General
1. Are programs menu driven?

    If 'YES' – can menus be bypassed once the user is familiar with the package?

2. Does the system maintain a log of usage?
3. Are informative messages produced on-screen whilst running?
4. Are error messages informative and easy to understand?
5. Is the system multi-company?
6. Is the original set-up straightforward?
7. Is there a copy/restore facility in the package?
8. Does the system cover disciplined taking of back-ups?

Documentation
(a) Manual
1. Is the manual clearly laid out and understandable?
2. Is the manual comprehensive and accurate?
3. Is there an index?
4. Is it easy to follow through all procedures?
5. Is it easy to locate specific points when required?
6. Are completed examples included?

(b) Help screens
7. Are help screens available?

    If 'YES' –

    Do they provide on-line instructions?

    Can they be edited or prepared by the user?

Supplier Details
1. What is the format of the supplier account code?
2. What other supplier details are held?

    Do these seem to be sufficient in general?

3. What is the maximum number of accounts that can be held?
4. Can supplier details be added/deleted/amended at any time?

	Y/N	COMMENTS

5 Is file re-sorted automatically when a new supplier is added?

    If 'NO' – can a re-sort be initiated?

6 Is deletion of a supplier prevented if the account has:

    an outstanding balance

    a zero balance but a b/f turnover

7 Is a hard copy of changes in supplier details automatically produced?

    If 'NO' – can a hard copy be taken?

Transactions
1 Can the system be open item?

2 Are the following inputs possible:

    invoices

    credit notes

    manual payments

    cash refunded

    discounts

3 Can an invoice be analysed to several different expense categories?

4 Are different VAT codes possible for different items within one invoice?

5 Are all transactions retained on file for at least one period?

6 Can a ledger date pre-date existing transactions?

7 Can 2 references be input for an invoice (own and supplier's reference)?

Matching/Allocations
(a) Balance forward
1 Is the balance b/f aged?

2 Can cash be allocated automatically?

    If 'YES' – how is the allocation made?

        – can this be overridden?

3 Can cash be allocated manually?

    If 'YES' – does the package check that cash allocated = amount paid?

    How is any such difference treated?

4 Can credit notes/journal entries be allocated to previous periods?

5 Can cash in advance be held and later allocated to subsequent periods?

	Y/N	COMMENTS

(b) Open item
6 Are outstanding transactions displayed for allocation?

7 Can cash be allocated automatically?

   If 'YES' – how is the allocation made?

   – can this be over-ridden?

8 Can cash be allocated manually?

   If 'YES' – does the package check that cash allocated = cash paid?

   How is any difference treated?

9 Can an over/under-payment of an invoice be recorded?

10 How often are settled items deleted from file?

11 Can credit notes be set against the invoices to which they refer?

12 Can journal entries be set against the invoices/credit notes to which they refer?

13 Can cash in advance be held and later allocated to invoice?

14 Can cash be held unallocated?

   – how is this treated?

Input Controls

1 Is password control used?

   If 'YES' – give detail

2 Is a hard copy automatically produced for all input?

3 Are batch totals automatically produced for all transactions input?

   If 'YES' – what is the procedure if this does not agree with a pre-list total?

4 Is it necessary that invoices, cash and adjustments are input in separate batches?

5 Are batches automatically sequentially numbered?

   If 'NO' – can they be so numbered?

6 Is a report produced at the end of each processing run to reconcile b/f total, transactions processed and c/f total?

   If 'NO' – is a control balance produced at the end of each posting run?

	Y/N	COMMENTS

7 Are the following validated:
   date
   supplier account number
   VAT code
   goods value
   analysis code

8 Is VAT calculated to check figure input?

9 Is the gross figure agreed to goods+VAT?

10 Is discount calculated to check the figure input?

11 Can the actual date of posting, or batch reference, be shown on hard copies of transactions input?

12 Does the screen always indicate that the Purchase Ledger, as opposed to the Sales Ledger, is running?

13 Do all input screens show clearly:
   type of entry
   the distinction between debits and credits

14 Is there any check that the same entry is not input twice?

15 Is there a warning if a supplier is overpaid?

16 Is it impossible for new accounts to be created during processing?

17 Is a reconciliation of numbers of accounts produced after amendment of the customer detail file?

18 Does the system prevent the abnormal termination of programs?

Integration

1 Can the purchase ledger be integrated with a job costing module?

2 Can the purchase ledger be integrated with a nominal ledger module?

3 Can the nominal ledger be updated as often as desired?

4 Is a hard copy automatically produced at the end of each nominal ledger update?

5 Is there a Purchase Ledger print-out (as well as a Nominal Ledger print-out) of the Nominal Ledger update?

Y/N	COMMENTS

6 Are the following automatically posted to the appropriate nominal ledger accounts:

    Discount

    Discount written back

    Contras with sales ledger

7 Are any invalid/unidentified entries posted to a suspense account?

    If 'NO' – how are they treated?

    If 'YES' – how is the suspense account treated?

8 Is the purchase ledger control balance agreed to the total of the balances in the purchase ledger?

9 Can current and future periods be maintained simultaneously?

10 Is there a check that transactions cannot be posted twice to the Nominal Ledger?

11 Must the Nominal Ledger be updated from the Purchase Ledger before the period-end is run?

12 Must the Nominal Ledger and the Purchase Ledger be in the same period for the update to be carried out?

13 Is there any report/warning that transactions posted to the Purchase Ledger have not yet been posted to the Nominal Ledger?

Output

1 Is it necessary to produce an audit trail before the period end procedure is run?

2 Does the audit trail enable all transactions to be traced fully through the system?

3 Can the actual run date, or batch reference, as well as current ledger date, be shown on reports?

4 Can the following be produced:

    List of Master File information

    Aged Creditors Report

    VAT Report

    Ledger Detail Report

    Remittance Advices

    Customer Name and Address labels

    Suggested Payments

    Cheques

	Y/N	COMMENTS
5 Can remittance advices show:		
individual invoices		
discount		
supplier's reference		
6 Can the following screens be seen:		
supplier details		
supplier transactions		
7 Can hard copies of the following be obtained for individual accounts/selected ranges of accounts:		
supplier details		
supplier transactions		
8 Does the Ledger Account Detail Report show:		
the source of all postings		
how part payments and allocations have been treated		
either the full account history or balance b/f together with the current period's transactions		
9 Is ageing strictly by transaction date?		
If 'NO' – how is ageing done?		
10 Does the Aged Analysis show unallocated cash separately?		
If 'NO' – how is it aged?		
11 Do all outputs show clearly the distinction between debits and credits?		
12 Are all reports adequately titled?		
13 Do reports provide totals where applicable?		
14 Can report production be varied by:		
printing a range of accounts		
printing by e.g. area		
15 Is the period number shown on reports?		
16 Are all report pages sequentially numbered with the end of report identified?		
17 Is a purchase analysis possible?		
18 Can reports be temporarily retained on file for subsequent printing?		
If 'YES' – are such files protected from deletion?		

	Y/N	COMMENTS

19 Is a report generator available for use with the Purchase Ledger module?

20 Can transaction files for previous periods be retained in the system to permit enquiries and reports?

Payments/Cheque Writing

1 Can the system write cheques?

    If 'YES' – is the payment posted automatically to the purchase ledger?

2 Is there an automatic cheque writing facility? If 'YES':

    is a list of suggested payments printed in advance of the cheques?

    is the total cash requirement printed in advance of the cheques?

    can the automatic payment routine be aborted if either of the above is not satisfactory?

3 Can the following payment/report options be selected:

    individual invoice selection

    supplier selection

    pay all invoices of a certain age

    pay according to due date

    pay all invoices except those marked not to be paid

    other (specify)

4 Is discount automatically calculated by the payment routine?

5 Can invoices be held as disputed?

    If 'YES' – can a report of disputed invoices be produced?

Appendix 3
Test Data

Company:	Rapid Retailers Ltd
Business:	Retailing of audio and visual equipment and accessories Commenced trading January 1975
Period of Test Data:	Accounts computerised at 31 October 1984 Transactions November 1984 Month end 30/11/84 Transactions December 1984 Year end 31/12/84
Address:	No. 1 The Arcade SALE
Telephone No:	0123 456 789
VAT No:	123 4567 89
Year End:	31 December

Trial balance 31/10/84

	DR £	CR £	Annual budget £
Sales – audio		500,000	(550,000)
Purchases – audio	300,000		300,000
Opening stock (1/1/84) – audio	30,000		
Closing stock (31/10/84) – audio		35,000	
Sales – video		300,000	(400,000)
Purchases – video	200,000		275,000
Opening stock (1/1/84) – video	17,500		
Closing stock (31/10/84) – video		20,000	
Discount received		1,000	(1,200)
Interest received		2,000	(2,500)
Administration expenses			
Directors' renumeration	60,000		80,000
Salaries – admin	60,000		65,000
Telephone	2,500		3,200
Posts and carriage	3,000		3,000
Printing	2,000		2,800
Stationery	1,500		2,000
Rent	1,000		1,200
Rates	4,650		5,500
Insurance	2,000		2,400
Audit fee	2,500		3,000
Depreciation – fixtures and fittings	1,750		2,100
Loss on sale of fixtures and fittings		500	
Repairs	6,000		5,000
Heat and light	10,000		8,000
Financial expenses			
Bad debts	5,000		5,000
Interest paid – loan	2,500		3,000
Interest paid – bank	1,200		1,500
Discount allowed	1,500		2,000
Selling expenses			
Salaries – selling	65,000		80,000
Motor expenses	13,000		10,000
Motor depreciation	4,510		1,875
Advertising	25,000		27,500
Entertaining	5,000		7,500
Fixed assets			
Property	50,000		
Property additions	—		
Fixtures and fittings:			
Cost	20,000		
Acc depreciation		8,500	
Additions	2,000		
Disposals – cost		1,000	

	DR £	CR £	Annual budget £
Disposals – acc depreciation	500		
Depreciation for year		1,750	
Motor vehicles:			
Cost	40,000		
Acc depreciation		17,500	
Additions		–	
Disposals – cost		–	
Disposals – acc depreciation		–	
Depreciation for year		4,510	
Current assets			
Stock	55,000		
Debtors	50,000		
Prepayments	2,200		
Bank – deposit account	10,000		
Bank – current account	2,500		
Cash	100		
Current liabilities			
Creditors		30,000	
Accruals		6,000	
Inland Revenue – PAYE & NI		6,500	
VAT		4,500	
Capital and reserves			
Share capital		10,000	
Share premium		2,000	
General reserve		20,000	
Profit and loss account		58,650	
Long term liabilities			
Loan – Mr Speedie		30,000	
	1,059,410	1,059,410	

Bank payments – summary

	November (Cash book page 84) £	*December* (Cash book page 85) £
Directors' remuneration (net)	5,185.00	13,650.00
Salaries – admin (net)	3,172.00	4,500.00
– selling (net)	5,978.00	9,120.00
Posts	480.00	620.00
Entertaining	75.00	175.00
Advertising	230.00	500.00
Inland Revenue	6,500.00	9,165.00
Petty cash	1,085.24	1,559.15
Purchase ledger	9,750.00 10/11	24,963.63 3/12
	22,743.13 25/11	10,450.00 15/12
		27,084.37 24/12
Motor expenses	21.74	
VAT	3.26	

APPENDIX 3   401

	November (Cash book page 84) £		*December* (Cash book page 85) £	
Property	25,000.00	New shop		
Motor vehicles	5,200.00	New car-balance		
Mr Speedie – loan interest	2,000.00	Mar–Oct		
Insurance	2,400.00	Yr from 1/11/84		
Bank interest and charges	320.00			
Rent			1,200.00	
Sales ledger – Rogues Retail			460.00	8/12
Purchases – Imports	audio		6,800.00	Tape recorders (4/12 8,500$ @ 1.25/£)
	video		3,684.21	TVs (6/12 10,500F$ @ 2.85/£)
	video		4,687.50	Video cameras (10/12 6,000$ @ 1.28/£)
TOTAL	90,143.37		118,618.86	

Bank receipts – summary

	(Cash book page 84)	(Cash book page 85)
Insurance claim – repairs	580.00	
Sales ledger	28,904.25	32,346.81
Cash sales	37,720.00	94,346.00
Purchase ledger – Paper Products		448.50
	67,204.25	127,141.31

Adjustments

Prepayments

	31 Oct £		*30 Nov* £		*31 Dec* £	
Insurance	—		2,200	11/12×£2,400	2,000	10/12×£2,400
Rent	200	2 mths	100	1 mth	1,200	12 mths
Rates	2,000	5/6×£2,400	1,600	4/6×£2,400	1,200	3/6×£2,400
TOTAL	2,200		3,900		4,400	

Accruals

Heat and light	1,200	E	—		800	E
Audit fee	2,500	10×£250	2,750	11×£250	3,000	12×£250
Loan interest	2,000	Mar–Oct	250	Nov	500	Nov–Dec
Telephone	—		250	Nov–E	500	Nov–Dec–E
Bank int & ch	300	E	100	Nov–E	200	Nov–Dec–E
Motor exp	—		550	Nov petrol–E	—	
	6,000		3,900		5,000	

Depreciation	30 Nov.	31 Dec.
	£	£
Motor vehicles	477	467
Fix & fttgs	175 (1/12×10% (20,000 +£2,000−£1,000)	175

Petty cash

	30 Nov.	31 Dec.
Entertaining	277.95	1,068.41
Motor exp	389.40	401.33
Stationery	95.20	25.40
Advertising	250.00	—
VAT	72.69	64.01
TOTAL	1,085.24	1,559.15

Stock	31 Oct.	30 Nov.	31 Dec.
	£	£	£
Audio	35,000	40,000	37,868
Video	20,000	25,000	29,510

Motor vehicles

Vehicle *sold* (Nov)		Vehicle *purchased* (Nov)	
	£		£
Cost	8,400	Paid	5,200
Acc depn	3,114		
WDV	5,286		
Trade in	5,000	⟶	5,000
Loss	286	Cost	10,200

	Cost		Depn	
	£		£	
Oct	40,000	Acc depn 1/1	17,500	
Disposal	(8,400)	Depn yr	4,510	
Addn	10,200	Disposal	(3,114)	
	41,800		18,896	1/12×25%(41,800−18,896)
Depn Nov			477	= £477
	41,800		19,373	
Depn Dec			467	1/12×25%(41,800−19,373)
	41,800		19,840	

PAYE & NI

	Nov	Dec
	£	£
Directors	3,315	7,350
Admin	2,030	3,000
Selling	3,820	6,080

	£
Year end adjustments	
Provision for corporation tax	3,250
Transfer to general reserve	5,000
Proposed dividend	1,000

Purchase ledger – balances 31/10/84

Name & address	Discount terms or days for payment	Date	Inv ref	£	Credit limit
P Pipe & Son Plumbers 4 Well Square SALE	30 days	1/10/84	1672/324B	340	
Sale Borough Council 1 Main Street SALE		30/9/84	1654/32446	2,400	
Video Productions Ltd 47 Main Street SALE	30 days	10/8/84 3/9/84	1489/233AS 1532/344AS	5,400 (3,840) ——— 1,560	10,000
Albatross Advertising 42 Sky Street SALE	2½% – 30 days	15/10/84 29/10/84	1691/425 1704/480	10,000 1,500 ——— 11,500	20,000
Audio Parts Country Lane LITTLE OAKS	20 days	13/8/84 14/9/84 15/10/84	1495/SS436 1545/SS552 1690/SS625	8,000 2,000 3,000 ——— 13,000	
Audio Visual Supplies 255 Heering Road LONDON	5% – 10 days 2½% – 30 days			—	30,000
Midland Gas Board 125 Main Street SALE				—	
Paper Products plc Mill Lane MUDSEY	2½% – 10 days	15/9/84 13/10/84	1601/3242 1680/4370	500 700 ——— 1,200	

Purchase ledger – invoices and credit notes

	Date	Own ref	Supplier's ref	Gross £	VAT £	( )=C/N Net £	
Audio Parts	4/11/84	1774	SS650	(2,000.00)	(260.87)	(1,739.13)	Faulty Recorders Ret'd Cancels Invoice SS552
P Pipe & Son	15/11/84	1775	375B	373.75	48.75	325.00	Plumbing
Video Productions	9/11/84	1776	451AT	920.00	120.00	800.00	Video Tapes
	10/11/84	1777	472AT	230.00	30.00	200.00	Video Accessories
Paper Products plc	4/11/84	1778	4923	343.88	43.88	200.00	Pricelists
						100.00	Envelopes
Audio Visual Supps	10/11/84	1779	1423	20,565.00	2,565.00	8,000.00	Radios
						10,000.00	TV's
BATCH 1				20,432.63	2,546.76	17,885.87	
Audio Parts	20/11/84	1780	SS701	2,300.00	300.00	2,000.00	Headphones
	28/11/84	1781	SS708	575.00	75.00	500.00	Miscellaneous Audio
Midland Gas Board	28/11/84	1782	476235678A	2,024.36	—	2,024.36	Gas September–November
P Pipe & Son	23/11/84	1783	384C	230.00	30.00	200.00	Plumbing
Audio Visual Supps	30/11/84	1784	1596	26,277.50	3,277.50	15,000.00	Amplifiers
						8,000.00	Videos
Video Productions	25/11/84	1785	594BS	8,050.00	1,050.00	7,000.00	Faulty Video Accessories
	30/11/84	1786	654CN	(230.00)	(30.00)	(200.00)	Ret'd Cancels Invoice 472AT
Audio Parts	30/11/84	1787	SS740	(460.00)	(60.00)	(400.00)	Faulty Radios Ret'd Against Invoice SS701
Paper Products plc	25/11/84	1788	5525	(573.13)	(73.13)	(500.00)	Incorrect Notepaper Ret'd Against Invoice 4370
	25/11/84	1789	5526	114.63	14.63	100.00	Envelopes
BATCH 2				38,308.36	4,584.00	33,724.36	

APPENDIX 3

	Date	Own ref	Supplier's ref	Gross £	VAT £	( )=C/N Net £	
Albatross Advert.	10/12/84	1790	520	573.12	73.12	500.00	Advertising
Sale Borough Coun.	15/12/84	1791	32446	57.50	7.50	50.00	Rubbish Collection
Audio Visual Supps	16/12/84	1792	1672	28,652.00	3,562.50	8,000.00	Radios
						17,000.00	TV's
Video Productions	20/12/84	1793	795BS	9,200.00	1,200.00	8,000.00	Videos
Audio Parts	21/12/84	1794	SS960	23,000.00	3,000.00	10,000.00	Turntables
						10,000.00	Amplifiers
Mudsey Motors	30/11/84	1795	R52	701.50	91.50	610.00	Petrol – November
	31/12/84	1796	R52	833.75	108.75	725.00	Petrol – December
	20/12/84	1797	404	287.50	37.50	250.00	Motor Repairs
	29/12/84	1798	498	552.00	72.00	480.00	Motor Repairs
				63,767.87	8,152.87	55,615.00	

Purchase ledger – payments and adjustments

Payments ( ) = CR

Date	Supplier	Net paid £	Discount taken £	Invoices paid
10/11/84	Albatross Advertising	9,750.00	250.00	1691
25/11/84	Albatross Advertising	1,462.50	37.50	1704
	Audio Visual Supplies	19,536.75	1,028.25	1779
	Paper Products plc	1,543.88	—	1601, 1680, 1778
	P Pipe & Son	200.00	—	Part Payment 1672 (work not satisfactory)
		22,743.13	1,065.75	

Adjustments

Date	Supplier	Net paid £	Discount taken £	Invoices paid
15/11/84	Audio Parts	8,000.00		1495 Contr with S/L

Payments

Date	Supplier	Net paid £	Discount taken £	Invoices paid
3/12/84	Audio Visual Supplies	24,963.63	1,313.87	1784
15/12/84	Sale Borough Council	2,400.00	—	1654
15/12/84	Video Productions	8,050.00	—	1785
24/12/84	Audio Visual Supplies	27,084.37	1,428.13	1792 £50 underpaid
		62,498.00	2,742.00	

Receipt

Date	Supplier	Net paid £	Discount taken £	Invoices paid
3/12/84	Paper Products	(448.50)	(10.00)	1789 & C/N 1788

Adjustment

Date	Supplier	Net paid £	Discount taken £	Invoices paid
15/12/84	Audio Parts	8,000.00		To A/C Contra with SL

Sales ledger – balances 31/10/84

Name, address, tel/contact	Date	Inv no	£	Credit limit £
Audio Parts	20/7/84	1689	4,000	
Country Lane	8/8/84	1725	10,000	
LITTLE OAKS	15/9/84	1762	2,000	
0155-6721	10/10/84	1890	2,000	
			18,000	20,000

Name, address, tel/contact	Date	Inv no	£	Credit limit £
Farmer Brown Home Farm MUDSEY 0133-4589	28/9/84	1784	3,250	5,000
Institute of Pseudo Accountants 27 King Street SALE Contact: Mr Bore	30/6/84 15/7/84 28/9/84 15/10/84	1503 1652 1785 2006	2,500 4,200 2,750 6,000 ——— 15,450	15,000
Mrs Mopp 46 Pail Road BRUSHTON 95-2395	15/10/84	2005	500	500
Hi-Tech School Learning Lane SALE 0123-987 654	15/10/84 30/10/84	2007 2413	5,500 (1,650) ——— 3,850	10,000
Murphy McGregor Esq 24 Scott Street MUDSEY 0133-7724	25/10/84	2357	950	1,000
Rogues Retail Chancery Lane SALE Cash With Order			—	0
Video Engineers Viewpoint Lane SALE 0123-522 4565	25/9/84 20/10/84	1780 2201	6,000 2,000 ——— 8,000	10,000

Sales invoices and credit notes

( ) = C/N

Date	Inv no	Customer	Sales type	£	VAT £	GROSS £
20/11/84	2500	High-Tech School	A–1	500		
			A–4	2,000		
			V–2	1,000		
			V–3	1,000		
			Carriage	20		
		(2½% discount – 30 days)		4,520	661.05	5,181.05
20/11/84	2501	Rogues Retail	A–1	2,000		
			A–3	700		
			V–2	3,000		
			Carriage	50		
				5,750	862.50	6,612.50
20/11/84	2502	Audio Parts	A–1	2,000		
			A–4	5,000		
			A–7	500		
			Carriage	30		
				7,530	1,129.50	8,659.50
20/11/84	2503	High-Tech School	A–1	(1,000)	(150.00)	(1,150.00)
20/11/84	2504	Video Enginers	V–1	2,000		
			V–2	1,000		
			V–3	4,000		
			V–4	1,000		
		(2½% discount – 30 days)		8,000	1,170.00	9,170.00
BATCH 1 SUBTOTAL				24,800	3,673.05	28,473.05

Date	Inv no	Customer	Sales type	£	VAT £	GROSS £
30/11/84	2505	Rogues Retail	A–1	1,500		
			V–2	1,500		
			Carriage	20		
				3,020	453.00	3,473.00
30/11/84	2506	Video Engineers	V–1	4,000		
			V–5	500		
			Carriage	50		
		(2½% discount – 30 days)		4,550	665.44	5,215.44
30/11/84	2507	Rogues Retail	A–3	(400)	(60.00)	(460.00)
BATCH 2 SUBTOTAL				7,170	1,058.44	8,228.44
31/12/84	2508	Rogues Retail	A–1	3,000		
			A–2	2,100		
			V–2	1,600		
			Carriage	50		
				6,750	1,012.50	7,762.50
31/12/84	2509	Mrs Mopp	V–4	(434.78)	(65.22)	(500.00)
		(To cancel Inv. 2005)				
31/12/84	2510	Audio Parts	A–1	3,000		
			A–4	2,000		
			A–7	5,000		
			Carriage	50		
				10,050	1,507.50	11,557.50
31/12/84	2511	Video Engineers	V–1	2,000		
			V–5	3,000		
			V–6	500		
			Carriage	75		
		(2½% discount – 30 days)		5,575	815.34	6,390.34
31/12/84	2512	College di Cablo	A–1	1,525		
		2540 Ampere	A–9	2,400		
		Flexiland	V–8	345		
		Cr Limit £5000		4,270	—	4,270.00
		(Pro-forma invoice issued 1/12/84)		26,210.22	3,270.12	29,480.34

Cash sales

	Sales type	£	VAT £	GROSS £
November	A–1	4,200		
	A–2	2,500		
	A–3	3,600		
	A–4	7,200		
	A–5	2,100		
	A–7	2,250		
	V–1	2,300		
	V–2	1,200		
	V–3	400		
	V–4	3,650		
	V–5	3,400		
		32,800	4,920	37,720
December	A–1	10,100		
	A–2	9,250		
	A–3	3,600		
	A–4	4,950		
	A–6	10,200		
	A–7	4,450		
	A–9	2,100		
	V–1	12,300		
	V–2	10,150		
	V–4	3,240		
	V–5	4,330		
	V–8	5,820		
	V–9	1,550		
		82,040	12,306	94,346

Sales ledger receipts and adjustments

( ) = DR

	Date	Customer	Rec'd £	Discount taken £	
Receipts	10/11/84	Farmer Brown	3,168.75	81.25	Invoice 1784
		Rogues Retail	6,612.50	—	In advance
	15/11/84	Video Engineers	6,000.00	—	Invoice 1780
			15,781.25	81.25	
	20/11/84	Institute Pseudo Accts	5,000.00	—	To A/C
		Video Engineers	1,950.00	50.00	Invoice 2201
	25/11/84	Rogues Retail	3,473.00	—	In advance
	30/11/84	Hi-Tech School	2,700.00	—	Inv 2007, C/N 2413, 2503
			13,123.00	50.00	
	Nov.	Cash Sales	37,720.00	—	
Adj	15/11/84	Audio Parts	8,000.00		Inv 1689 & part 1725 Contra with P/L
	30/11/84	Farmer Brown	(81.25)		Disc. taken not allowed
Receipts	10/12/84	College di Cablo	4,275.86		12400F$ @ $2.90/£
	12/12/84	Rogues Retail	7,762.50		In advance
	14/12/84	Institute Pseudo Accts	5,000.00		To A/C
	15/12/84	Hi-Tech School	5,051.52	129.53	Invoice 2500
	18/12/84	Video Engineers	8,940.75	229.25	Invoice 2504
	31/12/84	College de Musico 987 Staffa Largoland Cr Limit £5,000	1,316.18		895 L$ @ 0.68/£ (against pro-forma invoice for £1,400)
			32,346.81	358.78	
Adj	15/12/84	Audio Parts	8,000.00		Bal of 1725 & 1762 Contra with P/L
	31/12/84	Murphy McGregor	950.00		Bad debt w/off Invoice 2357
Payments	8/12/84	Rogues Retail	(460.00)		C/N 2507

Glossary

Account structure: This is the skeleton of the accounting system. It defines the number of accounts which can be used, the information to be held in them and the relationships between accounts.
Accounting functions: The accounting operations which should be carried out by the accounting systems.
Accounting packages: A ready-made set of computer programs to carry out standard accounting functions.
Accounting periods: Most businesses are required to produce a full set of accounts once a year. This is too infrequent for practical management purposes so it is common practice to produce accounting information at more frequent intervals or accounting periods. A calendar month or a four-weekly period is most often adopted.
Accounting software: Computer programs to carry out accounting functions. The software may be in the form of packages or written specially to meet businesses' own requirements. The term certainly covers Sales, Purchase and Nominal Ledger applications such as Payroll, Fixed Assets and Invoicing which have close links to the basic accounting functions.
Accruals: Accounting jargon for recording an expense already incurred but for which you have not yet received a bill.
Aged balance: Analysing the balance of an account by the dates of the transactions to determine which of these should be chased up. The term usually applies to customers' accounts and is used for credit control.
Allocation: Matching two financial transactions so that they can both be cleared from the system. For example, a cash receipt could be allocated to particular invoices. Any invoices which were completely paid by that allocation could then be removed from the system, minimising storage space and allowing the operator to concentrate on those still outstanding.
Alphanumeric: A computer format which allows an entry to be either alphabetic characters or numbers.
Applications: Tasks for a computer system to carry out. The term usually refers to a fairly broad area of a business, e.g. sales ledger, production control.

Audit trail: It is essential to be able to trace any accounting transaction all the way through an accounting system. The means of doing this is called the audit trail which is a detailed printout of all transactions at each stage of processing.

Back-order: Details of orders which cannot be met from stock are retained in the system and have priority when stock becomes available. Some systems can print an emergency stock order to be sent to the supplier.

Back-up: Copies of files which can be used in the event of any problems with the original data. Back-up copies of files should be made daily and stored safely and every now and again extra copies should be made and stored at a different site to guard against the possibility of a major disaster such as a fire which destroys the computer and all records.

BACS: This stands for Bankers Automated Clearing Services which is a system for the electronic processing of financial transactions between customers and suppliers. Some accounting packages provide links to this service.

Balance forward: A method of accounting where transactions are only shown for the current accounting period. Only the balance of the account is carried forward to the next period as in a bank statement.

Batch: The majority of accounting systems process data in batches of similar transactions. This is much more efficient than processing single transactions and allows for a greater degree of control. Batches are generally totalled before they are entered into the computer and the details recorded in a batch book. The computer can also work out the batch total as it processes the transactions. Comparing the batch totals acts as a check on the completeness of processing.

Bespoke: This has the same meaning as in tailoring i.e. the programs are written especially for a particular customer to exactly meet his requirements. This is expensive and not normally necessary to meet standard accounting needs.

Central processor: A term used to describe the main part of the computer to which other components (peripherals) such as terminals or printers can be attached.

Chart of accounts: A list of nominal ledger accounts used in a particular system.

Codes: In order to avoid ambiguity much data in a computer system is identified by unique codes. Thus, each customer will be given a unique code, each nominal ledger a unique code and so on. In many cases this makes a computer system less flexible than a manual one and the design of the coding structure adopted by a particular package is very important. The codes are the basis of all analysis in the system and much thought should be given to the meaning attached to each character which makes up the code to allow for a system which is flexible and easy to use.

Configuration: A technical description of the computer hardware which gives details of the size and type of equipment being used.

Contra: An accounting term to describe a transaction which is to be offset against another. For example, you may wish to offset sales and purchases from the same organisation.

Control: An accounting system is worse than useless if the information it produces cannot be relied upon. A large part of any system should therefore be devoted to ensuring that processing by the computer is both complete and accurate. The techniques used to do this are referred to as controls. The principles involved are covered in some detail in an Information Technology Statement entitled *Controls in Computer Systems* published by the Institute of Chartered Accountants of Scotland.

Control account: A summary account used for control purposes. It is most commonly used in the context of sales and purchase ledger control accounts where the sales and purchase ledgers are summarised in accounts in the nominal ledger.

Cost benefit analysis: The essential process of analysing the costs and benefits anticipated with any proposed computer system. The factors to be considered are explained in some detail in an Information Technology Statement entitled *Costs and Benefits associated with IT Projects* published by the Institute of Chartered Accountants of Scotland.

Cost centres: A sub-division of an organisation for which costs are separately recorded. A good accounting system should allow this to take place and also allow the figures to be amalgamated into an overall set of accounts for the organisation.

Data: Raw facts and figures fed into a computer. Once properly processed these are generally described as information.

Daybooks: Accounting expression for a list of invoices and credit notes recorded in the sales or purchases ledger.

Disk: Magnetic storage device which will hold your programs and data. There are two kinds in common use – hard disks, which have a large capacity and are permanently built into the computer and floppy disks, which have a rather limited capacity but can be removed from the computer and replaced with another floppy disk.

Documentation: The manuals which should accompany any package software. The documentation usually includes instructions on setting up and using the system. A reference manual is often included and dealers will generally have additional technical manuals which describe how the system works. Increasingly much of this material is built into the system as on-line help text. Bespoke software should be accompanied by very detailed documentation.

Dumb terminal: A screen and keyboard that cannot on its own run a computer program. It must be connected to a central computer.

File: A group of similar records usually held on a magnetic disk. Files are used to retain information in a computer and lie at the heart of any accounting system. A system will have a surprising number of these and procedures will have to be devised to take good care of them.

File locking: A technique used on multi-user systems to prevent two users working on the same file at the same time and thus corrupting the data.

Function key: A special key on the computer keyboard which initiates an operation specific to the system being used.

General ledger: Although purists may argue, for all practical purposes this is the same as a nominal ledger.

Generation number: This is used in some systems to indicate which version of a file is being used. Each time a file is updated the generation number is increased by one.

Hard copy: A computer print-out.

Hardware: The machines which make up a computer system.

Help screens: Instructions on using the system which can be displayed on the computer screen during the operation of the system. These are usually accessed by pressing a function key and save the user from thumbing through extensive manuals.

Hot-line: The telephone number of your software support service.

IBM compatible: A machine from a manufacturer other than IBM which has been designed to run IBM software thus giving it access to the largest library of programs.

Information Technology Statements: These documents have been issued by the Institute of Chartered Accountants to give advice on good practice regarding Information Technology to members and others.

Integrated systems: Software made up of a series of separate modules which can easily pass data from one to another.

Interactive processing: The alternative to batch processing where data is entered into the computer in response to a series of questions generated by the computer.

Interface: Something which allows two parts of a computer system to pass data to each other. The term can refer to either hardware or software.

Journal entry: An accounting transaction where the user has to input both the debit and credit side of the entry. A group of such transactions is known as a journal. It is usually used for making adjustments to the sales and purchase ledgers and entering transactions directly to the nominal ledger.

Ledger: A group of accounts. (*See* Sales ledger, Purchase ledger, Nominal ledger.)

Log: A record of operations carried out on the computer. This facility is usually only available on larger, more expensive systems.

Maintenance agreement: A contact with a supplier for supporting and repairing the computer hardware or software.

Manual: Essential part of the documentation of a system. They come in two main categories, user manuals which give instructions on how to operate the system and technical manuals which are available to programmers and others who wish to explore the system more deeply.

Master file: A file which contains semi-permanent information such as customer names and addresses.

Memory: The internal storage on a computer which can hold information temporarily.

Menu: A list of the options in a computer program available to a user. Menu-driven systems are generally simple to operate since the user merely has to select an option to proceed to the next stage of processing.

Microcomputers: Often referred to just as micros. These are the smallest and most inexpensive types of computers. They are generally single-user systems although a few of the more recent systems can support several users.

Minicomputers: Often referred to as minis. These are much larger expensive computers and invariably support a large number of users.

Modules: Most comprehensive accounting systems are broken down into a number of self-contained sub-systems, each dealing with a particular function. These are generally referred to as modules.

Multi-tasking: A system which allows a user to carry out several operations simultaneously.

Multi-user: A system which allows several users to operate on a system simultaneously.

Network: Short for local area network, a system of microcomputers connected together so that they can share programs and data files.

Nominal ledger: This is the set of accounts which contain details of all the financial transactions in an organisation, including a summary of information held in the other ledgers. Accounts in this ledger are identified by nominal codes and because of the wide-ranging nature of this ledger, the design of the nominal coding system is particularly important.

Nominal-update: The procedures used to transfer information from other modules into the nominal ledger.

Open item: All active transactions are carried forward from one accounting period to the next. This provides the user with much more information than with the alternative balance forward type of accounting.

Operating system: This is the software which operates the computer as opposed to some business application. It is an essential if rather technical part of a computer system and can be seen as fitting in between the accounting software and the computer hardware.

Package: Off-the-shelf set of computer programs designed to carry out some common application.

Parameters: Aspects of a software package which can be designed and set by the user when installing the system. They allow for some limited tailoring of a package to a user's own requirements.

Password control: This is the standard method of restricting access to parts of a computer system which are considered sensitive.

PC DOS: Effectively the same as MS DOS. The standard microcomputer operating system.

Period-end: At the end of each accounting period it is standard practice to run a number of computer programs and to make a number of accounting adjustments. These will allow the user to get an accurate picture of the accounting situation at the end of the period and will prepare the system for the start of the next accounting period.

Posting: An accounting term for entering an accounting transaction to a system.

Pre-list: A manual or calculator addition of the items in a batch prior to entering them into a computer.

Pre-payments: The opposite of accruals; that is accounting for an expense paid in advance and which you have not yet incurred. Most accounting packages have special facilities for dealing with these.

Programs: The instructions to tell a computer how to carry out any particular task.

Purchase ledger: The ledger which contains details of suppliers' accounts and all the financial transactions associated with them.

Record locking: A technique used in multi-user systems to prevent more than one user accessing any particular record at the same time. This is a more flexible technique than file locking.

Recovery procedures: Procedures which must be followed to restore accurate data to the system following a corruption of the original data.

Recurring journals: Journal entries which must be entered at regular intervals e.g. standing orders. Many systems provide a mechanism for doing this which avoids keying the same information over and over again.

Report generator: A set of computer programs or a module which allows the user to extract information from the system in a format of their own choosing.

Reversing journals: An accounting technique generally used at the end of an accounting period to account for period end adjustments and which reverses in the following period e.g. stock, accruals.

Sales ledger: The ledger which contains details of customers accounts and all the financial transactions associated with them.

Software: Computer programs.

Source code: The original coding used in a computer program. Without access to this code it is impossible to make any modifications to the program.

Spooling: Technique used to store output from a computer on disk from where it can be printed at a later or more convenient time.

Standing data: Data which will remain constant or will not be altered very often.

Support: Assistance available from the supplier of a computer system. It refers generally to help with a problem rather than the rectification of a fault.

Suspense account: An account where transactions are temporarily stored until their true nature can be determined.

System: A set of components and or procedures linked together to fulfil a given purpose. The term may refer to hardware or software or have nothing to do with computers at all.

Terminal: A screen and keyboard which allows a user to communicate with a computer.

Transaction: Record of an event in an accounting system.

Trial balance: A list of the debit and credit balances in the nominal ledger. Such a listing is often used by accountants to track down errors.

Turn-key: Term used to describe a system which has been completely installed by a supplier. In theory the user merely has to turn a key to begin operation.

Unix: A common multi-user operating system.

Upgrade: Transfer to a larger computer or more comprehensive piece of software.

Utility: Program which carries out some routine housekeeping on the computer system, for example, sorting data or copying files.

Vertical market software: Programs designed for a particular type of business, for example, estate agents.

XENIX: A common multi-user operating system which is a variation of UNIX.